Mike Squires

Class against class

Published by Manifesto Press Cooperative Limited 2025
© Mike Squires 2025
All rights reserved. Apart from fair dealing, e.g. for the purpose of private study
or research, no part of this publication may be reproduced or transmitted,
in any form or by any means, electronic, photocopying, recording or otherwise, without the
prior permission of the publisher.
All rights reserved

ISBN 978-1-907464-55-3
Typeset in Bodoni and Gill

CONTENTS

Preface *ii*

1. Introduction *1*
2. The road to the New Line *9*
3. The Prophets Outcast
   the Party Line in transition 1927–29 *33*
4. Party membership in the Class against Class years *57*
5. Fighting 'social fascism' at election time *75*
6. *The Daily Worker*: weapon of the New Line *100*
7. The struggle against imperialism *121*
8. 'Down with the Colour Bar': *144*
   anti-racism and the New Line
9. The end of the New Line *163*
10. Class against class: the formative years
    of British communism *173*

Index *181*

Preface

MOST BOOKS of this kind have acknowledgements, and this is no exception. The usual protocol is to thank all those who have contributed in some way to the book's production, either through help rendered in the research, in the editing, or in giving moral and physical support in the writing process. Often there is no order of importance, and individuals help the author in any number of ways, as every assistance is of value. What sometimes gets missed out in the accolades is the subject or subjects of the book itself. I don't want to go down that path.

So first and foremost in my acknowledgements I would like to thank all those communists who passed through the ranks of the Communist Party of Great Britain during the period under review. Without them this book would not have been possible.

They were, in the main, ordinary working class people who will have no epitaph. There were often unemployed, disproportionately male, and largely drawn from Britain's bedrock industries: coal, engineering, textiles. They were trade union members, if employed, or active in organisations of the unemployed.

They were spied upon by Britain's not so secret police, their mail was opened, and meetings were bugged. Many were imprisoned and the party's leadership was interned before the outbreak of the General Strike. Their press was on occasions closed down and police raids took place on their premises. Communists working in industry were regularly black-listed by employers. Every instrument of the state was used to isolate and denigrate the communists, their only crime, to which they willingly pleaded guilty, was to work for a new form of society.

They were also internationalists, not only in their support for the Soviet Union but in their backing for liberation movements throughout the world. At a time when the ideology of Empire had a grip on the thinking of even the most advanced sections of the Labour movement it was the communists who virtually alone denounced colonialism and gave support to those in India, Ireland, Africa, Asia and the Caribbean who were struggling for freedom. It was not an easy fight. The decision by communists to oppose the annual Empire Day celebrations was an act of bravery, as the recollections of communist miners' leader Will Paynter cited in the book will testify.

Racism in 2020s Britain is officially frowned upon. Discrimination in sport is outlawed and there are laws banning the propagation of racist ideas. It wasn't like that in the 1920s and 30s. Racism was endemic and underpinned the rationale for Empire. Racist ideas were commonplace and early on in its history the CPGB passed a congress resolution that 'imperialist prejudices' amongst the working class must be combated. It was easier said than done, but communists did have an advantage. One of their foremost orators, and for a time MP' was Shapurji Saklatvala. 'Sak', as he was known, was spellbinding as a speaker and single-handily recruited thousands to the ranks of the CPGB. His eloquence must have done something to offset the 'imperialist prejudices' referred to by the party.

In the newly founded *Daily Worker* positive images of black workers were a constant feature of the paper and the communist press propagated ideas of integration and solidarity. In all this they were very much on their own. Ideas of Empire and white superiority were the mainstays of the national press.

Socialist ideas too were keep alive by the communists in this period which included two very disappointing Labour governments. The Labour party through the 20s and early 30s moved steadily to the right culminating in the split in 1931 and the formation of a national government with Ramsay MacDonald as the nominal head. Former Labour leaders in the government supported cuts in benefits to an already impoverished working class.

No wonder the communists, and they were not alone, felt little but contempt for a Labour Party that they saw as little different to the Tories. It was the communists who with pamphlets, leaflets and other propaganda outlined socialist solutions to the problems of capitalism, something the Labour Party had apparently abandoned.

So these acknowledgements include thanks to all those men and women whose efforts and dedication to a better world made this book possible. You are gone but not forgotten.

Communists of another era may form the backbone of those who made this book possible but without other people still alive it would never have been completed. Lots of people have helped me and I cannot name them all. However, I would like to mention a few whose contribution has been outstanding. They are in no particular order of merit.

David Horsley is a very old friend (and now I am pleased to say comrade) who encouraged me from the very beginning to seek publication. Without his constant prodding I might have given up.

Phil Katz, generously gave his time to read the first draft and with his encyclopaedic knowledge gave me almost another book of useful recommendations. Thank you Phil: I didn't use all of them, principally because that would have made this work a two volume edition.

My old comrade Nick Wright, as the chairof Manifesto Press, has devoted his talents both as an editor and designer to left wing publications. I hope your faith in me is rewarded with sales numbers.

Pat Squires, my dear sister, who with patience and dedication read through the entire script, made numerous grammatical corrections and attempted to rein in my eccentric approach to sentence construction and capitalisation.

Finally, my partner of forty years, Robin Solomon. What would I do without her? She has always encouraged me in everything I do. This book was no different. Thank you, as always.

Dr Mike Squires
March 2022

1 Introduction

THE COLLAPSE of the Soviet Union and the subsequent opening up to public view of the archive of the Communist International has lead to a burgeoning interest in the history of world communism. The Communist Party of Great Britain has been no exception to this close scrutiny. There has emerged over the past few years a proliferation of interested parties and institutions each intent on profiling individual British communists and more generally the CPGB's culture, history, and contribution.

This opening of the temple of gold that is the CI archive has led not only to an increase in published work by academics and others, but also to a growth in the number of students pursuing theses directly related to the CPGB, or some of its satellite bodies. What previously was almost an untouched arena for fields of study, has now become a growth area with people almost falling over themselves to chart the course of a party that at some stages during its history had fewer members than those who are now interested in its progress. There has been established a network of historians interested in the CPGB where the old lags and the new arrivals can swap information and gain new ideas. There are regular conferences that look at different aspects of the CPGB's history. All this has come about as a direct result of the changes that have taken place in the old Soviet Union.

While none would deny that the CI Archive and its contents will not give us a better insight into the workings of British communism, a certain fetishism can develop that attributes to the archive more than it can deliver. For even when all the relevant documents are scanned, filed, and pawed over, they are documents, letters, observations and minutes appertaining predominantly to the leadership of the CI and the leading bodies and personnel of the British party. The archive can tell us about the machinations of leadership and how policy was arrived at by the CPGB's Central Committee. It can tell us about the final decisions, and how they were made, but it cannot tell us the influences that individual leading communists were under, or how their views were changed by their interactions with their friends and workmates, or the changing situation in the labour movement. We know for example that Pollitt wanted a change of policy towards the Labour Party in 1928 and that there was pressure from the CI on him and the Executive of the British party to adopt a more hostile approach. What the archive cannot reveal is the development of Pollitt's thinking about the issue. It cannot reveal the cumulative effect of seeing his comrades expelled from the Labour Party, watching fellow communists give their all on behalf of the locked-out miners in 1926, only to see both the communists and the miners increasingly deserted by the labour and trade union movement. At this time there was euphoria amongst working people at the election of the first Labour government, which was welcomed by the CPGB, whose members had participated so willingly in Labour's election campaign, but within a few months it became clear that the government would do virtually nothing for those who had elected them and even less for the millions in the colonies who suffered under British rule. The effect of none of these things on Pollitt, or other British communists' thinking, can be gauged by merely looking at the records of the CI.

Another even more dangerous spin-off is that, by concentrating solely on leadership records and reports, the CPGB can be neatly packaged as a willing vassal of an international body which itself, according to many commentators, was by the early 1920s nothing more than a tool of Soviet foreign policy. British communists can thus be effectively dismissed as uninterested in Britain's internal affairs and only concerned with trying to implement policies that were in accord with the aspirations of the USSR.

The CPGB is presented, even by the friendliest of historians, as an organisation that despite its small numbers, throughout its one hundred years existence played an important part in the labour movement. It is presented as a party which was often led astray by its devotion to the CI, and after that body's disappearance in 1943, by its unstinting support for what came to be known as 'real existing socialism'. When the CPGB did make a positive contribution, many historians argue, it was by its own endeavours, with a policy that seemed to be arrived at, not by any CI pressure, but by the experiences of British communists, reflecting the changing moods and patterns of the labour movement. Throughout the party's history, certainly during the twenty-three years that it coexisted with the CI, there have come to be 'good' and 'bad' periods designated by the experts. The positive periods, particularly the united front era from 1935-1939, are attributed by almost all historians to the earthy good sense of rank and file party members who saw the necessity of working with all those who were opposed to fascism. As a result of this homespun wisdom, CPGB membership increased and party influence in a whole number of spheres began to grow. This policy was terminated when the CI decided, at the outbreak of war in 1939, that the CPGB was wrong in its assessment of the war as anti-fascist and ordered that the policy should be changed to one of anti-war. A compliant CPGB leadership agreed, with one or two honourable exceptions, and for almost two years the party swam against the stream of the pro-war majority of the British public.

If 1939 is viewed as a disastrous turnabout by the CPGB, the change of policy a decade earlier is considered an even greater fiasco. This involved the CPGB jettisoning its traditional support for the Labour Party and adopting a policy of outright opposition, with the Labour Party and its membership being viewed by the communists as the allies of capitalism and fascism. This new strategy of 'class against class', or 'the new line', is generally perceived by almost all commentators on British communism as the worst period in the party's entire history. Membership slumped, they declare, and the party's influence in the trade union and labour movement, so painstakingly built up since its formation, hit an all-time low. It was only when the policy was abandoned that the CPGB emerged from its years of subterfuge and again began to play a positive role in working-class politics and the labour movement. Also, these same commentators would have us believe that the class against class policy, which was part of a worldwide communist strategy, was thrust on a reluctant British party by an omnipotent CI. They argue that, working first on the Central Committee, and then on the rank and file, the apparatchiks of world communism pressurised the CPGB membership, much against their better judgement, into accepting the new line.

The theme running throughout the work of all writers on the period, be they Marxist or non-Marxist in their approach, is that the strategy of the CPGB was determined more by external factors than by internal ones. One of my objectives in the following pages is to combat this line of reasoning, arguing that the CPGB, although a disciplined section of the CI, changed its policy not simply because of directives from that body, but because of changes that were taking place within the British labour movement. Why British communists came to embrace the new line can only be understood in the light of their preceding history. The developments that took place between 1920 and 1927 were an important prerequisite for this new policy, and by 1927, several important policy changes had already taken place in the British party, due to disenchantment with the Labour Party. All this had happened without any CI intervention.

There were two factors involved in the CPGB's changing assessment of the situation between 1920 and 1935. One was undoubtedly the world-wide strategy of the CI, but the other, and equally important one, was the party's appraisal of the objective situation in Britain. So far, all labour historians have concentrated on the first factor. This book, therefore, will attempt to redress the balance and show that there was a relationship between both these factors.

A serious deficiency in trying to interpret the period has been the lack of any planned attempt to tape the reminiscences of party activists of the time. There have been no oral history projects that have made a concerted effort to relate the experiences of Communist Party members in the period preceding the new line, and how their attitudes affected the Communist Party's policy. Some work has been done, for example with the South Wales Miners Oral History Project, including CPGB members recounting their experiences in the broader movement, in this case with the South Wales Miners' Federation. But nothing significant has been accomplished in the field of oral history that attempts to discover why communists during the 1920s underwent such a radical change of attitude towards the Labour Party. Because of this neglect of rank and file feeling, historians of the period have interpreted the CPGB's policy changes as a result almost entirely of a change of view by the Executive Committee. In doing so, these historians have incorrectly balanced the impact on policy of the Executive Committee and the party rank and file. This study will argue that policy changes, particularly the change of line towards the Labour Party, came about because of dissatisfaction amongst the communist rank and file. The EC responded to the pressure from party members as well as to pressure from the Executive Committee of the Communist International. This should come as no surprise. The leadership of the CPGB was, after all, in close communication with party activists in every sphere of work. The EC throughout most of the 1920s was elected by an open vote at National Congress, of which there were eleven between 1920 and 1929. The CPGB was very small and close-knit, and throughout the period its membership never rose above 10,000, except for a brief period after the General Strike. Because of these factors, there was a close liaison between the party membership and the leadership, and the Central Committee, which always included a number of labour movement activists, reflected rank and file feeling. There was a relationship between the leadership and the party membership, and policy did not change because of a sudden decision by the EC. Complete reversals of strategy did occur, but that was, in part, because of the demand for change from within the party.

That is not to say that the CI did not have a tremendous influence on the CPGB. It organised the work of communist parties throughout the world and British communists were expected to carry out the agreed line of the world communist movement. The British party was proud to call itself the British Section of the 3rd International. CI policy was decided at world congresses, of which there were six between 1919 and 1928. At these congresses delegates from the world's communist parties met to discuss strategy and tactics. In between such congresses, there were plenary sessions at which the problems of a particular party could be discussed in depth. In addition to this, communist parties often had permanent representatives in Moscow, and the CPGB had members of its Central Committee situated there throughout the period. There was also attached to each party a representative of the CI, whose job it was to inform the ECCI of the developments which were taking place in the respective country. When there were problems with a particular party or the question of a policy change, often the entire central committee would go to Moscow to discuss the issues. The CPGB Central Committee made several such visits during the period. The ECCI was very well informed of developments in Britain, and when they issued a directive, it was only done after there had been widespread consultation with the British party. The policy changes urged on the CPGB by the CI were made by a body that was in close touch with both CPGB thinking and the situation in the labour movement, and when they urged a change of strategy it was done with these two considerations in mind.

Policy changes in the CPGB, when they occurred, were not just a sudden process. The idea that the CI ordered a change of strategy one day and the British party implemented it the next, is without foundation. There were two major strategic changes by the CPGB during the period under review, the new line and the united front, and neither policy change came about overnight. The discussion around the new line, even after the CI's intervention, took almost two years before it was resolved, and that around the united front only a little less. These changes were slow to take place, precisely because the British party was responding to a changing internal situation.

It is fashionable amongst historians of British communism to portray the CI as an inflexible organisation, where the party line once agreed was implemented by national parties irrespective of national conditions or traditions. The CI was not a rigid body. The ECCI was careful to emphasise that communists must be constantly aware of their own country's characteristics and situation. There was no absolute and rigid line of approach that was the same for every party. On the contrary, the CI urged each of its sections to take into account their own national circumstances. At the Fourth Congress the delegates were told, "it stands to reason that the tactics of the United Front should be applied in the different countries in various forms in accordance with the actual circumstances."[1]

It was argued that only by careful study of the national situation could a communist party correctly apply CI strategy. Two years later the same point was made in the programme of the CI adopted by the Fifth World Congress:

"being the united world party of the proletariat, the CI makes it incumbent upon a section carefully to weigh all the peculiarities of the situation in their respective countries. Only by studying these peculiarities is it possible to conduct a real Marxian policy."[2]

Even communist party organisation during this period was remarkably flexible. The ECCI recommended no standard structure. In the outline for the 'Organisation and Construction of Communist Parties', the Third Congress declared:

"there can be no absolutely infallible and unalterable form of organisation for the Communist Parties. The conditions of the proletarian class struggle are subject to change in a continuous process of evolution, and in accordance with these changes the organisation of the proletarian vanguard must be constantly seeking for the corresponding form. The peculiar conditions of every individual country likewise determine the special adoption of the forms of organisation of the respective parties."[3]

Equally, the function of national parties was not defined. The general purpose of all communist parties, as laid down by the ECCI, was to "conquer the bourgeoisie and to wrest the power from its hands."[4] This rather non-specific aim was "for all of them until further developments the determining and guiding main goal".[5]

Even the role of communist parties, particularly communist parties like the British one, operating in advanced capitalist countries, were not spelt out, other than to demand of them that they conquer state power: "The determining factor in the organising activity of the Communist Parties in the capitalist countries must be the upbringing of such organisations as will make the victory of the proletarian revolution over the possessing classes both possible and secure."[6]

It certainly seems that during the first united front period which lasted until 1928, communist parties were left very much to work out their own tactics in line with CI strategy. The importance for communists of applying Marxist theory to their own national situation was referred to on numerous occasions by the ECCI. It was expected of communists that they creatively adapt CI policy.

Although throughout the early 1920s the CPGB was operating within the general guidelines of the CI's united front strategy, there were still differences. These differences arose precisely because it was left very much to the national sections to implement and interpret CI policy in their own way. The ECCI encouraged communist parties to creatively apply Marxism to their own national situation. It begs the question of how much changes in CI strategy were determined by the ECCI, and how much changing conditions in each of the sections forced the CI to alter its line. A veteran CPGB member, Bill Moore, talking some years later about the CBGB's about-turn at the outbreak of the war, argued that British communists made policy turns at this time because of their experience, which corresponded with the desires of the ECCI:

"I listened very carefully to what Monty had to say, but with all the qualifications it still amounts to this in my mind; that the changing line was due to the intervention of the CI, when Joe turns we all turn; and I just don't believe it. It would not have had, as I remember, total acceptance unless it corresponded with the experience that I think all the Party had over the previous ten years."[7]

Although he was referring specifically to 1939, Moore encapsulates my own view concerning the earlier period. Changes in CPGB policy from a united front to class against class, were as much due to developments in the internal situation, as they were to the CI's change of line.

The author's aim in this book therefore is two-fold. First, to show that the policy of class against class, although the strategy of the world communist movement, was not simply accepted in Britain because of imposition by the CI. There was a groundswell of support for the new line because it was in accord with the experiences that many communists had gone through in the preceding years. The membership of the CPGB welcomed the change of approach because it was in keeping with the thinking and direction in which the party had been moving since the mid-1920s.

As well as looking at the reasons why policy changes occurred, this book will also attempt to redress the balance concerning the class against class years. So far, the period has had a very bad press. All historians have pointed to the new line's isolating effect on communists. They have also claimed that the policy led to a decline in support for the CPGB. Whilst I accept the first premise, the evidence shows that the new line, far from leading to a drop in membership in the CPGB, actually resulted in an increase.

During the period Britain's communists initiated campaigns against the colour bar and carried on an ideological struggle against what they referred to as 'imperialist prejudices' – racism. They were probably the only political party that organised meetings to recruit non-white members.

The liberation movements in Britain's colonies were given support and coverage in the party press. It was during the class against class years that emphasis was placed on the idea that British workers could not be free unless their class brothers and sisters in the Empire were free as well. The party sent members to the colonies to agitate and it was in response to this that the famous Meerut conspiracy trial took place.

Elections during the period took on new importance as the CPGB sought to replace

the Labour Party as the workers' party. To do this the party adopted, at least at the local level, a set of realistic policy proposals, proposals that were implemented by all parties after the war. It was also this period that laid the basis for the election of Britain's longest-serving communist MP.

One of the new line's greatest achievements was the establishment of a daily communist newspaper, the *Daily Worker*, which still survives under a different name. Had it not been for the change of policy it is unlikely that the paper would have started when it did: to become the leaders of the labour movement, the communists needed their own daily voice.

In all, they are many positive aspects to this short period of communist history. They were formative years for the British party and during the period that the new strategy was operable there was a renaissance of British communism and the basis was laid for the party's subsequent rapid growth and emergence as a mass organisation during the Second World War.

Notes

1   *Resolutions and Theses of the Fourth Congress of the Communist International.* Held in Moscow Nov 7-Dec3, 1922. CPGB page 31
2   *Programme of the Communist International.* Draft adopted at the Fifth Congress of the Communist International June 7-July 8, 1924 CPGB p37
3   *Decisions of the Third Congress of the Communist International Moscow*, July 1921. CPGB p29
4   *Ibid* p 29
5   *Ibid* p 29
6   *Ibid* p 29
7   *1939 The Communist Party and the War*. Edited by John Attfield and Stephen Williams. Lawrence and Wishart pp 54-55

| How the Strikers Fought the Bosses— | **Sunday Worker** SUNDAY, MAY 9, 1926 | And How the Bosses Fought the Strikers |

HISTORIC SCENES IN THE GREAT INDUSTRIAL STRUGGLE

Armoured cars and armed troops patrolled the streets. These were used in London to protect blackleg traffic.

Submarines were sent for the first time to the London Docks. Four were sent to the Victoria and Albert Docks as a result of the strike.

THE BALDWIN GOVERNMENT USES FULL POWER OF STATE AGAINST STRIKERS

Tanks and armed soldiers at Wellington Barracks, London.

Lady members of idle class "caught" doing something useful in Hyde Park.

Welsh Guards in full war kit and tin hats at Hyde Park.

ORGANISED MASSES IN THE STREETS HOLD UP BLACKLEG TRAFFIC

Mounted and foot police make a baton charge upon strikers in South London.

A striker arrested after a thrilling battle at Hammersmith, London.

WORKERS GREET THE GENERAL STRIKE WITH ENTHUSIASM

When the General Strike was declared on May 1 the masses hailed it with amazing demonstrations. Scene in London.

The SUNDAY WORKER banner was carried to the London May Day demonstration by Richard Hampton.

2 The road to the New Line

THE REASONS for the adoption of the new line were complex and as much due to internal conditions as to external factors. Why British communists came to embrace such a strategy can only be understood in the light of their preceding history: he developments that took place between 1920 and 1927 were an essential prerequisite for this new policy.

By 1927, several significant policy changes already had taken place in the British party, due to disenchantment with the Labour Party. This was before any attempt at intervention by the Communist International.

To understand why the CPGB so readily adopted the policy of class against class in 1929 and why the party retained the strategy, virtually intact, until the end of 1934, twenty months after Hitler had come to power in Germany and the CI had issued its call for a united front, it is necessary to come to terms with the internal dynamics of British communism during the period preceding the new line. It was during the seven years from the CPGB's formation in 1920 until 1927 that the groundwork for class against class was prepared. The growing hostility towards the Labour Party felt by communists, reinforced by the experience of the first, brief, Labour government, helped shape their later, and comfortable, conversion to the slogan of 'Social Democrat equals Social Fascist'. It was a response, first to the Labour Party's ostracism of the CPGB as a party, and later of communists as individuals, that pushed the party in the direction of class against class.

The main strategic aim of the CPGB until 1927 was to gain Labour Party affiliation, and virtually everything the party did was subordinated to this goal. This objective also determined the communists' electoral strategy. It was not until the Ninth Congress in October 1927 that the CPGB finally came to accept that it was unlikely to gain Labour Party affiliation. This congress also recognised that the expulsion of communists from the Labour Party, as a result of the implementation of the 1924 Annual Labour Party Conference decision that had deemed them ineligible for membership, was likely to be a permanent feature of political life. Once these unpalatable facts were realised, the CPGB began a radical reassessment of its strategy. Its policy towards the Labour Party altered fundamentally, and it was in the process of changing before there was any indication from the CI that a new strategy was desirable. As it transpired, the new policy was welcomed by many of the communist rank and file who wanted their hostility towards the Labour Party taken to even more extraordinary lengths than either the CI or the party leadership, in the early stages, were prepared to go.

CPGB strategy 1920-24

From 1920 to 1924 communists could be individual members of the Labour Party. They could stand as Labour candidates at either local or national elections. They could be elected as delegates to Labour Party National or Regional conferences. Local CPGB branches could be affiliated to their local Labour Party and Trades Council. Communists were often the backbone of their constituency Labour parties, they enjoyed full rights, and for the four years after the CPGB's foundation, there was little attempt to discriminate against them. The affiliation of the CPGB to the Labour Party was another matter, and this was continually rejected both by the Labour leadership from 1921 onwards when it was first raised, and by successive Labour Party annual conferences.

That communists should be individual members of the Labour Party was not unnatural. The British Socialist Party, which was the primary grouping that formed the CPGB, was affiliated to the Labour Party, and so too was the Independent Labour Party. When the ILP rejected CI affiliation at its 1921 Annual Conference, about 500 or so members of its left wing joined the CPGB. In the maelstrom of socialist politics around the First World War, it was not unusual for socialists to belong to several different socialist organisations. When the CPGB was formed, members of the new party retained their Labour Party membership, and it was one of the problems of the CPGB in its early days that party members were often more active in the Labour Party than in the CPGB.

Labour Party affiliation was the most controversial question discussed at the CPGB's founding conference in August 1920. A motion in support was only carried by 100 votes to 85, and many communists were opposed to any representations being made to the Labour Party. The majority of delegates were members of the British Socialist Party, and many BSP delegates wanted affiliation to the Labour Party to continue after the CPGB was established. The party chairman, Arthur MacManus, was a member of the Socialist Labour Party who was opposed to affiliation. The two trends within the CPGB regarding affiliation can be seen in the communists' first approaches to the Labour Party soon after the conference finished.

The first application for affiliation was sectarian in the extreme. A short letter from the CPGB Central Committee to the Labour Party NEC made three points. It announced the communists' belief in, " the dictatorship of the proletariat as a necessary means for combating the counter-revolution during the transition period between Capitalism and Communism ......" [1] It also explained the new party's view of its elected representatives:

> "...... the tactics to be employed by representatives of the Party elected to Parliament or local bodies must be laid down by the Party itself, according to national or local circumstances. In all cases, such representatives must be considered as holding a mandate from the Party and not from the particular constituency for which they happen to sit. Also, that in the event of a representative violating the decisions of the Party as embodied in the mandate which he or she has accepted, or as an instruction that he or she is called upon to resign his or her membership of Parliament or municipality and also of the Party......" [2]

Emphasis on the dictatorship of the proletariat and the CPGB's right of control over its MPs were hardly demands that were likely to be sympathetically received by the Labour leadership. The response by the Labour Party NEC was to reject the communists' first application for admission. [3]

This rejection resulted in the first of many changes of tactics by the communists in pursuit of their affiliation aim. They now adopted a different approach and were far more conciliatory in tone. They sent a further letter to the Labour Party NEC, and this time couched their demand for affiliation in much more reasonable terms. They emphasised the federal structure of the Labour Party and the rights of affiliated groups, however critical, to operate within it:

"...... it (the CPGB) understood the Labour Party to be so catholic in its composition and constitution that it could admit to its ranks all sections of the working class movement that accepts the broad principle of independent working class political action, at the same time granting them freedom to propagate their own particular views as to the policy the Labour Party should pursue or the tactics it should adopt..." [4]

The Labour Party NEC's reply was interesting. They too recognised that there were conflicting trends within the CPGB between those who saw Labour Party affiliation as an absolute priority and those who were antagonistic to the idea. Their response was to quote from an article in the party's weekly paper, *The Communist*. MacManus, writing about the founding conference, had written:

"one impression that I should like to definitely make clear as gathered from Sunday's experience, and that is, that those arguing for affiliation to the Labour Party did not argue for, nor contemplate working with the Labour Party. The antagonism to the Labour Party was general, but those for affiliation held the opinion that such antagonism would be best waged within the enemy camp." [5]

The Labour Party NEC concluded that, "the Communist Party is less concerned with the "broad principle of working class political action" than with disrupting the Labour Party and conducting an intensified campaign within its ranks against its policy and methods." [6] The CPGB was forced onto the defensive and repudiated its chairman to show that the body of opinion represented by McManus was a minority within the Party. In a further conciliatory letter to the Labour Party NEC, the Central Committee declared that the communists were prepared to accept, albeit critically, the Labour Party constitution, by declaring," in deciding to affiliate we accepted the constitution of the Labour Party in the belief that the Communist Party would have the common right of every other section to advocate its own views as to the policy and tactics the Labour Party should pursue." [7] This was the first time that they had made such an admission. It was, however, a case of too little too late, and the Labour Party NEC again informed the communists that their application had been rejected and that the matter was to be referred to the 1921 annual Labour Party conference.

This early exchange of correspondence shows the inconsistency of British communists in arguing their case. Throughout this first period, they were undecided in their strategy towards the Labour Party, and it was this indecision that led to changes of policy. Primarily, they were unsure of their role concerning the larger organisation. Was the CPGB to replace the Labour Party as the party of the working class? This certainly seemed to be the opinion of many in the party, and this was expressed in the first letter of application when the communists spelt out their own distinct views of achieving power. These views were very different from the Labour Party's conception of a parliamentary road to socialism, and it meant that the labour movement was now offered a clear choice of two opposing strategies. It could opt for the CPGB or the Labour Party – there was no middle course. The alternative view in the CPGB and this was the one that dominated at least until 1927, was that the party, like the British Socialist Party before it, should become an affiliated part of the Labour Party and strive within that organisation to push the labour movement in a revolutionary direction. It was this view that found expression in the later applications for affiliation when the federal structure of the Labour Party was given greater emphasis.

In the debate at the 1921 annual Labour Party conference, Arthur Henderson, the General Secretary, quoted a communist statement on the Woolwich by-election in February 1921 to defend their non-affiliation to the Labour Party. This was the CPGB's first intervention in an election since the party's foundation. Ramsay MacDonald was the Labour candidate and the CPGB called on the electors to abstain from voting. In a party statement entitled, 'The Communist Party and the Woolwich by-election' the communists argued that there was no difference between the Labour Party and other capitalist parties:

> "remember workers of Woolwich that where the coalition candidate stands openly and avowedly for capitalism in all its ramifications its industrial autocracy its attacks on trade unions, its exploitation, its predatory imperialism, the Labour candidate stands for capitalism and all its manifestations, none the less surely because its purpose is hidden under high sounding words." [8]

This kind of statement was hardly different in tone to that being issued ten years later during the class against class period. It shows that hostility to the Labour Party was never far below the surface even during the period of communist overtures towards the larger body. It did not help their case for admission, and although the communists had some influential support at the conference, notably from A J Cook, the miners leader, and from the London Trades Council, their application for affiliation was rejected by 4,115,000 votes to 224,000.

This antagonism towards the Labour Party, particularly in the electoral sphere, was still very dominant in the British party a year later. In the same month as the 1922 annual Labour Party conference, at which CPGB affiliation would again be discussed, the communists issued a statement outlining their parliamentary policy and electoral programme. They made clear their determination to stand against Labour candidates and particularly Labour leaders.

The communists were in a contradictory position: although no rule in the Labour Party constitution outlawed affiliated organisations from standing against Labour candidates, it made the communists' case for affiliation that much more difficult to argue if they were trying to win an independent electoral base separate from the Labour Party.

Harry Pollitt, speaking at the 1922 conference, dealt with the issue of CPGB candidates. In his speech, Pollitt was much more reasonable than the previous party statement, and he articulates the arguments of those in the party that saw affiliation as a priority. He was, he said, prepared to negotiate over the withdrawal of CPGB candidates standing against Labour. Pollitt, who was a delegate to the conference from the Boilermakers Union, stated, "... it was true it (CPGB) had candidates in the field who were opposing official Labour Party candidates, he happened to be one of them, but these were matters which could be made the subject of negotiation..." [9] If the communists were hoping to use the withdrawal of their candidates as a bargaining point for affiliation, it came to no avail. A large majority again rejected their application for affiliation.

Also, the conference decided to add a new rule to the Labour Party rulebook that was explicitly aimed at the communists. The new rule stated

> "... no person shall be eligible as a delegate who is a member of any organisation having for one of its objects the return to Parliament or to any local governing authority of a candidate or candidates other than such as have been endorsed by the Labour Party or have been approved as running in association with the Labour Party...." [10]

If the Communist Party now stood candidates in opposition to Labour, communists would be ineligible to be elected as Labour Party delegates. Although their party had been rejected as an affiliated organisation, communists were still individual members of the Labour Party and enjoyed the same rights as other Labour Party members.

Although Pollitt at this conference may have said that CPGB candidates were the subject of 'negotiation', when faced with a choice of either dropping those candidates or of losing fundamental Labour Party rights, the party decided on the former. The EC of the CPGB, meeting soon after the Labour Party conference had taken place, decided to establish a subcommittee to review the new situation and particularly whether or not to comply with the new rule which would mean the withdrawal of all CPGB candidates where they were in opposition to Labour. The subcommittee was split 6:6 over the issue, and the party leadership in response decided to appoint a commission that would 'represent all points of view'. Surprisingly, there was little hint of a compromise in the commission's recommendation, which was that the CPGB comply with the new Labour Party rule.

The initial split in the subcommittee over the issue was also reflected in rank and file opposition to the measure. In response to an EC circular notifying branches of the decision to withdraw party candidates, nineteen branches responded, and all of them, to a greater or lesser degree, were hostile. Five lodged a formal protest, four agreed to carry out the decision, though they strongly disagreed with it, and ten branches demanded a referendum of the membership or a special party conference – neither of which happened.

This sharp reaction to the new election strategy was an indication that both at leadership and branch level, there was considerable opposition to a policy that was viewed by many communists as being too soft on Labour. Yet it was a policy that was to remain intact for the next five years. When it changed, it did so as a result of a congress decision, a decision that was taken quite independently of any pressure from the CI.

In August 1922, two months after the conference, the party declared in a public statement that it would no longer stand in opposition to Labour. It had decided to forfeit its electoral independence for fear of jeopardising its claim for affiliation. The party reasoned that if there were no communists present at Labour Party conferences because of ineligibility, the struggle for affiliation would be that much more difficult. In making this decision, the CPGB had decided that affiliation and electoral strategy were interwoven. For the next six years, the party kept to its pledge of not standing against Labour candidates. That decision was only reversed when the CPGB's strategy towards the Labour Party changed, and affiliation was no longer considered a priority.

That the decision was taken at all indicates that for the first time since the CPGB was formed, there was some consistency in the communists' approach towards the Labour Party. For the time being anyway, the view in favour of Labour Party affiliation as the principal strategic objective was in the ascendancy. But there was still a great deal of hostility from within the party towards this approach, and this was expressed in several ways. MacManus, when giving his report on the British situation to the fifth congress of the Communist International, in 1924, made it clear that the dropping of communist candidates was nothing more than a tactical ploy. [11]

The divergent views within the CPGB about the Labour Party can be seen in the disparity between the communists' public statements about affiliation, and their private reservations concerning the way this issue was pursued. When arguing their case at Labour Party conferences, the communists were at pains to show that they were prepared to abide by the Labour Party constitution. Pollitt, at the 1922 conference, almost like an honest broker, had informed the delegates that affiliation was likely to be a recurring issue and that the way to resolve it was to ask the CPGB if it accepted the Labour Party Constitution. [12]

On both occasions, by massive majorities, the Labour Party delegates showed that they did not believe the communists and did not accept their reassurances about the Labour Party constitution. They voted overwhelmingly against accepting the CPGB as an affiliated organisation. Although the CPGB had been continually refused admission, individual communists who were members of the Labour Party were not discriminated against in any way. At the 1922 Labour Party conference seven CPGB members were delegates, and by the 1923 conference, this figure had increased to thirty-eight.[13] The Labour Party NEC made no attempts to restrict the rights of communists, and the question of their expulsion did not become an issue until the Labour Party conference of 1924. At the 1922 general election, four communists were Labour candidates, and by the general election of the following year, this figure had risen to seven. The Labour Party had endorsed five of these nationally, and the other two received local Labour

Party and Trades Council support. Most of the communist Labour parliamentary candidates all agreed to abide by the Labour Party constitution and policy.

Whilst unconditional support for Labour may have been the public stance of most of the communist Labour candidates this was certainly not the prevailing view within the CPGB. Privately, the party was concerned that its members, who had made sufficient impression within the Labour Party to become adopted Labour candidates, should at all times be seen to be advocating CPGB policy. At the fifth congress of the Communist International, the British delegation statement made clear that this was their priority:

> "...Communist Candidates should be nominated and selected only on the basis of a clear and fighting Communist Policy. Our candidates should in no way be selected simply as left wing representatives of the Labour Party. It should be made definitely clear from the commencement of the campaign what the Communist Candidate fights for. It should be remembered that it is of even greater importance to win the masses over to Communism than to win a Parliamentary Seat on a vague opportunist platform..." [14]

This may have been the CPGB's proclaimed policy, but clearly, no attempt was made to impose such a discipline on many of the communist Labour candidates. The fact that at the 1923 general election five CPGB members standing as Labour candidates received National Labour Party endorsement meant that whatever the communists may have said about their own independence, in most cases they were prepared to forego this independence to win the Labour nomination. The disagreements in the party are highlighted at this election by the decision of two other party members, Geddes at Greenock and Ferguson at Glasgow Kelvingrove, who were also both Labour candidates not to accept the conditions laid down by the national Labour Party and thus to be deprived of national endorsement.

The indecision over this issue by the CPGB was itself a further indication of the conflicting views within the party regarding Labour Party affiliation. At Labour Party conferences, party members, like Pollitt and Shapurji Saklatvala, who was the communist Labour candidate for Battersea North, were prepared to emphasise the similarities between the Labour Party and the CPGB. Many communists worked within the Labour Party and were ready to accept its rules and constitution. A whole number of Labour councillors were also communists – at least two of the Poplar councillors sent to prison in 1921 were CPGB members. In many ways, the communists were an integrated part of the Labour Party, and their public utterances in support of affiliation emphasised the unity of purpose. Yet at the same time, there was within the party hostility towards Labour, and this hostility grew as the communists saw their attempts at affiliation continuously rebuffed.

The consistent rejection of the communists by the Labour Party, coupled with their experiences of the first Labour government, laid the basis for a change of policy within the party. Even in the first phase of the communist campaign for affiliation, up until their expulsion began in 1925, there were all the signs of an antagonism towards the larger organisation that was later to find expression during the class against class years. In many ways, the new line of 1929 was not so new. It was there in substance if not in form at a much earlier date. The other side to the communists' pronouncements in favour of the Labour Party was that they were often coupled with a denunciation of that party. These denunciations became sharper, particularly after 1924 and the failure of the first Labour government. During the period of that government and immediately following can be discerned a perceptible reappraisal by the communists. The policy towards Labour does not change, but it is decidedly much more lukewarm. That strand of communist thinking that since the party's formation was in outright opposition to Labour had been given a boost by the changing circumstances.

1924 – A crucial year

1924 was a turning point for the CPGB. It began with the formation of the first-ever Labour government, a government that was dependent on Liberal support but whose formation was nevertheless supported by the communists. Halfway through that government's uninspired term of office, the CPGB's sixth congress took place, and the first experiences of Labour in power began to be discussed. Towards the end of the year came the historic 24th annual conference of the Labour Party at which a decision to expel the communists was approved.

Since the CPGB's formation, one of the aims of the communists in relation to the Labour Party was to turn that party to the left and make it a significant force for socialism. Many communists argued that the right-wing Labour leadership should campaign for socialist policies or it would have to be replaced by a leadership that was committed to revolutionary change. Gallacher, at the opening session of the party's sixth congress, explained their overall strategy:

> "... the Communist Party does not attack the Labour Party. The Communist Party strives all the time to make the Labour Party a useful organ of the workers in the struggle against Capitalism, but we do attack the leadership of the Labour Party and will go on attacking it until the Labour Movement has forced it, either to prosecute a working class policy or to make way for a leadership that will do so." [15]

Whilst Gallacher may have maintained that it was possible to influence the Labour leaders and to bring pressure to bear on them from the labour movement, the congress resolution on, 'Relations With The Labour Party', held out no such prospects. Here the communists' aims were spelt out in no uncertain terms:

> ".... the Communist Party considers it its duty to enter into the ranks of the Labour Party in order to strengthen the militant and fighting elements of the Labour Movement and to unmask the treacherous elements in the Labour Party and free the workers from their influence..." [16]

The Labour leadership was castigated not only as treacherous, but also as middle class, and the resolution declared it was the communists' duty to enter the Labour Party in order to expose them and their policies. [17] At this Congress, for the first time, the communists suggested that the Labour Party, if it continued on its present course, without communist participation, would not be a Labour Party in the real sense:

"... if the middle class leaders of the Labour Party continue to keep the communists out of the ranks of the Labour Party and to transform it into a sham Labour Party and a close corporation of their own, they thereby will only hasten the disillusionment of the workers and their own downfall." [18]

Later on, after the adoption of the new line in 1929, this was precisely what the communists did argue. During the class against class period they maintained that the Labour Party was not a workers' party, but the third party of capitalism. The ideas for that analysis were formulated five years before and were not new to the politics of the CPGB.

While the communists may have supported the formation of a Labour government even they were surprised by its actions. Their criticisms became sharper, and by the time of the fifth congress of the Communist International, in July 1924, they declared that the Labour government was just another capitalist government and consequently the CPGB should take a sharper line concerning the Labour Party. [19]

This was not just the view of those in the party that had always been hostile to Labour. At a meeting of the Executive Committee of the CPGB just after the sixth congress, a resolution on the newly formed 'Left Wing Movement' also referred to the Labour government as an imperialist government. The resolution, which was a mixture of old and new, urged the communists to unite with Labour left wingers to rid the Labour Party of its right wing leadership. [20] The resolution also reasserted the party's independent role, but again stressed the importance of working within the Labour Party. [21]

Although the communists were becoming increasingly critical of the Labour Party, and this criticism was being expressed by the EC, and at party congresses, the strategy was still to gain Labour Party affiliation and to work within the larger body. The 24th annual Labour Party conference, coming as it did just three weeks before the general election, was recognised by the communists as crucial. Yet again CPGB affiliation was on the agenda, but so too was a recommendation from the NEC to exclude CPGB members as Labour candidates. If passed, this would be a severe setback to the communists' hopes of influencing the Labour Party, particularly at parliamentary level. At this conference, the arguments in favour of affiliation were articulated by communist delegates and once again, the emphasis was on the unity of purpose that existed between the CPGB and the Labour Party.

The decisiveness of the conference for the CPGB was reflected in a letter sent by the Polit Bureau to all party members who were attending the conference.

They were informed that they must attend a Polit Bureau meeting on Monday,

October 6th, and urged to cancel all other engagements. At the meeting, the speakers would be appointed to come in on various items on the Labour Party Executive Committee's Report and also on the main resolution on the agenda. [22]

It was evident from the letter that the CPGB members were extremely disciplined, and the message outlined who should be supported for the Labour Party NEC and how party members should vote on various resolutions. The Polit Bureau considered the conference as of the utmost importance, and it warned against party members' non-participation in the conference discussion. [23]

The NEC's proposals were in two parts: first, that the application for affiliation from the CPGB be refused, and second, that no member of the party wouldbe eligible for endorsement as a Labour candidate for Parliament or any local authority. [24]

The arguments utilised by both sides were a reaffirmation of their previous positions. The Labour leadership argued that the CPGB's strategy for achieving power was incompatible with the Labour Party's belief in parliamentary democracy. Frank Hodges, an NEC member, emphasised this point. When moving the resolution, he argued throughout his speech that the CPGB did not accept a peaceful road to socialism. His speech was friendly in tone, and he called on the CPGB to establish itself as an independent organisation, without seeking the protection of the Labour Party umbrella.

The argument that the Labour Party was a federation was emphasised again and again by the communists and their supporters. Harry Pollitt, again representing the Boiler Makers Union, accused Hodges of splitting the Labour movement. [25] William Paul, another communist representing Rusholme Labour Party, concluded his speech by saying that the differences between the two parties were not differences on matters of principle, but only on tactics. [26]

The NEC's case for banning communists standing as Labour candidates revolved around their commitment to expound Labour Party policy. This was in part a response to the communists' own indecision in setting out guidelines to their members who were Labour candidates. Some communist Labour candidates did accept the NEC's instructions; others did not. To resolve this dilemma, which in many ways was not of their making, the NEC urged the conference to empower it to refuse endorsement to members of the CPGB as Labour Party candidates because Labour candidates should wholeheartedly support Labour policy. [27]

When the two motions were put to the vote, they were passed overwhelmingly. The CPGB's application for affiliation was turned down by 3,185,000 votes to 193,000. The proposal that communists should no longer be eligible as Labour candidates received a smaller majority, 2,465,000 votes to 654,000. [28] It was yet another setback for the communists but by no means a disaster. Apart from remaining outside the Labour Party as an organisation, the rights of communists within the party remained very much intact. They could not stand for local or parliamentary office, but that apart, they still enjoyed the same rights as other Labour Party members. It was the third motion on the agenda concerning the CPGB that was to be the most crucial and to have the most long-term effect. It was a resolution submitted by the Sutton Divisional

Labour Party which moved that no member of the CPGB should be eligible for membership of the Labour Party. [29] Over this issue, there was a much greater division of opinion and the motion to expel the communists were only carried by 1,804,000 votes to 1,540,00077

At their first post-conference meeting, the Labour Party NEC decided to establish a select committee of three NEC members which included the ex-communist A J Cook. The subcommittee was to examine the resolution's implementation and to make a further report to the NEC. The subcommittee met the following month and agreed on a resolution which was to be submitted to the next NEC meeting. The effect of the subcommittee's recommendation, if passed, would be to delay until the next annual conference any exclusion of the communists. At the full NEC meeting in January 1925, the recommendations from the subcommittee were accepted. Even at this stage, there was some trepidation by the Labour Party leadership upon engaging in a witch-hunt before the constitutionality of the communists' exclusion had been thoroughly discussed.

This, however, was not the interpretation put on the delay by the CPGB. They maintained that the conference decisions were not being carried out because there was widespread resistance. *Workers Weekly* argued that the conference decision was not being carried out because it couldn't be carried out. [30] A similar assessment was made at the party's seventh congress by J R Campbell, who argued that the support for communists within the Labour Party was so great that their expulsion was impossible.[31]

The communists were consistent in this analysis, at least until their ninth congress in 1927. They continued with over-optimistic and incorrect assessment of their chances of re-admittance to the Labour Party, based on the false assumption that they could gather sufficient support from the Labour Party rank and file to overturn the decisions.

The initial delay by the Labour Party in working out the implementation of the conference resolutions was overcome by the following year. At the June meeting of the NEC, the subcommittee again reported on their progress. The recommendations were in two parts. Here also, there was a certain reluctance to pursue the vendetta against the communists, particularly in the trade union side of the movement. The subcommittee reported:

> "...... we have considered the Sutton Resolution that no member of the Communist Party be eligible for membership of the Labour Party. We have made an examination of the correspondence from affiliated organisations and do not anticipate very much difficulty in applying the resolution to the individual membership of the Party. With regard to its application to accredited representatives of affiliated trade unions, your committee are convinced that it would be very difficult, as trade unions resent interference with the delegates who are the duly elected choice of their members."[32]

The subcommittee recommended to the NEC that it should intimate to the annual conference that, in its opinion, affiliated trade unions could only act consistently with the decisions of the annual conference in its relation to the communists by appealing to their members when electing delegates to national or local Labour Party conferences or meetings, to refrain from nominating or electing known members of non-affiliated political parties, including the communists.[33]

The recommendations were accepted, and they showed that the Labour Party NEC was not prepared, at this stage, to engage in a wholesale witch-hunt of the communists. Because of this, communists were still eligible to attend Labour Party conferences. The Boilermakers Union, for example, rejected the NEC's advice and sent Harry Pollitt to conference for the next two years. This was only possible because of the NEC's reluctance to dictate to the trade unions over who they should elect as Labour Party delegates.

The recommendations of the NEC were endorsed at the 1925 annual Labour Party conference by overwhelming majorities. Even the somewhat controversial advice to the trade unions was accepted by a vote of almost six to one. This conference effectively ended the first phase of the communists' campaign for admission. They had been defeated on every count. Not only was the party consistently rejected as an affiliated organisation, but now communists as individuals could no longer be Labour Party members. It was a severe setback that would have far-reaching consequences for the CPGB.

The passing of the resolutions marked a historic turning point for the communists in their relationship with the Labour Party. It meant that they were now isolated from the larger organisation and no longer could they seek to influence the Labour Party as individual accredited members, or as parliamentary or local candidates. It would now be much more difficult to recruit members or to disseminate the party's propaganda from within. Its effect over the long-term was that it contributed to the CPGB's increasing antagonism towards the Labour Party and its leadership. This, in turn, was fuelled by the Labour leadership's lack of commitment to socialism – an assessment that was shared by many on the left and not just by the communists.

That the decisions were taken at all was partly due to the CPGB's own strategy in conducting the fight for affiliation. It was clear from the beginning that there was likely to be some opposition to this from amongst the more anti-communist Labour Party members, and the conflict internationally between the Second and the Third International did not help the communists' case either. If, after its formation and in its subsequent dealings with the Labour Party, the party had been more flexible in its approach and had emphasised the federal nature of the larger body, both parties commitment to socialism, the similarities rather than their differences, there would have been a much greater chance of success. Instead, in response to the latent and growing anti-Labour feeling within the party, the communists demanded virtual autonomy, attacking the notion of a democratic advance to socialism and denouncing the Labour leaders as middle-class traitors. These were hardly measures that were likely to endear them to the Labour rank and file. Yet the CPGB's greatest weakness was its inconsistency when challenged over these issues. At numerous Labour Party conferences, communists declared their support for the Labour Party constitution, their belief in using the electoral process and their willingness to abide by the Labour Party rules and regulations. The CPGB, at its conferences and meetings and in its press, adopted a much more intransigent approach than when its members were arguing for affiliation at Labour conferences, where communist delegates were less adamant in their approach and based their appeal more on the issues that united the movement, rather than on their disagreements.

The prelude to the new line

This early period, which was marked by inconsistencies on both sides, was now at an end. The Labour Party had, at last, a coherent policy towards the communists and over the next few years, this would be rigorously applied. The communists, for their part, despite their crushing defeat, did not attempt any significant policy reversal. For the next two years, the party's strategy towards the Labour Party in many respects remained virtually unchanged. What was notable, however, was that the anti-Labour views within the party had been considerably reinforced. During the next two years, although the communists were adamant that their setbacks were only temporary, there was a marked increase in their attacks upon the Labour Party. This was coupled with a continuance of their already changing assessment of the Labour Party as a working-class party. By 1927 the communists' appraisal of the Labour Party was very much in the new line mould. Although the slogan of 'Social Democrat Equals Social Fascist' had not yet been adopted, in many essential areas the communists had already accepted the class against class philosophy. This was without any intervention by the CI and was solely due to internal conditions.

After the setbacks of the 1924 and 1925 Labour Party conferences, Shapurji Saklatvala, the communist MP for Battersea North was one of the most prominent of party members to urge a change of policy. Within a week of the conference closure, he had written to the Central Committee demanding a change of line. In the wake of the conference defeat, he urged the adoption of a far more hostile attitude towards the Labour Party:

> "... I feel that the extraordinary circumstances prevailing at the moment call for extraordinary measures to be taken by our Party. There is not much doubt in my mind that without drastic measures to build up our Party, we shall be submerged into insignificance in Great Britain. Parliamentary customs and traditions have still a very great attraction for the masses. In order to overcome this, we must adopt merciless measures to fight the Labour Party. We will not succeed to the point of actually wiping it out, but we do not require to do that. What we shall succeed in doing is to give a dangerous shaking to the Parliamentary position of all the Right Wingers and it would then be their turn to patch a peace with the Communist Party at any price, and the Left Wing will be forced into an open fight against the Right."[34]

He argued, in what was to become new line phraseology, that the Labour Party was no longer a workers' party and had abandoned the struggle for socialism. The CPGB had therefore to establish itself as the only anti-capitalist party:

> " we must appeal to the Central Committee at Moscow to let us work temporarily along the lines I am suggesting. We should adopt the attitude that the Labour Party has now deserted its original function and turned itself into a Liberal Reformist Group, like the Irish Nationalist Party, and that the real political crusade for Socialism has been abandoned by the Labour Party, therefore the Communist Party must now set itself up as the only avowed anti-Capitalist party to take such action inside and outside Parliament as will lead to the taking over of the means of production and the abolition of imperialist exploitation." [35]

He further advocated that the trade union movement should be split from the Labour Party and that trade union branches should affiliate to the CPGB instead.[36] The purpose of this was to be another feature of the new line, the standing of communist candidates against Labour.[37] In virtually every respect the course of action recommended by Saklatvala (right) was later to become party policy after 1929.

Saklatvala's reaction to the conference decisions was symptomatic of the growing demand for change from amongst the membership. This demand was given a further boost by the outbreak of the General Strike and its aftermath.

The General Strike strengthened the disillusionment with the Labour Party that was now widespread within the CPGB. The events leading up to the dispute, and the strike's conduct, and ultimate betrayal by the Labour leadership had a lasting effect on communist thinking. Even on the eve of the strike, however, communists still retained a mixture of feelings towards the Labour Party.

Saklatvala, who by now was firmly in the camp of those who wanted a more independent role for the CPGB, could still maintain in a speech to the Commons:

> "...... I myself am a child of the British Labour Party. I am the product of the teachings of the British Trade Unions. I am a member of the Communist Party because rightly or wrongly it honestly appears to me to be pointing the way through which the objects laid down by the Labour Party are to be achieved." [38]

After the strike's conclusion, he was to proclaim no such liberal notions, and this change of feeling was reflected in a shift in stance by the CPGB leadership.

The part played by the CPGB during the dispute was without parallel. Although there was a pre-strike membership of less than six thousand, communists were active in a wide range of activities in solidarity with the miners. They were the instigators, and often the local activists, in the network of 'Councils of Action' that sprang up across the country. They published their daily paper, the *Workers Bulletin*, throughout the stoppage, , the production of which was itself no mean task, given the close police scrutiny. For their contribution to the struggle they faced particular police harassment, and the CPGB, more than any other labour movement organisation, was dealt with harshly by the state. At its eighth congress, held not long after the end of the strike, the CPGB estimated that about 1200 party members had been arrested during the strike, about a quarter of the entire party membership. This was a proportion no other political body in the labour movement could remotely approach.[39]

Six months before the strike began, in anticipation of the coming dispute, twelve leaders of the CPGB were arrested, including eight of the ten members of the Polit Bureau. Six were sent to prison for a year and the remainder for six months. By their action, the government had effectively silenced some of the movement's most militant and articulate voices. It was in this repressive climate of opinion that the General Strike took place. The full weight of the state machine which was brought to bear on the miners and their sympathisers, was almost without precedent. For the communists, it reinforced their view that when the capitalist class was challenged, even over such a non threatening issue as miners' wages, it was prepared to resort to force to maintain its rule. The notion, so dear to the heart of many labour leaders of a constitutional advance in socialism was, in the eyes of the communists, dealt a severe blow by the events of May 1926. The Labour leadership's constant calls during the dispute for respect for law and order damned them in the eyes of the CPGB. The General Strike led to increasing antagonism between the Labour Party and the CPGB, not only over their respective analyses of the strike but also because of the labour leadership's conduct during the dispute. This conduct pushed the communists further towards a position that did not differentiate between the Labour Party and other capitalist parties.

The calling off of the strike after only nine days by the TUC General Council was considered by the communists to be an act of betrayal towards the miners. In a statement published in the *Workers Bulletin*, the Central Committee of the CPGB declared, "...... the General Council's decision to call off the General Strike is the greatest crime that has ever been permitted, not only against the miners, but against the Working Class of Great Britain and the whole world ......"[40] In the wake of this surrender the communists' strategy was, on the one hand, to urge the miners to refuse to return to work, and on the other, to win the rank and file of the labour movement for a continuing struggle on the miners' behalf. The CPGB called for immediate emergency meetings of all strike committees and councils of action, to continue the battle and force the leaders to do so.[41] The miners did continue with their efforts for a further six months, but without the support of the leadership of the labour movement, they had little chance of success, and they were ultimately starved back to work at lower wages and longer hours.

The CPGB, for its role in the dispute, won some acclaim from amongst the most militant sections of the working class. In the mining areas particularly, the party grew in numbers and influence. By the time of the eighth congress in October 1926, the CPGB had doubled in size, (to ten thousand) and for the first time since the party's formation, the membership was into five figures. The five thousand recruits, many of whom were miners, did not stay for long. They had been recruited on a wave of enthusiasm generated by the strike, and once that collapsed, they left the party equally as quickly.

Apart from generally strengthening the anti-Labour Party views held by the communists, the strike also led to an essential change in CPGB policy. Since the party's establishment, the communists had consistently argued for the return of a Labour government. This had been their policy at three general elections. On the eve of the strike, a party statement linked the ensuing struggle with the need for a change of government. The communists argued that the strike could not be brought to a successful conclusion unless the Tories were defeated and a Labour government returned.[42]

By the strike's termination, this was no longer CPGB policy. The Executive Committee in a full statement entitled 'Why the Strike Failed', dropped from its list of demands the return of a Labour government. Instead, the party called, as a priority, for a change of leadership in the labour movement. The communists, again using new line rhetoric, called the Labour leaders, "agents of Capitalism within the Labour Movement".[43] It was no longer considered desirable that the Labour Party, under its present leadership, should be returned to power. The communists argued that the strike had shown that the leadership was incapable of utilising parliament for progressive change.[44] After the General Strike, the communists no longer demanded the return of a Labour government. Three years before the policy of class against class was officially adopted, the communists had already scrapped a vital plank of their pre-new line strategy.

The strike also led to a continuation of the reappraisal of the Labour Party that was already underway in the CPGB. The communists, at their first post-strike congress in October 1926, advanced the theory that the Labour Party was becoming a third party of capitalism. They maintained that the Labour leadership was preventing the Labour Party from becoming a working-class party, "...... It must be recorded, therefore, that both at the Liverpool Conference and since, and both politically and organisationally the reformist leaders have advanced a step towards their aim of preventing the evolution of the Labour Party into a class organisation, and of transforming it into a definitely Liberal Party, the third Party of the Capitalist Class." [45] The idea that the Labour Party was another prop of capitalism was intrinsic to the new line, and here once again, an essential concept of that strategy was already present in CPGB thinking some years earlier.

The effect of the strike was that it acted as a catalyst on CPGB thinking. It speeded up and crystallised many of the notions that were already prominent in the party. It led to changes in strategy and increased the criticisms of the Labour Party.

Above: The imprisoned Communist Party leaders on release

James Klugmann, in an excellent summary of the decisions of the eighth congress, linked these criticisms with the events of the nine days:

> ".... to understand the bitterness of this criticism it is necessary to remember the context in which it was being made. The greatest Strike in British Labour history had been sold out, and one of the greatest fighting forces of the British Workers – the organised miners – were being betrayed and left to starve. In October when this resolution was passed, hunger, internal breakaways, the pressure of the general council, were gradually, inexorably, pushing the miners to retreat and defeat. And to the militants and communists who were given everything they had to help the miners, those who claimed to be Socialists, militants, and yet did little or nothing to help seemed to be the greatest traitors of all ......" [46]

It was not long before the CPGB did castigate the entire Labour Party as enemies of the working class, and the communists' march in this direction had been greatly accelerated by the betrayal of the miners.

The fight back against the expulsions

Despite the impact of the General Strike, with all its attendant repercussions, the policy of the CPGB in one crucial aspect remained unchanged. The communists still adhered to their goal of Labour Party affiliation, despite their reservations about the changes that were taking place within that party. The CPGB's assessment of the 1925 annual Labour Party conference resolutions affecting the rights of communists was that these decisions were only temporary, and could be reversed if a good fight back was conducted. This optimistic approach can be seen in the parliamentary report given to the party's eighth congress. The report argued that the exclusion of the communists has not been as successful as was anticipated. In every part of the country, local Labour Parties were refusing to operate the Liverpool decisions.[47] This feeling of optimism was widespread within the party.

The principal hopes of the communists for a reversal of Labour Party policy rested with the newly emerging Left-Wing Movement. This movement, which started soon after the 1925 Labour Party conference, consisted of many local Labour Parties conducting an organised fight back against the conference decisions. The movement was particularly strong in London, and at its peak, it had the support of a large number of constituency Labour Parties. The South West Bethnal Green Labour Party called the first London conference in November 1925. It was attended by ten local London Labour Parties and issued a manifesto – 'The Left Wing – Its Programme and Activities'. From these relatively modest beginnings, a national Left Wing Movement emerged.

The movement grew rapidly during the following year. A second conference was held in Bethnal Green in January 1926, and by this time the number of Labour Parties represented had grown to 50. There were also delegates in attendance from left wing groups in right wing-dominated local parties.[48] The Left Wing Movement over the next few months grew in size and influence, but its most potent base always remained in London. It held two other conferences in 1926. The first in June, was for Labour Parties in the Greater London area and was attended by 148 delegates representing 40 London Labour Parties, 23 left wing groups, and 4 women's sections. The second conference, in September, was a national conference and was attended by 150 delegates. Of these, 73 were representatives of London Labour Parties, and again it indicates how strong the movement was in London compared with the rest of the country.[49]

The movement's rapid growth enthused the CPGB, and the Executive Committee berated communists for not playing their full part. The political report to the eighth congress underlined the importance of the movement for the party and urged party members to play a more significant role.[50]

The same congress continued with the theme that the expulsions and disaffiliations would never work. The communists were, however, concerned that the Labour leadership was attempting to undermine their influence within constituency Labour Parties. They were quite open about their continued involvement in the Labour Party. Only three weeks after the final decision to expel them at the 1925 annual Labour Party conference, *Workers Weekly* reported that twenty two communists had been chosen by the Labour

Parties in London to run as candidates for the municipal elections.[51] The paper even named those boroughs in which the communists were standing. It was an open invitation by the CPGB to the Labour leadership to disaffiliate, if they dare, those constituency Labour Parties where the communists were still very well entrenched.

Throughout 1926 and into 1927 the communists still maintained that their exclusion from the Labour Party was just a temporary set-back. They were optimistic about the impact of the Left Wing Movement, and also of their own success in maintaining communist factions within the Labour Party. In a blatantly open way, they publicly revealed the way the party organised and operated within the larger organisation. The parliamentary report to the 1926 congress spelt out for all to see the communists' achievement in this field. There were, according to the report, something like 150 groups and factions all operating within the Labour Party, and this was by no means a complete total. In London alone there were eighty seven factions as compared with thirty the year before. Sixty-five of these operated and reported regularly as compared to a mere two in the previous twelve months. Forty eight Labour Parties had endorsed the left wing programme.[52] The communists were hopeful that the decisions of the two previous conferences could be reversed in 1926 and the Executive Committee reported that twenty eight different organisations had sent resolutions to the Margate conference calling for the Liverpool decisions to be rescinded.[54] This did not happen, and after 1926 it was to be nine years before communist participation in the Labour Party was again discussed by a Labour Party conference.

The communists were wrong in their assessment of how easy it would be to persuade the Labour Party to revert to its previous position. They overestimated their own influence and also the capacity of the Left Wing Movement to change Labour Party policy. Most serious of all, they underestimated the Labour Party's ability to act on the expulsions once the decision had been made. The CPGB was sceptical about the NEC's ability to enforce a policy of disaffiliation.[54] Their estimation was based partly on the Labour Party's previous reluctance to act against the communists. However, once a decision had been made, and had been approved of at two conferences, the Labour leadership did act and acted decisively.

In London, where resistance to the expulsions was strongest, by February 1927 eleven London Labour Parties and trades councils had been expelled. Disaffiliations continued, both in London and elsewhere, throughout 1927. By the end of the year, it was recognised, both by the communists and the Labour left, that resistance to the expulsions was no longer feasible. Many communists were still members of the Labour Party and remained so even after 1927. But organised opposition was by now virtually at an end, and it was in recognition of this that the communists again continued with their reappraisal of the Labour Party.

The party's ninth congress, held in October 1927, was a particularly decisive one. It was the last congress before the two 1929 congresses at which the new line was adopted. The CPGB was continually reassessing its attitude towards the Labour Party. This reassessment continued at the ninth congress, and contrary to what most historians of the CPGB have claimed, this congress did make essential policy changes towards the Labour Party.

The most important contribution the congress made was that the communists recognised that their exclusion from the Labour Party was emphatic, and the fight back against that decision was now nearing defeat. They admitted for the first time that the threat of disaffiliation was forcing many Labour Parties to operate a ban on communists and that local Labour Parties had applied the Liverpool decisions. Twenty four Labour Parties and Labour Party sections had been disaffiliated for refusing to do so, or on other pretexts. However, a few relatively important Labour Parties had not yet applied the decisions and had so far managed to avoid disaffiliation.[55] This recognition, that for the time being they could no longer operate within the Labour Party led the communists to revise their strategy further. On two important issues, the ninth congress marked a complete break with previous communist policy. These issues were electoral strategy and the need for a Labour government.

The 9th Congress decided that in future the return of a group of communist MPs was a significant priority, even if this meant challenging Labour candidates. The resolution on the 'Labour Party and Parliamentary Action' declared:

> ".. in order to effectively combat the policy of disruption and reaction so rapidly developing in the Labour Movement it is of first importance that the Communist Party specially concentrate on establishing a group of leading party members within Parliament at the earliest opportunity. Immediate attention must be directed towards securing favourable constituencies and all the available resources of the Party must be utilised to secure success for our candidates." [56]

The reasons for this electoral challenge, particularly to the Labour leadership, was bound up with the communists' increasing antagonism towards the Labour Party, which took a further step forward at the ninth congress. In arguing the case for communist candidates the same resolution declared:

> "...At the same time the growing middle class and bureaucratic control of the Labour Party which is directed towards making the Labour Movement safe for Capitalism must be energetically combated. This corruption of the Labour Movement has been especially evident in the Parliamentary Labour Party in the support given to the Baldwin Government, in all its anti-Working Class activities.... it makes it imperative for the Communist Party, in conjunction with the steadily developing National Left Wing would haveMovement to make a determined and organised effort to get the most reactionary of these middle class and bureaucratic leaders repudiated by the organised workers in their constituencies, and to have them replaced by militant working class fighters." [57]

Given the Labour Party's 1922 rule change, the communists' new electoral policy would have effectively ended any hopes they may have entertained of gaining Labour Party affiliation. Although it did not say so in the form of a resolution, this decision meant the end of the affiliation campaign. Whatever line the CI may have adopted after 1927, CPGB strategy towards the Labour Party would have had to alter fundamentally.

Utterly unaware of each other's thinking about electoral strategy, the delegates to the CPGBs ninth congress and the CI had come to very similar conclusions. A letter from the ECCI to the congress, which did not arrive until after the congress had finished, had declared that the CPGB: "must make the necessary preparation for participating in the next General Election as an independent Party with its own platform and candidates even in cases where so-called official candidates of the Labour Party will be brought forward against the candidates of the CP. For this purpose it is essential for the CP to make an immediate start with its preliminary work, at least in 20-30 constituencies where the influence of the Party is the greatest" [58]

Apart from specifying the number of candidates, the ECCI letter is precisely similar in tone and content to the resolution passed by the ninth congress – congress, it must again be emphasised, that knew nothing of the CIs desire for a change of line.

The other significant policy change the congress made was over the demand for the return of a Labour government. Since the General Strike, the communists were equivocal over their support for a Labour government. At the ninth congress, these doubts were carried even further. The communists now argued that a Labour government would only be worthwhile once there had been a change of leadership in the labour movement. They did not give unqualified support for the return of a Labour government, as their congress resolution made clear. On the contrary, they argued that the Labour Party was fast becoming a capitalist party, and a Labour government under such leadership was undesirable:

> "... This Congress records that the decisions reached at the Labour Party Conference at Blackpool marked the zenith of the liberalising process that has been steadily increasing in the Labour Party. A strong and powerful Labour Government can only be realised when the Labour Party and the TUC fight in a united manner for the immediate demands and the necessities of the Working Class. This involves a complete change in the present leadership and the replacement of those Liberal Leaders by honest working class fighters prepared to utilise the whole resources of the Movement to defend the workers from the attacks of the Capitalists. Only in this way can the spirit and energy be developed that will ensure the return of a Labour Government basing its whole strength upon the organised power of the working class." [59]

To summarise, then, from the CPGB's formation, there were, within the party, doubts about the primary strategic objective of Labour Party affiliation. Many communists, because of their membership of the British Socialist Party or the Independent Labour Party, were also members of the Labour Party. They saw no conflict of interest in operating in both organisations. Their conception of the role of a revolutionary organisation was in many ways similar to that envisaged by the ILP, ie to push the Labour Party in a more left and socialist direction. For four years, from 1920 – 1924, many communists continued to operate in the way that they had always worked: they combined their activity in the new party with their activity in the Labour Party.

It was the Labour Party conference decision of 1924 that made British communists begin to rethink their ideas about their own role. In many ways, the decision was a shock to the system. The communists did not expect to be banned as individuals; they expected to be able to continue to operate openly in the Labour Party just as revolutionary socialists had done before them. When the decision for their expulsion was made, it forced the communists into a reappraisal of their role. Although they believed that their exclusion was only likely to be temporary, they did begin to rethink their strategy. If communists could not operate within the Labour Party, then the CPGB took on new importance. A vital repercussion of the Labour Party conference decision was that it strengthened the hand of those in the CPGB who advocated the party's leading and independent role.

Hostility towards the Labour Party from the CPGB was further enhanced by both the experiences of the Labour government and the betrayal of the General Strike. Both these events added to the demands for a change of policy that was being expressed by an increasing number of party members. Saklatvala's letter to the Polit Bureau was a reflection of this growing antagonism. The failure of the Labour Party to give leadership in parliament, or outside, led to the communists making a reappraisal of their assessment of the Labour Party as a workers' party. This reappraisal gathered momentum after the events of the nine days. The net effect of the communists' expulsion, coupled with the increasing exasperation at the Labour Party's lack of action, meant that by the time of the CPGB's ninth congress in 1927, severe misgivings were being expressed within the CPGB about the policy towards the Labour Party.

The cut-off point of 1927 was chosen by the author for very definite reasons. Before that year no-one has suggested that the CPGB, within the confines of Communist International perspectives, was not responsible for working out its own strategy. It is only after 1927 that it is alleged that the CI took a more assertive role, and urged changes of policy on the British party. I have argued that policy changes had already taken place and that on several key questions, communists had moved considerably from the stance they took in the early 1920s. By 1927 their electoral strategy was different and would preclude any attempt at affiliation, and there were no longer calls for unreserved support for a Labour government. The Labour government was denounced as an imperialist government, which played a role inpropping up capitalism. In another crucial area as well, the communists were making a reassessment. The Labour Party was increasingly denounced as a party in which the reactionaries were gaining control, intending to turn it into the third party of capitalism.

The relationship between the Labour Party and the CPGB during this early period is the key to understanding why communists so readily adopted the class against class strategy. In many ways, this policy was not such a radical new departure for British communists. Many of the ideas had already been expressed and received support at numerous party congresses. The Labour Party was not yet seen as social fascist, but the communists' estimates of that party were rapidly moving in that direction. All this happened before there was any talk of a change of line from the Communist International.

Notes

1. Report of the Twenty-First Conference of the Labour Party, Brighton, June 21st-24th, 1921, The Labour Party, 1921, p18
2. *Ibid*, p19
3. *Ibid*. p20
4. *Ibid*.
5. *Ibid*
6. *Ibid*
7. *Ibid*, p21
8. *The Communist Party and the Woolwich By-Election*, Communist Party Statement, 1921
9. *Report of the Twenty-Second Annual Conference of the Labour Party*, Edinburgh, Jue 27th-30th, 1922, The Labour Party, 1922, p196
10. *Ibid*, p177
11. *Fifth Congress of the Communist International*. Abridged Report of meeting held in Moscow, June 17th-July 18th, 1924, CPGB. No date of publication,p87
12. *Report of the Twenty-Second Annual Conference of the Labour Party*, p 196
13. Noreen Branson, *History of the Communist Party of Great Britain, 1927-41*, Lawrence and Wishart, 1985, p5
14. *Fifth Congress of the Communist International*, p87
15. Speeches and Documents of the Sixth Conference of the Communist Party of Great Britain, May 17th-19th, 1924. CPGB, 1924, p11
16. *Ibid*, p32
17. *Ibid*, p33
18. *Ibid*
19. Fifth Congress of the Communist International, p86
20. Is it a Labour Government? Report of the Open Session of the Central Committee of the CPGB held at Socialist Hall, Openshaw, on Sunday, September 28th, 1924, CPGB, 1924, p25.
21. *Ibid*
22. Letter from the Polit Bureau to 'All communists attending the Labour Party Conference, contained in 'Report on Revolutionary Organisations in the UK. Report No 275, dated October 9th, 1924. Issue by Special Branch, New Scotland Yard, housed at Public Record Office, PRO/30/69/1/220 (McDonald Papers)
23. *Ibid*
24. Report of the Twenty Fourth Annual Conference of the Labour Party, London, October 7th-10th, 1924. The Labour Party, 1924, p 129
25. *Ibid*, 127
26. *Ibid*, 126
27. *Ibid*, p40
28. *Ibid*, p131
29. *Ibid*
30. *Workers Weekly*, February 6th, 1925
31. Report of the Seventh National Congress, Communist Party of Great Britain, May 30th-June 1st, 1925. CPGB, 1925, pp 32-33
32. Minutes of the Labour Party NEC Sub Committee meeting held on June 23 1925

33 *Ibid*
34 Letter from S. Saklatvala to the Polit Bureau of the CPGB dated October 7th 1925. Contained in Communist Papers. Documents selected from those obtained on the arrest of the Communist Leaders on the 14th and 21st October 1925. HMSO, 1926
35 *Ibid*
36 *Ibid*
37 *Ibid*
38 *Hansard* Vol 194 – 1338, April 21st 1926
39 *Report of the Eighth Congress of the Communist Party of Great Britain*, held at Battersea Town Hall, October 16th- 17th 1926. CPGB, 1927, p 13
40 *Stand by the Miners*, An appeal by the CPGB, May 13th, 1926
41 *Ibid*
42 The Political Meaning of the General Strike. Statement by Executive Committee CPGB, May 5th, 1926, contained in *Workers Bulletin* No 2, May 5th, 1926
43 *Why the Strike Failed*. Statement adopted by Executive Committee CPGB at its extended meeting on May 29th-31st 1926, contained in '*Workers Weekly*', June 4th 1926
44 *Ibid*
45 *Report of the Eighth Congress CPGB*, p 32
46 *Ibid*
47 *Report of the Eighth Congress CPGB*, pp43-44
48 *Ibid*
49 *Ibid*
50 *Report of the Eighth Congress CPGB*, p44
51 *Workers Weekly*, October 30th, 1925
52 *Report of the Eighth Congress CPGB*, p44
53 *Ibid*
54 *Ibid*
55 *Report of the Ninth Congress of the Communist Party of Great Britain*, held at Salford Town Hall, October 1927, CPGB, 1927 p 17
56 *Ibid*, p 96
57 *Ibid*
58 Wire to the 9th Congress from Political Secretariat of the Communist International, October 1st 1927. It did not arrive until well after the Congress had finished. Contained in James Klugmann's notes at CPGB Archive. Folder 8 495/100/392
59 *Report of the Ninth Congress CPGB*, p 97

3 The prophets outcast: the Party Line in transition 1927–29

THERE WAS no attempt by the Communist International to persuade the Communist Party of Great Britain to change its policy towards the Labour Party until the end of 1927. The first full discussion about the British situation did not take place until the Ninth Plenary session of the Executive Committee of the Communist International in February 1928. The Executive Committee of the Communist Party of Great Britain was present during the deliberations and a full report of the plenum's findings, and recommendations were published by the British party. Before that discussion took place, the CPGB had already recognised the significant changes that had occurred over the past year. Due to these changes, the Central Committee argued, the party should continue with its reassessment of the Labour Party and assert its independent rule. This was very much in line with the anti-Labour direction in which the party had been travelling over the past three years. The Central Committee outlined the significance of 1927 in a letter to the membership in which they called for yet another renewal of policy. This letter was sent out over a month before the Ninth Plenum took place. It was called, 'On the Lessons of the Past Twelve Months' and pointed out the changes during the past few years. These were that the workers had learnt from Labour's betrayals, the Labour government (1924), Red Friday (1925) and the General Strike (1926) which had all had an impact.[1] The EC argued that the events of 1927 had proved that the opportunities were there for communists to defeat the reformist leadership of the labour movement.[2] The party's aim must be, said the EC, to become the undisputed leaders of the working class.[3]

At the Ninth Plenum, there were two sets of proposals. A Majority Thesis from the Central Committee of the CPGB, and a Minority Thesis submitted by Dutt and Pollitt. The Majority Thesis argued in favour of continuing with the campaign for Labour Party affiliation and of supporting Labour candidates where there was no communist standing. Dutt and Pollitt's proposals were for an all-out campaign against Labour – to drop the affiliation campaign and to urge voters to abstain from voting where there was no communist candidate. In the discussion that took place a compromise formula was arrived at: although this went some way towards meeting Pollitt and Dutt's demands, it by no means encompassed all their proposals. The idea that the CI intervened in favour of the minority of the Executive Committee of the CPGB in order to change party policy does not give a true reflection of events. This is the argument pursued by most historians of the CPGB during the period.

The result of the Ninth Plenum was not a dramatic departure from CPGB strategy. It confirmed and reinforced existing party policy and made suggestions for a number of changes. As it transpired, the proposals did not go far enough to meet the demands of the communist rank and file. Such was the hostility towards Labour that had built up over the preceding years, that ultimately the membership demanded changes that went even further than the CI or Dutt and Pollitt wished to go. The plenum rejected the view put forward by Pollitt and Dutt that the campaign for affiliation to the Labour Party should be dropped. They urged the continuation of this campaign although it was couched in anti-Labour rhetoric. The CI maintained that the Labour Party had not yet had a complete metamorphosis into a Social Democratic Party of the European type. There was still hope, and therefore British communists should not, "abandon the slogan of affiliation to the Labour Party, as the latter has not yet completely transformed into a Social Democratic Party in organisational structure. The fight for affiliation, however, must be converted into an offensive fight against the treacherous leadership of the Labour Party". The plenum also spurned the idea of telling the voters to abstain from voting where there was no communist candidate. What the plenum did propose was that there should be the maximum number of communist candidates at the next general election. The Ninth Party Congress in October 1927 had already decided that the election of a group of communist MP's was of paramount importance so that the decision of the Ninth Plenum merely reinforced this earlier proposal. What was new was the call for the formation of a 'Revolutionary Workers Government', but even then the communists, at their Ninth Congress, had dropped their demand for the 'Return of the Labour Government'. It was clear that a new slogan was necessary, and this one should be in keeping with their anti-Labour stance.

The Ninth Plenum reaffirmed and strengthened the CPGB's hostility towards the Labour Party and the need for British communists to assert their independent leadership of the working class – but it left many questions unanswered. In the months that followed the membership of the party pushed the leadership, against the advice of the CI, into an even more aggressive approach towards the Labour Party, and nowhere was this more apparent than over the question of Labour Party affiliation. This was the primary strategic objective of the CPGB from its formation until 1927. Even after the Ninth Plenum, with CI approval, it was still the party's aim to achieve affiliation. As it transpired, it was not an ambition that was welcomed by the communist rank and file. They were much more sympathetic to Pollitt and Dutt's ideas.

'Orders from Moscow'

It is generally agreed by all historians and commentators on the CPGB that by the Eleventh Congress of the CPGB, in December 1929, the CPGB had wholly accepted the New Line and had in control a leadership that was fully committed to the new policy. During the two years preceding that congress, the ECCI discussed the British situation at two Plenary sessions (the Ninth and Tenth). Discussions also took place at the Sixth World Congress of the Communist International in July 1928. In February 1929, the ECCI sent a 'Closed Letter to the Executive Committee of the CPGB,' urging changes in the leadership.

There was also one meeting between a British delegation and the ECCI in June 1929, at which a further discussion about the leadership took place. It is not the author's contention that the CI did not make an important contribution towards changing CPGB policy. They did intervene and helped push the CPGB in a more 'left' direction. My argument is that the CPGB was already well along this path without any help from the CI. Some of the important changes recommended by the CI in 1928 had already been substantially incorporated into CPGB strategy. Secondly, the suggestions made by the CI, far from being imposed were often not far-reaching enough for the rank and file of the CPGB, who rejected them as not sufficiently anti-Labour. Finally, throughout these almost two years of discussion, the decisions arrived at by the CI concerning the British party, were made, not based on some abstract universal principle, but on the concrete situation in Britain. This last point was taken up by the CPGB itself, which went to some lengths to refute those who alleged that the New Line was imposed on British communists, in contradiction to the internal political situation. The preface to 'Communist Policy in Britain' (1928), which was a party statement on the New Line, stated:

> "…… this report explodes all the fairy tales and the mischievous assertions of the enemies of the working class that the British Resolution of the Comintern Plenum, as well as all the resolutions of the staff of the World Revolution are 'Orders from Moscow', forced on the sections of the Comintern in the various countries. This report shows clearly in what manner and by what means the Plenum came to the conclusion that it was necessary to change the tactics of the British Communist Party in conformity with the changes which were taking place in the correlation of class forces in Great Britain, as well as in the relations with the British Working Class. This report will show to all unprejudiced readers that, in fulfillment of its function of general staff of the forces of world revolution, the Plenum of the Comintern discussed very carefully not only the general lines of the development of class forces, but also all concrete problems brought to the fore by the interest of the British proletariat at the given stage in the development of its struggle." [4]

The statement shows quite clearly that even after CI intervention, it was Britain's changing situation that was responsible for the change of line. The overriding issue was the party's falling membership, which since the end of 1926 had slumped quite dramatically. According to Pollitt and Dutt, the decline in membership since 1927 made a change of policy a matter of urgency.[5] It was a view which had found expression even before the 9th Plenum, and some party members well away from the leadership had doubts about the softly-softly approach to Labour. In the month before the 9th Congress, one delegate to the Birmingham district congress argued that the united front strategy was responsible for the party's lack of growth, "now that the reformist trade union officials were more and more acting as agents of the capitalists there was room for a review of the Party's 'United Front' tactics, thanks to which many hundreds of revolutionary workers had left the Party in the past." [6]

It was a view shared by the respected woman communist, Fanny Deakin, who had the distinction of being one of the first communist councillors elected in the Midlands.[7]

This idea that it was the changing situation in Britain's labour movement, rather than anything else which led to a change of strategy, was articulated in an important article in *The Communist*, entitled, 'Why Did We Change Our Policy'. The author argued that the new policy had been forced upon the party by the reformist Labour leadership who were intent on driving communists out of the Labour Party.[8] In the face of this new situation, and with no other option, the communists had no choice but to change their policy.[9] It was a view that had been expressed in *Workers Life* some months before. An editorial in the paper, 'Orders from Moscow' claimed that at the January meeting of the Central Committee a majority had been opposed to standing communist candidates against Labour except in certain circumstances. Now, barely three months later, there was general agreement that this should be the case. Why, the paper asked, had such a change of heart occurred? The paper concludes that the answer was to be found in both CI persuasion and the changes affecting the Labour Party:

"It cannot be said that the British delegation and the Executive of the British Party were converted to this point of view solely by the arguments of the comrades attending the Ninth Plenum of the Communist International. The Labour Party Executive played a considerable part in their conversion.

At a time when the Plenum was actually taking place, the Labour Party Executive – in pursuance of its splitting policy – expelled a group of left-wingers in Tottenham, not because they had violated any Party decisions, but simply because they were left-wingers.

"These things in addition to the arguments of the Ninth Plenum have now convinced the whole of the British Executive that even if the Ninth Plenum had adopted its thesis, they would have had to scrap that thesis and adopt the new one three months later."[10]

The ten months, from the Ninth Plenum in February 1928, until the 10th Party Congress in January 1929 was a period of much soul searching by the CPGB. During this time it became apparent that the active party membership was keen for the new line to develop. The communist rank and file effectively pressurised the leadership into taking their anti-Labour hostility to its logical conclusion. By the end of 1928, the Central Committee of the CPGB had taken on board some of the demands of the membership, who were becoming increasingly belligerent as a result of what they perceived as a too softly-softly approach towards the Labour Party by their leaders.

This groundswell of opposition to Labour from the communists was reinforced by the Labour leadership's increasing determination to root out any communist influence within the party. This took the form of further measures against any remaining links that the communists still maintained with the larger organisation.

In the trade unions too the communists were subjected to vilification. Throughout 1928, bans and proscriptions against members of the CPGB and the Minority Movement were adopted by many trade unions, and even trades councils were not immune from the increasing tide of anti-communist legislation sweeping the labour movement.

No contact with Communist International
The CPGB was buffeted like a ship in a storm. The more the Labour leadership moved to the right, the more communist militants demanded a harder line, each pushing the other into a more intransigent position. The result was that by the time of the Tenth Congress, much of the new line strategy was firmly in place and was not to be replaced until well after the CIs turn to a united front.

This internal dynamic within the CPGB which characterised much of 1928, was taking place against a background of almost complete ignorance amongst the party membership of what was the CIs approach towards the evolving strategy. Far from being goaded by the international body into the new line, some in the party leadership thought that the membership was blissfully unaware of the CI's wishes. Orders from Moscow there may have been, but the message clearly failed to get through.

William Rust, a belated convert to the new line, but subsequently one of its most belligerent supporters complained that, "the Party membership did not know that the CI had any opinion with regard to the situation in Great Britain. During the last twelve months hardly any communications whatsoever have been sent regarding the work of the British party."[11] It was a view shared by the leadership of the CI which was also critical of the lack of information passed on to CPGB members about the new policy. The decisions of the 9th Plenum, according to the ECCI, were hardly dealt with in the party press and at party meetings.[12] It adds weight to the view that during this critical time, 1928, the British party was more influenced by internal changes in the labour movement than by pressure from outside.

Rank and file hostility to Labour grows
In order to acquaint the membership with its new policy towards the Labour Party, in March 1928 the Central Committee decided to call several district conferences. These conferences reveal the extent to which, not only was the CPGB rank and file ready for a change of strategy but was also eager to carry the momentum of the class against class policy even further.

The first real shock came at a meeting of the party's largest district, London. An amendment to the ECCI resolution from the district party committee called for the abandonment of the affiliation campaign. Many speakers argued that it was inconsistent to continue with the affiliation campaign and that the Labour Party was already a fully-fledged Social Democratic party of the continental type. One delegate claimed that the rank and file had been faced with problems,' insoluble on the old line'. He cited the example of the Stepney branch where they had been driven to adopt the new policy before the ECCI resolution.[13] It needed all of Pollitt's oratory as the CC representative at the conference to keep the troops in place, and even then the amendment was only defeated by 62 votes to 44. This conference must have sorely tested Pollitt's commitment to democratic centralism. He had to put the CC's case knowing full well that his own view, which he had expressed at the January CC, was to abandon the affiliation fight. Support for the political levy also came in for criticism at the London conference, and many speakers pointed out the inconsistency of urging the workers to give financial support to candidates that the CP was opposing. There were also murmurings against the continuation of the Left Wing Movement, but both these planks of the old party policy were successfully defended.

The revolt against affiliation was put down in London but there were also minor rebellions at other party meetings in Scotland, Liverpool, Newcastle and Sheffield. All reaffirmed their support for the new line. However, again there was some opposition to the continuation of the affiliation campaign and criticism of the political levy and the Left Wing Movement which were both seen as part of the old strategy. As the year progressed, this revolt was to gather momentum, fuelled by the drive against the communists by the Labour Party and trade union leadership.

No sooner had the membership registered its support for the policy change but the strategy was given a fillip by the local election results in Wales in April 1928. In the first electoral test of the new policy, the communists were overjoyed by the results. If they were to supersede the Labour Party as the workers' party, then an important first step must be to win the workers' electoral allegiance. In South Wales, a key area, where party growth during and after the General Strike had been phenomenal, they achieved a mini triumph. In the seats they contested, the communists received almost half the Labour vote. In the election for the Rhondda District Council, the heart of the coal mining area, the communists polled 1689 votes compared to Labour's 2738 – a very credible performance. This was despite the party's apparent lack of any electoral organisation. As *Workers Life* commented, in South Wales the number of votes cast for communist candidates was remarkable, since in most cases not a word of printed matter was used and hardly a penny spent.[14] Although small, this decisive electoral breakthrough helped reinforce faith in the new policy – a faith that was to be given a further bolster by the actions of some trade unions later in the month.

The Executive of the Boilermakers Society, the very union which had sent Pollitt to numerous Labour Party conferences as one of its delegates, decided to ban CPGB members from representing the society. This was in April 1928. Two months later the ban was extended to exclude CPGB members from being elected to any official position in the union.[15] Other trade unions were quick to follow. The Amalgamated Engineering Union, the Boot and Shoe Operatives, the Shop Assistants' Union, and the National Union of General and Municipal Workers, all introduced anti-communist clauses and measures into their constitutions. The London Co-operative Society Political Committee was not to be outdone and decided to send a circular to all members denouncing the CPGB and the Minority Movement.[16]

Labour Party becomes a social democratic party

The Central Committee of the CPGB, in response to this increasing anti-communism, began to waver in its commitment to Labour party affiliation, a strategy still supported by the ECCI. The support for affiliation, which was evident in the early part of 1928, began to falter as the year progressed. At the June/July meeting of the Central Committee, the leadership was split 9:9 over whether or not to continue with what was left of the affiliation campaign. Opposition to the campaign was to harden even further under the impact of the communists' modest success in the Aberdeen North by-election in August, and after the results of the Birmingham Annual Labour Party Conference a month later.

The by-election in Aberdeen was the first communist parliamentary contest since the adoption of the new line. Aitken Ferguson, the communist candidate, did very well (see Chapter 5) and his success increased enthusiasm for the new policy and its electoral fruits throughout the party. The membership, if not already convinced of the wisdom of the new line, was given a further push in its direction by the 1928 Annual Labour Party Conference in October. This conference was described in the communist press as the one that 'rounded off' the work of turning the Labour Party into a Social Democratic Party of the continental type.[17] At the conference further measures were taken against the communists, the most significant being to deprive them of the right to be elected as trade union delegates to Labour Party management committees. This proved to be the straw that broke the camel's back. At the Polit Bureau meeting in October, immediately following the conference, a memorandum from Rust claimed that the Labour Party after Birmingham had been completely transformed into a Social Democratic party, and consequently he argued that the campaign for affiliation should be dropped. His views touched a chord, and the resentment against Labour spilt over. The Polit Bureau the following month, unanimously recommended that the documents for the forthcoming Tenth Party congress exclude the demand for Labour Party affiliation. That decision was unanimously ratified at the November Central Committee meeting, the last one before the congress. This went entirely against the advice of the CI. On two other contentious issues, the payment of the political levy, and support for the Left Wing Movement, the Central Committee decided to continue with the present policy. The leadership notified the CI of the change of policy and were sorely vexed that they did not respond until 48 hours before the Congress. If the CI was pressurising the CPGB into a strategy change, they were rather lackadaisical at ensuring that the changes they wanted were being implemented.

In the short space of fewer than four months the leadership of the CPGB, from being evenly divided over whether or not to pursue the goal, since the party's formation, of Labour party affiliation, was now in total agreement that this should no longer be the party's aim. It was a historic decision and one that owed much to developments that were taking place in the labour movement.

Importance of elections
As if to ratify the party's leadership's change of heart the results of the local elections the following month further convinced them that the new line offered the party a new lease of life. An editorial in *Workers Life* emphasised the importance of the electoral struggle in the implementation of the new line, stating "it is very fitting that the immediate reply of the Communist Party to the Birmingham Conference should be energetic preparations for independent participation in the November municipal

elections on an unprecedented scale "[18] Although the contests were limited, once again the communists did sufficiently well to support their belief that the new line held potential, and that they could surpass the Labour party as the party of the working class.

Political levy and Left-Wing Movement must go.

If the CPGB leadership was hardening in its approach towards the Labour Party, this was merely a reflection and response to the wholesale race in that direction by the party membership. Long before the Central Committee's belated change of heart about affiliation, the membership was expressing reservations about continuing with that part of the old strategy. They also had misgivings about the leadership's support for payment of the political levy and the retention of the Left Wing Movement, both of which were advocated by the ECCI.

In the lead up to the Tenth Party Congress, which took place in January 1929, the pages of *Workers Life* were thrown open to a discussion about the new line. From the letters that appeared, it was evident that the membership was unhappy about the apparent contradictions in the new policy. To continue with the demand for Labour party affiliation was particularly offensive to many of the writers. One reader wrote, ".. part and parcel of the former line was our demand for affiliation to the Labour Party and our support of the Labour party political levy. Our attitude towards these two points is incompatible with the New Line and should now go by the board." [19] This point was raised again and again by those who wished to push the New Line to its logical conclusion, "... it should be obvious to all trained members of our party and of the Young Communist League that after the acceptance of the new party line in the Spring of this year, and the Swansea and Birmingham Conferences we should definitely drop the struggle for affiliation to the Labour Party".[20] Many writers argued that it was a contradiction for the CPGB to fight for the leadership of the labour movement and yet go on supporting the campaign for affiliation, "... no-one welcomed the new party line more wholeheartedly than myself, but what is illogical about it is the demand for affiliation and payment of the political levy. Neither of these can be defended from a tactical standpoint and are a source of danger for the party in the future "[21] Some of the depth of the anti-Labour feeling can be gauged from the following letter:

> ".... can a Workers Revolutionary Party support a party that has been guilty at home and abroad of supporting the enemies of the workers by massive laws, bombs, bayonets and machine guns ? Or can a Workers Revolutionary Party make excuses to the workers on behalf of that party. Certainly not. The Communist Party must fight that party as an anti-Working Class Party. Therefore the Communist Party should not apply for affiliation to the Labour Party." [22]

Many writers felt that for the CPGB to advocate the payment of a political levy by the trade unions to the Labour Party was a contradiction. How could the party implement the new line and smash the Labour Party while at the same time urge workers to give financial succour to 'an anti-working class party'.

One incensed reader wrote, "I have from the commencement of the change of party policy criticised the absurdity of continuing the political levy. My question is are we fighting 'Labour' in earnest or only playing with it." The writer argued that to continue paying the levy was giving ammunition to the enemy. [23] It was an argument that was difficult to counter. The letters published in *Workers Life* were overwhelmingly in favour of the new policy and wished the leadership to go even further. One writer even claimed that the Labour Party served capitalism and was not the third but the first capitalist party. [24] It was a view shared by many of those who contributed to the pre-congress discussion.

If the letters in *Workers Life* were a reflection of the views held by the communist rank and file, then the membership was clearly out of step with both their own Central Committee and the CI. It could be argued of course that letter writers to *Workers Life* did not reflect the feelings of the average party member. Nevertheless, there is other evidence to show that an increasing section of the party was more hostile to the Labour Party than the national or international party leadership. At district conferences held on the eve of the National Congress resentment was widespread, and the prevailing view was that the new policy was not being pushed to its logical conclusion. London, the largest district, which in March had voted 62 to 44 in favour of affiliation, was now opposed. Such had been the swing in opinion against the Labour Party that not one of the conference delegates favoured continuing the affiliation campaign. The London conference voted by eighty one to nil against affiliation. Opinion had also hardened since the March conferece about both the political levy and the retention of the left-wing movement. Previous support had now turned into one of opposition, and the London delegates voted forty five to thirty nine against support for the political levy and sixty three to eighteen against continuing with the Left Wing Movement. [25]

It was not just in London where a perceptible change in party opinion had taken place. In Sheffield, a much smaller district, there was opposition to the limitations placed on the new strategy by the party leadership. Although the Sheffield delegates, at their December conference, voted in favour of affiliation they were opposed to the other two critical issues of payment of the political levy, and the Left Wing Movement. This was despite both the Central Committee and the CI's support for their continuation.[26]

So concerned was the Secretariat of the CPGB at the criticism that the new line was not being carried out, that it issued a statement that was published just two days before the commencement of the . Responding to the attacks in the party press, and at the recent district conferences, the statement implied that any opposition to the leadership was opposition to the CI – which was undoubtedly true. The ECCI, and the Central Committee of the CPGB, were agreed that the political levy should be continued and the Left Wing Movement should be retained, at least until the Labour Party had broken up. The Secretariat statement took to task those who in the course of the discussion had suggested that there was considerable hesitancy on the part of the majority of the Executive Committee to apply the new line completely. This, the leadership maintained, was not the case. The statement argued that the Central Committee, still favoured the political levy and the Left Wing Movement, and these were decisions supported by the 9th Plenum. In a sideswipe at critics of the political levy the secretariat claimed that advocacy of non-payment would put communists in the same category as Liberals and Tories, none of whom would have a say in the Labour Party. In a final, almost defensive move, as if anticipating the belligerence of the congress delegates, the secretariat pleaded that the leadership should not be straitjacketed with a policy that was too anti-Labour or to use the code word, too 'sectarian'. [27] In their view of the direction the congress should take, the Central Committee were in unanimity with the ECCI. The Comintern delegation at the 10th Congress was instructed to urge the party to render all possible support to the Left Wing Movement. This was hardly likely to be a popular demand amongst the delegates. Besides, unlike many of the party rank and file, the ECCI wanted the continuation of the payment of the political levy.

The first New Line conference

The CPGB's 10th Congress took place from January 19th-23rd 1929. The decisions arrived at by that congress provide further evidence that British Communists were dissatisfied with the stance taken towards the Labour Party both by their own Central Committee and the Communist International. The Congress resolution was somewhat equivocal towards the Labour Party. On the one hand, it condemned the Labour Party as a bourgeois party. Yet, on the other hand, the issue of affiliation was effectively shelved, with the delegates informed to prepare for the abandonment of the affiliation tactic. [28] This was despite the previous commitment of the Central Committee to drop any demand for affiliation and that, according to Tom Bell, due to technical rather than political reasons. Bell told the Presidium of the Communist international at their post-congress discussion of the British situation that the Central Committee's resolution on the Labour Party to be submitted to Congress had been shelved because it had some faulty formulations and contained many repetitions which appeared in the other resolutions. [29] This was hardly a convincing argument, given that this was undoubtedly the most important of items to be discussed by the delegates. On one issue, however, the resolution was exact, and that was that the CPGB must become the undisputed leader of the labour movement.[30] On this question, all three groups were unanimous: the ECCI, the Central Committee of the CPGB, and the party membership, were all adamant that the party must assert its independent role. The differences arose as to how that leadership should be asserted.

The rank and file of the CPGB showed its independence during the congress discussion that took place around the retention of the Left Wing Movement. For many communists, it was a contradiction that they should condemn the Labour Party, yet at the same time, support a movement that had as its aim the readmittance of communists to the Labour Party. The Central Committee of the CPGB recommended support for the Movement, and this had been agreed to at the Ninth Plenum. The party membership rejected the advice both of its own Central Committee, and the ECCI and delegates voted narrowly to disband the Left Wing Movement. It was a move that was supported by those in the party who had been most involved with the Labour left. Ralph Bond, who had been the secretary of the National Left Wing Movement, spoke in favour of its disbandment. It was yet another indication of the antagonism towards Labour that was felt, even by those most associated with the affiliation campaign.

'Right Mistakes'

On many issues, the results of the 10th Congress were unclear. The campaign for affiliation was left in limbo, and support for the political levy, although policy, was hedged around with certain conditions. The Left Wing Movement had been abandoned. Communists were determined that the Labour Party must be broken, but they were as yet unsure as to how this was to be achieved. Their conference resolution might confidently declare, "...... the New Line involves a far reaching change in the methods and forms of struggle against reformism in general and must be expressed in the everyday struggles of the working class as well as in general political questions." [31] Yet they had not as yet carried the new line to its logical conclusion. It was the CPGB membership that played a significant role in the following year, along with the CI, in pushing the party leadership into outright opposition to Labour. At the same time, the rank and file demanded a Central Committee that would be committed to the new policy. That this would be a possible option was hinted at by *Workers Life* soon after the 10th Congress. The paper told its readers that at the congress there were 'right mistakes and hesitations' and the New Executive would go into office conscious of the fact that the party membership supported the vigorous application of the New Line. [32]

No sooner had the congress finished, but the up and coming leaders were making optimistic estimates of its results. With an eye on the CI, both Pollitt and Rust were adamant that the congress had been a great success. Rust claimed that the delegates were far in advance of the leadership in both their understanding and support for the new line. This theme of his that the Central Committee was holding back the new line supporting membership was one that he was to develop further as the year progressed. In Rust's view, there was a marked difference between the congress delegates, who gave 'militant support for class against class', and the leadership. So different were the attitudes that for Rust the defining theme of the congress was the division between the leadership and the membership:

> "I can tell you that after three days of the Central Committee, to go into the opening of the Congress was just like a breath of fresh air. The attitude of the delegates was so different to the attitude of the Central Committee, that right throughout the Congress we saw the Central Committee versus the delegates".[33]

For Rust, the solution was a change of leadership. He believed this would reactivate the party and stem the loss of membership – party membership had fallen by 50% in the past year This was a view he stuck with doggedly throughout the internecine struggles of 1929. Pollitt was also pleased with the outcome of the congress, and described it as 'the best ever', although like Rust he was concerned at the party's decline. For Pollitt, this was not so much due to a lack of leadership, although he wanted a more proletarian Central Committee, but rather the low quality of the party press, notably *Workers Life*. Pollitt thought the paper concentrated too much on high political questions.[34] Instead, it should be giving leadership and inspiration in the day to day struggles of the workers. It was a criticism that was too little too late, as Pollitt surely knew. *Workers Life* was not long for this world, being discontinued within the year in favour of the *Daily Worker*. One of the demands of both the congress delegates and the CI had been for a *daily* communist paper, which was an essential requirement of the new line.

'Falls outs' on the Central Committee

Although there were public pronouncements by the party leadership on the merits of the congress, there were still serious disagreements. These first emerged publicly in *Workers Life* in March 1929. A bitter ideological opponent of Bill Rust was JR Campbell, who queried Rust's view that the new line was built on the swing to the left of the working class.[35] Campbell, in response to a letter from Rust where he argued this theme, claimed that although there was a swing to the left, this was not always in a straight line. Campbell's idea – and it was to be graphically illustrated a few months later when Labour won the general election – was that workers do not immediately stop supporting social democracy and instantly switch to communism – it was more of a gradual process. What emerges from the disagreement is not so much the fine line of inner-party struggle, but the lengths to which one of the protagonists would go to make a point. Rust complained to the editor that his letter had been cut by a third, and in recompense he was allowed to submit, not another uncut letter, but an article. Campbell was given no such privilege. However, Rust was not to have it all his own way. An editorial comment in the paper accused him, and others, of selfishness. His original letter was, the editor claimed, too wordy – that was why it was cut. In addition, the paper commented, "we fail to see why he and other comrades should expect us to print their discourses in full when letters from workers in the factories and mines are crowded out."[36] It was a telling jibe at someone who repeatedly demanded more workers' participation in the running and leadership of the party.

More disagreements were to follow. At two March meetings of the Central Committee called to discuss a closed letter from the ECCI to the CPGB, there were personal attacks of a particularly vindictive nature. The 'Closed Letter', which was issued on February 17 1929, was very critical of the CPGB leadership. Campbell, when introducing the letter, suggested that the ECCI letter, plus the leadership's response, be sent to all party members. Despite disagreement from Tapsell, the leader of the Young Communist League who wanted wholesale acceptance of the ECCI recommendations, this was agreed. It was in the discussion around its acceptance that some of the most biting remarks were made. Arthur Horner, the South Wales miners' leader, in a scathing comment, said of Rust:

"to my knowledge (he) has never had any normal party life, has never seen the working class except in pictures and from platforms, and is certainly not entitled to take up the attitude he is taking up of conscious opportunism aimed at getting into a position in this party, he is not properly entitled to." [37]

These remarks were made in response to pleas to co-opt Rust onto the Central Committee after he had been defeated at congress in elections to the CC. Such a move was also opposed by Andrew Rothstein, who claimed that it was "suspiciously like political blackmail." Rothstein was not too happy with Robin Page Arnot either, commenting that he "personally never had any high opinion of his political capacity."[38] Arnot had just scraped on to the CC after being absent in Moscow for two years. He had not been recommended for inclusion by the Polit Bureau because he was unable to play an active role in the British party.

These heated exchanges amongst the party leaders were to continue throughout 1929, and the struggle around the implementation of the new line was to reach crisis proportions with the calling of a general election for May of that year. On the issue of elections, the Tenth Congress had been clear about the need for a number of communist candidates to contest the general election. It was the participation of communists in the General Election that led to a further development of the new line, and at the same time highlighted the problems posed by this new strategy.

Don't Vote Labour

The Communist Party decided to field twenty-five candidates in the May election, and where there was no communist standing voters were urged to abstain from voting. An editorial in *Workers Life* made clear that the communists supported this policy because of the changes that had taken place in the Labour Party,

"...... the Labour Party was at one time a body with a semi-socialist programme, revolutionary workers were in its ranks as well as the reformist leaders and those masses who are as yet not clear enough in outlook to belong to either camp, it was possible for the revolutionaries to support Labour at the election in order to try to establish through the Labour Party and on the Parliamentary field unity of the Working Class movement – every shred of socialism has now been purged from the Labour Party programme. The process has been gradual but with the publication of the Election Programme at the beginning of this month it has become complete. The Revolutionary Workers have been carefully combed out of the Labour Party – the workers can no longer express themselves in action through the Labour Party. The Labour Party has become a ruling capitalist party, carrying out 'continuity of policy' in every field of work. It is no longer possible for those who wanted a workers fight against Capitalism to support this party. That is why the Communist Party is coming out in open opposition to the Labour Party at this election..." [39]

It was the first time since 1922 that such a call had been made. The decision to abstain had been taken at the Executive Committee meeting in March, and once again was against the advice of the Ninth Plenum. There a similar suggestion had been rejected by the CI. [40]

The ECCI was extremely critical of the CPGB's electoral policy and in a 'Closed Letter to the Central Committee of the CPGB', the International commented on what it saw as a confused, and confusing, approach:

"...... put up candidates, removed them, urged people to vote for members of the Labour Party, to refrain from voting etc., that not only the sympathising workers, but even party members could not make head nor tail of what was our New Line in practise and the Central Committee did not explain to the members what were the causes that led to these vacillations ......" [41]

The policy of abstention was a logical development of the new line and was generally acceptable to the communist rank and file who were looking for some consistency in strategy. It was not, however, a policy that was likely to be sympathetically received by the communists' allies amongst the Labour left. AJ Cook, the miners' leader, summed up the shortcomings of such a policy in a letter to Arthur Horner:

"...... in regards to the tactics of the Communist Party in opposing Labour candidates, I have always opposed this and I feel sure that you can't agree it is the right thing to do. It divides the workers and gives power to our enemies – as you know the next election means either putting the Tory Party or the Labour Party in power. I can't believe you want to return the Tory Party, after the experience we have just gone through ......" [42]

1929 General Election and more 'fall outs'

Cook was right, and the election proved a disaster for the CPGB. When confronted with a clear choice of which of the two parties they wished to govern them, the working class, even the most militant sections, opted for the Labour Party, with all its failings and inadequacies. Saklatvala was defeated in Battersea, his percentage of the poll cut from 50% to 18%. Only three other communist candidates managed to save their deposits. One was Arthur Horner in Rhondda East, who gained 15% of the vote. Another was Alex Geddes in Greenock, who, like Saklatvala, had contested the seat since 1922 and was for a time supported by the local Trades and Labour Council. He polled 20%. William Gallacher also gained 20% of the vote in the contest for West Fife. Nineteen of the other candidates received votes ranging from 0.6% to 5.5%, and two candidates received votes of 7.7% and 6.5%. The total CPGB vote was 50,000. All in all, it was not a particularly impressive performance in the party's first major electoral challenge since its formation. A Polit Bureau statement said that the election showed that the uppermost thought of the mass of the people and the working class, in particular, was the defeat of the Tory Baldwin government. It was of the opinion that the workers wanted to give Labour a chance, but the Labour government would betray them and would be the enemy of the workers. [43]

The poor showing at the general election led to mounting criticism of the leadership by the CPGB membership. The CI too was concerned at the party's lack of support. At the Tenth Plenum, in July 1929, there was yet another discussion of the British situation. Campbell, thoughtful as ever, and in a reflective mood, stated that he, along with others on the CC, had too readily accepted the new line, stating that it was this that had led to failings in its implementation. He felt that although many in the leadership accepted the new line in theory, they did not do so in practice; and he counted himself in that number. [44] Campbell concluded that the party had done poorly in the general election because it had not changed its strategy earlier.[45]

Rust used the plenum meetings to further his case for a change of leadership. Returning to the familiar theme of 'lions led by donkeys', he used the opportunity to applaud the 10th Congress delegates for their unswerving support for the new policy. This, of course, was in marked contrast to the blinkered view of the CC. At the congress, he said the "delegates were more critical and saw the new line more clearly than the leadership. "[46] Horner could not resist the obvious retort that if this were so, why hadn't the congress delegates elected Rust, the guardian of the new line, to the leadership, saying "Comrade Rust has not explained that the Conference which he considered overwhelmingly left did not place him on the Executive in spite of the fact that he claims to be the highest expression of the correct line that we have in the British Party." [47]

However, most were agreed that there ought to be changes in the party leadership. Pollitt was particularly unhappy that the great majority of the CC were party functionaries, and only two worked in factories. The ECCI suggested leadership changes. The present Executive Committee, it declared, was not committed to the new policy, it did not reflect the feelings of the rank and file, and there were not enough industrial militants in leading positions. It was a view shared by the leadership of the CPGB.

More 'Right mistakes'.

In their criticisms of the British party, the CI was actively supported by the CPGB membership, and this is reflected in the views expressed in the party press, and the resolutions passed at a number of important District Congresses. Even the party's official organ, *Workers Life*, admitted to the misgivings felt by many party members. In an editorial, it claimed that the party was in an unsatisfactory situation mainly due to the 'right mistakes' of the leadership.[48] The paper published numerous letters from readers that were critical of the party leadership. The most common accusation was that the Executive Committee was out of touch with the rank and file. One writer complained that the Executive Committee was "apart from the membership"[49] Another argued that Party members were demanding a harder line towards the Labour Party long before it became party policy.[50] But the most common criticism was that the present leadership did not have sufficient faith in the new policy to secure its implementation. One reader summed up the feelings of many when he said, "...... I do not believe the present leadership have any faith in the party's ability to operate the independent line ...." [51]

Coupled with these attacks on the leadership in correspondence in the party press, there were further indications of dissatisfaction in the critical motions passed by several district meetings. At an aggregate of London Communists on July 20 attended by over 300 London party members, a resolution was passed critical of the CC for failure to conduct an energetic fight against the Right danger. So bad was the situation that the aggregate demanded a special congress in October. At another aggregate in Tyneside held a week before the London one there were similar demands. The Tyneside party members went even further, and called for the removal of Pollitt, Horner and Campbell from the Central Committee because they were too 'Right Wing'. They wanted to know who had voted which way at Executive Committee Meetings in order that those who had voted to support Labour Candidates where there was no communist standing, could be removed. [52] In addition, the Tyneside communists were appalled at the 'social democratic general election campaign'. In their view, the severe decline of the party was due to the failure to operate the new policy. A resolution calling for a special congress within three months was carried almost unanimously, as was the call for the election at the congress of a party leadership committed to the new line.

The Young Communist League too added its voice to those who wanted change. At its National Congress in August, the YCL condemned the 'right danger both in the party and the YCL'. The delegates called the present Party Executive Committee 'weak and vacillating in its application of the new line', and there was a call for a renewal of the leadership 'to draw more militant elements into leading positions'.[53]

Demand for a Special Party Congress

Such was the clamour for change from within the party that the Central Committee, soon after the critical motions from Tyneside, London and the YCL had been received, did decide on a special congress. At a heated CC in August the decision was taken to call this congress for November, subsequently changed to December. In the discussion, Gallacher made the interesting observation that he had proposed to the party leadership way back in November 1926 that they pursue an independent line and stand candidates against the Labour leaders. Gallacher claimed that the CC refused to discuss his suggestions, but this was emphatically denied by Campbell. This exchange emphasises that the new line – far from being imported into the British party via the CI – was very much on the minds of at least some in the leadership well before any international pressure for a change of policy. Both Gallacher and Saklatvala, who had made similar proposals a year earlier, were long-established and respected members of the leadership.

Apart from Gallacher's hindsight view of the need for the new line, the August Central Committee also opened up further cracks in what Manuilsky had described as a 'society of friends'. Exacerbated by deep ideological divisions, the personal squabbles amongst the party leaders went from bad to worse. Wal Hannington claimed that there was definite faction work taking place and sited the similarities between the demands emanating from Tyneside, the YCL and London. The London aggregate meeting he called a 'disgraceful affair', a view echoed by Aitken. Hannington's accusations of factional activity were later denounced in an article in *Communist Review* by the Tyneside district organiser, Maurice Ferguson. [54] TA Jackson, in an effort to pour oil onto troubled waters, claimed that there were no significant differences amongst the party leaders, saying "I am of the opinion that here is no fundamental political division in the ranks of the Party – though comrade Tapsell has worked like a hero to create one ". [55]

Jackson, who was to be dropped from the CC at the special congress, wanted a more comradely discussion and urged restraint, "if the idea is that you are revolutionary if you are a hooligan, and are being oppressive, the sooner it is abolished the better . . . . It will cripple the party if it is not stopped."[56]

For his pains, he was accused by Rust of attempting to smother debate: "Jackson, in his street corner speech showed the demagogical attitude of mind which helps to stifle political discussion". [57] It was all too much for JR Wilson, another casualty of the Special Congress. He accused Rust of unprincipled behaviour in trying to persuade Willie Gallacher to connive in the destruction of members of the Polit Bureau and Central Committee who were perceived as too right-wing. Defending Jackson against Rust's allegations, Wilson declared, "it is not half so unprincipled as writing letters to comrade Willie Gallacher suggesting that certain members of the PB and CC should be destroyed." [58] Despite the misgivings of some of the Central Committee the majority, sixteen, voted in favour of a special congress and also to call a series of conferences and district aggregates to discuss the difficult situation in the party.

These decisions were conveyed to the party membership through *Workers Life*. The leadership also agreed to issue a statement concerning the 'right mistakes' of the CC. In the lead up to the special congress, the criticisms expressed at the grassroots level were now articulated by those in the leadership who wanted to harness the dissatisfaction amongst the rank and file and push the CPGB's commitment to class against class to what they saw as its logical conclusion.

The key to this was the election of a new party leadership, but this itself posed problems. Both the CC and the rank and file were keen on changes that would make the leadership more proletarian and, as if the two were inseparable, more committed to the new line. Serious misgivings had already been expressed about the composition of the Central Committee. Concrete proposals now began to emerge from the districts as to how positive changes could be brought about. The West Wales regional Council of the party suggested that the forthcoming congress had a duty to elect "an honest, trustworthy, proletarian Executive, not from the ranks of the intellectuals, but from the ragged trousered toiling and suffering membership." [59] According to the West Wales comrades 50% of the Central Committee should consist of workers and the Politbureau should be 80% workers. JT Murphy went even further: he wanted the leadership to be composed of 50% factory workers.[60] This was a view shared by the Liverpool party district, who also wanted the party leadership to maintain its links with the membership by working in the districts. The CC of the CPGB had already made its position clear about the need for a more proletarian CC, and this too was the position adopted by the ECCI. What was not so simple was how this demand for change could be translated into action by the special congress.

Pollitt, at a meeting of the Presidium of the CI in February, had outlined the problems confronting the delegates at the 10th Congress when trying to elect a more proletarian CC:

> "In the last two or three years at our Party Congresses we have been so democratic that we have taken the nominations for the Central Committee from the floor of the Congress. These nominations have been circulated and every delegate has had the right to vote for whom he pleases......... there was from the delegates an insistent demand that the leadership should be based more on comrades coming from the workshops and the trade union movement, but when they had the opportunity to vote for such comrades they did not vote for them......... delegates expressed the demand that the leadership should be working class and comrades who have not been for so many years away from the workshop, and when they had the chance to vote for such men, because they were not such well known figures, have not been prominent in the Party press and not known to the Congress, these comrades were not elected to the Central Committee." [61]

Pollitt's suggestion for overcoming this problem was a recommended list of candidates for the Central Committee which was to be drawn up by the retiring Central Committee. This was the only way he claimed that new, but less well known party members could be brought into the leadership. [62] Pollitt was supported in his stand by Tom Bell. The latter explained to the comintern leadership the difficulties the CPGB leaders faced in trying to overcome what he called, the 'democratic tradition' within the party. Bell was confident though that after the failings of the 10th Congress in this respect the party membership was ready for a new method of electing their leaders.63

While Bell may have wanted a new leadership, one drawn directly from the factories and the workshops, he did not take too kindly to such criticisms of the CPGB coming from CI functionaries. It showed that the leadership of the CPGB, far from being acquiescent playthings of the CI, often argued stoically for their own political position, and were not afraid to confront even those at the top of the international pyramid. In one exchange Bell castigated Khitarov of the EC of the Young Communist International for his attacks of the British party and called him nothing more than a 'Party clerk.':

> "Comrade Khitarov also severely attacks the Central Committee because of its composition and says that the Central Committee is composed of Party clerks. Since when Comrade Khitarov did you work in a factory or a workshop. Since when have you been anything else but a Party clerk? The Central Committee of our Party are workers to a man, coming from the working class......This is absolutely irresponsible

talk. There is not a single comrade here in this Presidium against whom you could not level the same charge. They are functionaries, 'clerks of the CI'"[64]

In the run-up to the special congress, the conflict on the CC was sharp and acrimonious and reflected the sense of urgency felt by the membership for a new leadership. Neither the CC nor the rank and file questioned the correctness of the new policy. It was the implementation that was the problem, not the soundness of the strategy. It was felt that as soon as a leadership could be installed that was committed to class against class, all would be well, and the party would grow. To get that leadership meant a falling out amongst the 'society of friends', and in the process, new faces were to emerge and old ones disappear.

'Battlegrounds'

The CC meetings preceding the special congress were veritable battlegrounds with harsh words being spoken on all sides in the struggle to ensure a leadership worthy of class against class. At the September meeting so tense was the atmosphere that Pollitt proposed an adjournment for an hour in an effort to cool things off. He was defeated. Campbell, earlier on in the meeting, had warned that the way the discussion was progressing could lead to factionalism along the lines that had happened in the American Communist Party. Frank Bright, who was to be a casualty of the special congress, also tried to pacify the proceedings. He claimed, "it is a scramble for positions and jobs," and reminded the rest of the leadership that they had all changed their positions over the past few years. He urged his fellow CC members to stop indulging in personal squabbles, but his pleas fell on deaf ears. Arthur Horner could not resist the opportunity to make a jibe at J T Murphy. Murphy, he claimed, was "the outstanding so called left, who left to go on holiday to 'Royal Bognor' during the Textile Strike ". But Horner too was worried about the way the discussion was going. So concerned was he that he asked to be relieved of his duties at party centre. In a cry from the heart, he said, "I have been driven into a position of disrepute for the honest expression of opinion". For Horner, it was not just personal but political as well. The inner-party struggle was, in his view, paralysing the party's activity. He argued that in the last three months, the party had been less active than at any time in its history. [65]

The 'Recommended List'

Despite the acrimony, the September CC did at least agree upon one thing, and that was that there should be a recommended list of candidates for the leadership that would be proposed to the special Congress.

The struggle around who should appear on the recommended list dominated the October and November meetings of both the Politbureau and Central Committee. Arguments raged back and forth over who was left and who was right. Tapsell and Rust, the most outspoken supporters of the new line, complained that there must be no surrender to the vacillators and that the new CC must be dominated by the left, or class against class adherents. Even Horner, who was, to say the least, equivocal in his support for the new strategy, wanted to include on the new CC those, 'consistent left elements from the old CC'. This did not, however, include Rust, who Horner called "...an automaton. I have never heard him say anything save a recitation." Instead Horner suggested that Rust be sent to do local party work in order to experience working-class life. In that way, Rust would "see the working class elsewhere than on the pictures" So incensed were Rust and Tapsell by these type of comments that they wrote letters to the Politbureau complaining about the character of the discussion. Tapsell maintained that the leadership was capitulating to the right, while Rust accused Pollitt of encouraging the opportunist elements and allowing a "torrent of personal abuse let loose against me." [66]

At several acrimonious October meetings the Polit Bureau finally decided on a list of candidates that at least a majority of the Polit Bureau were agreed upon. This list was then sent to the ECCI for its opinion. What followed was a body blow to those who wanted a clean sweep of all the old CC. The ECCI suggested changes that were anathema to Tapsell. He claimed that the proposals from the international body would shift the balance of the Party leadership to the right. It was "a worse list than the list of the CC." [67] If it was adhered to, Tapsell claimed that it would leave the leadership in the hands of the 'old right.' [68] Not that apparently the ECCI view was the all-important one. Idris Cox made this clear at an eve of congress meeting when he told the CC that the ECCI's view was that the congress must decide on all matters and that there must be no attempt to impose the wishes of the ECCI.[69] Within hours of the pre-congress meeting, the CC finally decided on a list of candidates. It comprised national party leaders and militants from the rank and file. Even at this late stage, Pollitt explained that there was to be no rigidity. The recommended list was only that, and they, the leadership, should test out the feelings of the delegates before making a final decision.

At the special 11th party congress, the demands of the membership were finally adhered to. The old leadership was firmly rejected, and the congress elected a Central Committee that was committed to the new line. Many old faces were rejected by the delegates including Tom Bell, Arthur Horner, TA Jackson, Albert Inkpin, and Andrew Rothstein. In all, only twelve of the previous Executive Committee were re-elected. Wal Hannington, although not on the recommended list, was elected to the new CC by the congress. JR Campbell came in for some scathing criticism from the London delegation who opposed his re-election to the CC. He was accused of associating with the most right-wing elements in the party. He and Gallacher, against whom similar charges were made, survived, but not so Arthur Horner, despite support from the South Wales delegation. This was probably no hardship for the Welsh miners' leader who had already expressed a wish to return to the pits. Pollitt took over as General Secretary, a post he was to fill, with one minor interruption, for the next twenty-seven years.

Even the change of leadership was not without its bloodletting, and an interesting postscript to the whole affair was the treatment of the now redundant party leaders by the young Turks. Albert Inkpin, J R Wilson and Beth Turner, all members of the previous CC were recommended for removal from work in the party apparatus by the Polit Bureau. This was for 'definite political reasons'. Inkpin, on being told of his fate, retaliated, "if there had been a free vote at Congress many comrades in the present leadership would not be there at the present time. "[70] The secretariat, in a more kindly frame of mind, had recommended to the Polit Bureau that Inkpin, who had never worked in industry and had been a party functionary for twenty-three years, be found work in one of the party's auxiliaries. The Politburo rejected this suggestion. Pollitt at the CC pleaded the dismissed comrade's case. He was incensed at what he called "scandalous rumours" being circulated, particularly at the Lenin School in Moscow, that Inkpin kept a pub. Pollitt obviously knew this not the case and defended Inkpin vigorously against the accusations. Pollitt was keen for the party to utilise the experience of the dismissed comrades, but in that he was almost a lone voice. The CC voted by 27 to 2 to uphold the decision of the Polit Bureau, and the three former leaders were made redundant.

The Eleventh Congress was the final part in the radical rethinking that the CPGB had subjected itself to in the previous two years. The party was now totally committed to a strategy of exercising its own leadership in every area of struggle. Thus the CPGB entered the 1930s with a strategy fundamentally different from that which it had adopted throughout much of the 1920s. It was a policy which in hindsight Pollitt believed they should have adopted three years before in the wake of the general strike. He explained to the congress delegates that the turn to the new line had little to do with CI strategy and much more to do with class politics in Britain:

> "to us 1926 has the same significance as 1905 had for our Russian comrades. We should have seen this. The turning point for us was the betrayal of the General Strike, not the 9th Plenum, and, if we had taken then the turn we took in February 1928, we should have been greatly stronger today" [71]

The strategy of class against class and the independent leadership of the CPGB was the world wide strategy of the CI. It is not the author's intention to look at how other communist parties received that strategy, but certainly, in Britain, it was a policy that found a ready response amongst communist activists. British party members, because of their experiences of the Labour Party during the preceding years, were ready for a change of line, but they were by no means passive recipients of such a change. Since the party's formation in 1920 British communists had been steadily moving towards a new policy and it was their call for change, as much as anything else, which was the decisive factor in why the new line was so readily acceptable in Britain.

In bringing about such a change of policy, the CI had played an important part. It did intervene and made several suggestions, both about strategy and the quality of the CPGB leadership. But it was not the sole or even decisive factor in the transition. By 1927 the CPGB had dropped its previous friendly attitude towards the Labour Party and had made many important new line policy turns, before CI intervention. By 1927 British communists were referring to the Labour Party as a 'bourgeois party', two years before the Eleventh Congress. The expulsion of the communists from the Labour party which by that year was becoming a reality meant that a drastic reappraisal of policy was necessary. The decision by the 9th Congress to stand communist candidates in opposition to Labour was the final straw. It meant that the old strategy of Labour Party affiliation would now have to be jettisoned. The Labour Party had made it clear soon after the CPGB's formation that it would not tolerate beneath its umbrella any organisation that sought to take votes from Labour.

In addition, the increasing attacks on the CPGB from within the labour movement led to the party's adoption of a more isolationist and defensive position. This affected the thinking of the dwindling party membership. They were unhappy with the strategy of turning the other cheek. For them, the only way forward was to go over to a full-scale attack on the Labour Party. Once the 9th Congress had started the ball rolling the membership took it up. It carried it with occasional prods from the CI until finally the faltering CPGB leadership, after a suitable purge of its ranks, embraced the new line and carried it to the goal line. The goal was a regenerated CPGB, standing alone and winning the hearts and minds of the working class. Just how successful the new policy was we shall see in subsequent chapters.

Notes

1. Letter from Executive Committee CPGB to all Party members, contained in *Workers Life*, January 27 1928
2. *Ibid*
3. *Ibid*
4. *Communist Policy in Great Britain: The Report of the British Commission of the Ninth Plenum of the Comintern*. CPGB 1928, p7
5. *Ibid*,p161
6. *Workers Life*, September 30 1927
7. *Ibid*
8. *The Communist*, December 1928
9. *Ibid*
10. *Workers Life* March 30 1928
11. CI Presidium Meeting February 13 1929.
12. Instructions for the Comintern delegation to the Conference of the CPGB's 10th Congress Jan 1929
13. *Workers Life* April 16 1928
14. *Workers Life* April 13 1928)
15. *Workers Life* April 20 1928, and June 15 1928).
16. *Workers Life* June 15 1928)
17. *Workers Life* Oct12 1928
18. *Workers Life* Oct12,1928
19. *Workers Life* October 26 1928
20. *Workers Life* October 19 1928
21. *Ibid*
22. *Workers Life* November 2 1928
23. *Workers Life* October 26 1928

24 *Workers Life* December 7 1928)
25 *Workers Life* December 14 1928
26 *Workers Life* December 21 1928
27 *Workers Life*, January 18 1929)
28 *The New Line: Documents of the Tenth Congress of the Communist Party of Great Britain*, held at Bermondsey, London, on January 19-20th, 1929. CPGB 1929,p81
29 ECCI Presidium meeting, February 13 1929
30 The New Line: Documents of the Tenth Congress of the Communist Party of Great Britain, op cit *Ibid*
31 *Ibid*,p59
32 *Workers Life* January 25 1929
33 *Ibid*
34 *Ibid*
35 *Workers Life* March 1, 1929
36 *Workers Life* March 29
37 CPGB Central Committee Meeting March 23-25 1929
38 *Ibid*
39 *Workers Life* May 14 1929
40 Communist Policy in Britain op cit p144
41 Closed Letter from the Presidium of the ECCI to the Central Committee CPGB, dated February 27, 1929
42 Arthur Horner, *Incorrigible Rebel*, Mc Gibbon and Kee, 1960, p206
43 *Workers Life*, June 7 1929
44 ECCI Political Secretariat July 1 1929
45 *Ibid*
46 ECCI Political Secretariat July 11 1929)
47 *Ibid*
48 *Workers Life* August 16 1929
49 *Workers Life* October 4 1929
50 *Workers Life* October 11 1929
51 *Ibid*
52 *Workers Life* December 20 1929
53 *Workers Life* August 9 1929
54 *Communist Review* October 1929
55 CPGB Central Committee Meeting, August 7 11 1929.
56 *Ibid*
57 *Ibid*
58 *Ibid*
59 *Workers Life* September 20 1929)
60 *Workers Life* October 11 1929
61 ECCI Presidium 13 2 29
62 *Ibid*
63 *Ibid*
64 *Ibid*
65 See August, September and October 1929 CPGB Central Committee Meetings and also meetings of the Politbureau. Contained at CPGB Archive
66 CPGB Polit Bureau meeting October 31 1929
67 CPGB Central Committee meeting November 29 1929, on the eve of the Special Congress
68 *Ibid*
69 *Ibid*
70 CPGB Central Committee meeting January 11-12, 1930
71 *Ibid*

DAILY WORKER

Workers of the World, Unite!

The Organ of the Communist Party of Great Britain (British Section of the Communist International)

THE STORY OF "TURK.-SIB." (SEE PAGE 5)

No. 103   THURSDAY, MAY 1, 1930   One Penny

ALL OUT ON THE STREETS TO-DAY!

**Employed and Unemployed Together,
Rally to the Red First of May.
Fight for the Seven-Hour Day!
Aid the Woollen Strikers!
Long Live the Indian Revolution!
Defend the Soviet Union!**

KARL MARX
Founder of the 1st International

Down With the Labour Government

MANIFESTO OF THE COMMUNIST INTERNATIONAL

V. I. LENIN,
Founder of the Communist International

J. STALIN,
Leader of the Communist International

EXECUTIVE COMMITTEE OF THE COMMUNIST INTERNATIONAL

4 Party membership during the Class against class years

WHOEVER HAS written about the history of the Communist Party of Great Britain, from whatever perspective, is clear about one thing – the class against class years were a disaster in terms of party membership. So unanimous have all surveyors of the period been, that this assessment has gone almost unchallenged, and is now an accepted part of the historiography of British communism. Even those historians sympathetic to the CPGB, many of whom are ex-party members, have accepted this orthodoxy. It makes for rather a neat package. The strategy was imposed on the British party by Moscow, via the Communist International, and therefore must have been a disaster.

Membership of the CPGB during this period has not been closely scrutinised. This chapter aims to do just that and to show that, contrary to what others have said, far from the new policy leading to a decline in numbers it actually resulted in a historic upturn in CPGB membership. From 1929 until 1933 thousands passed through the ranks of the party on a scale previously unknown. The problem was not one of recruitment but of retaining the recruits once they had been made. The new line years were extremely productive ones for the new party. At the end of the period, CPGB membership had risen dramatically, and the spiralling decline evident from the beginning of 1927 had been halted.

CPGB membership 1920-28

CPGB membership, since the party's formation in 1920-21, had always been small. For the most part, we are talking about a party that throughout the twenties never exceeded eleven thousand members, and for much of that decade was no more than half that number. On paper, the membership, at the time of the party's second unifying Congress in January 1921, may have been 10,000. However, Tom Bell, the party's first secretary, concluded that actual membership was more in the region of 2000-2,500.[1] Bell's assessment was confirmed by the commission set up at the Fourth Party Congress in March 1922. This commission, which consisted of Harry Pollitt, Rajani Palme Dutt and Harry Inkpin, was instructed to examine, and report on the new party's organisation and structure. Early on they discovered that actual membership was around 2,000, and nothing like the paper figure of 10,000 first mooted by the Communist International the year before.

Throughout the middle years of the twenties, CPGB membership began a steady increase, and by 1924 it was around the 4000 figure. This was in part the result of a recruitment drive at the latter end of 1923 and the early part of 1924. It did not resolve the enormous gender imbalance, and only 14% of the membership were women. In addition, unemployed members made up almost one-third of the membership. A steady trickle of recruits continued throughout 1924 and 1925, again with special membership drives being organised by the party leadership. By the time of the Seventh Congress in

May 1925 party membership had increased by 25% and now stood at 5000 members.

What boosted CPGB membership during the twenties, and led to a dramatic increase, was the General Strike. The nine days of the stoppage in May 1926 and the subsequent lockout of the miners had a catalytic effect on recruitment to the young party. Communists paid dearly for their support for the miners. The well-documented arrest of twelve communist leaders before the strike began was undoubtedly carried out to paralyse the party and intimidate the membership. It had the reverse effect. Such was the new party's mobilisation on behalf of the miners that almost twenty-five per cent of the membership suffered arrest and in many cases imprisonment in the course of the dispute.[2] The party was organising support for the miners throughout the working-class movement and was giving practical assistance to the locked-out miners and their families. The feeling of betrayal amongst many labour movement activists which set in with the calling off of the strike, only added to the communists' credibility.

Party recruitment, particularly in the mining areas, was prolific. By July 1926 CPGB membership had increased by over fifty per cent, with three thousand new recruits joining the party within three months. New members continued to join and by the time of the CPGB's Eighth Congress in October 1926 membership stood at 10,730. Of these, 3,767, or 35%, were miners. The membership peaked at 11,127 in December 1926. This last figure was based on an estimate after returns from party locals (branches) were reported to the Central Committee in the early part of 1927.[3] A census of the membership which took place in August 1926 revealed that just 14% of the membership were women. The party had doubled in size in the space of six months. But the factor that had led to such an astronomic increase was now in recession. The miners, who had formed the backbone of the new recruits, were now drifting back to work in their thousands, and by the end of 1926, all the coalfields were working. With the ending of the miners' lockout, recruitment into the CPGB began to plummet.

The downward spiral in the membership began in 1927. By September of that year, membership was down to 7,377, which signified a loss of about one-third of members. By the time of the CPGB's Ninth Congress, a month later in October 1927, a further dramatic fall had taken place. Another 1800 members had left the party and membership – at 5,560 – was little more than the pre-General Strike figure of 5000. Throughout 1928 the decline continued. At the beginning of the year, an embarrassed party leadership reported to the 8th Plenum in February that membership was now down to 5000. The first discussions about the new line were taking place against a background of plummeting party membership. There was even more embarrassment a year later at a meeting of the ECCI Presidium, where the differences amongst the leadership over the falling membership were all too apparent. There were disagreements amongst the party leadership as to the reasons for the decline, but whatever the rights and wrongs of the protagonists what was inescapable was that CPGB membership continued to decline, and by January 1929, the time of the first new line Congress, was down to 3500.

Membership of the party's youth organisation, the Young Communist League, which had been established in October 1921, paralleled that of its parent organisation. In 1924 there were 500 members of the YCL, and by the time of the YCL's third Congress in July 1925 membership had increased to around 600.[4] Like its adult counterpart, the YCL also benefited from the General Strike. Membership trebled throughout the dispute, and seventy-five per cent of the recruits were young miners. At the YCL's Fourth Congress in December 1926, membership was reported as being 1800. After that, its decline was even sharper than that of the CPGB. YCL membership by March 1927 was down to 1300 members, and by February 1928 it had declined even further to 1000. So serious was the situation that Bob Stewart, who attended the 1928 YCL Congress on behalf of the party's Central Committee, concluded that in future the YCL representatives should keep the party leadership 'more fully informed of the situation in the YCL'. Stewart reported that the YCL was in a 'bad state of affairs'.[5] This dire state of affairs reached a crisis at the start of the class against class period. In March 1930 the YCL was on the point of liquidation with less than 100 members.[6]

Throughout the latter part of the twenties, since the ending of the miners' lockout, membership of both the CPGB and its youth organisation had been in severe decline. It was precisely this question of falling membership that the new strategy of class against class was meant to address, and resolve. At the very beginning of the discussion about a change of policy, this point was emphasised by both the party leadership and the Communist International.

This was to be the acid test of the new class against class strategy. Would it stop the continual decline in membership, and would it lead to a bigger CPGB? All those historians of British communism, friend and foe alike, have argued with one voice that the new line led to a slump in membership.

There is no doubt that during the first year or so of the new line, membership did continue on its downward spiral. By the time of the Eleventh Congress in December 1929, which installed a leadership fully committed to the new policy, membership had fallen to 3,200. Throughout 1930 the trend continued. Rust told the British Commission of the Comintern in 1930 that the party was in a dangerous situation and was isolated from the masses.[7] Party membership by then had dropped to 2800, and for the first time, Rust hinted at the large fluctuations in membership that were to be a hallmark of the period. He reported to the Commission that since the Leeds Congress 230 members had left the party, over 7% of the membership, while another 180 had joined. In London, the largest district, with one-third of the total party membership, there had been an even more significant percentage turnover during 1929. With a District membership of just a thousand, 250 (about a quarter) had left, while 150 had joined, in the space of a year. It was all too obvious that with the onset of the new line, the CPGB was capable of making recruits but could not retain them. It was a pattern that was to continue throughout the period.

So serious had the membership situation become that on his return from Russia, after attending a meeting of the CI, Pollitt wrote a series of articles for the *Daily Worker*, entitled 'How to improve the work of the Communist Party'. Pollitt's solution to the lack of recruitment was not to scrap the policy but to improve it and to make sure that it was applied correctly. Pollitt posed the question to the paper's readers, "Why in the favourable situation does the CP not grow? Is the line of the Party wrong?" His answer was an emphatic 'no'. He contended that what was wrong was that throughout the whole party the new line was not being applied correctly: the policy of class against class, the policy of independent leadership was being interpreted in too narrow a sense so that the danger of isolation came from a wrong application of the new line.[8] Pollitt was both resounding and transparent as to why he thought the strategy was correct. In the article, he attacked what he called both the right and the left dangers in the party. The right dangers were members who did not believe in the policy. The left dangers were those who interpreted it so narrowly that it could lead to the party's isolation. Pollitt used the paper to fight against both these trends and to reassert to the dwindling membership his conviction that the strategy was a good one and would eventually result in a greatly expanded party.

Just how small the Communist Party was at the start of the new line can be gauged from the following exchange that took place in the pages of the *Daily Worker*. To encourage the embattled membership the paper, soon after its foundation, decided to use the ploy of a 'mystery man' whose task it was to tour the country and to expose those CP locals who were not 'pulling their weight'. The Battersea local was revealed as one such branch. In reply to the criticism, the branch made a spirited response, and the correspondence showed both the dedication and commitment of communists at this time to their party and also the workload that was taken on by a tiny number of people.

The accusation levelled against the local by the party paper, was that in a constituency where over 6000 people had voted communist at the 1929 General election there was no drive for sales of the *Daily Worker*. The assumption was that this was a promising area with an influential party local. However, this was not the case, as the branch in its letter to the paper made clear. There were only nine active party members in the Battersea local and of these several lived in Balham which was a 3d train ride from Battersea. Even in an area which had twice returned Saklatvala to Parliament, the local CPGB was tiny. Yet for all that the effort put in by this small number of dedicated individuals was prodigious. In the two previous months, they had carried out an average of three-door to door canvasses on behalf of the *Daily Worker* per week. They had organised two big indoor meetings and secured several names for a *Daily Worker* committee. Over two hundred posters had been fly posted all over the area. Chalking the streets advertising the paper had been carried out two or three nights per week. The local had distributed over 2000 *Daily Worker* bills. Finally, an effort had been made to persuade local railwaymen and bus workers to read the paper, and a special leaflet aimed at these two groups of workers had been distributed.[9] Clearly, even though isolated and seemingly swimming against the stream, the small party could still enthuse its membership with a sense of purpose.

The one bright spot for British communism in 1930 was that the YCL seemed to have been saved from extinction. In March, the organisation was down to a hundred members. At the May Central Committee meeting, Idris Cox told the party leadership that, despite a previous Central Committee resolution passed in January to help the League, nothing had happened, and the YCL was now in a worse position than at the beginning of the year. Bob Massie, the leader of the YCL, reported that it was in a 'catastrophic situation' and was on the verge of liquidation. The League had ceased to function in Fife, Tyneside, South Wales and Manchester. The only district where progress had been made was in Yorkshire, and that was mainly due to the cotton strike. Even in Bradford, where there were supposedly 150 members of the YCL, these only existed on paper. The League representative at the May meeting was critical of Tapsell and Rust and their leadership of the organisation. He claimed that the YCL had been declining for several years and Tapsell and Rust were responsible for its decline.[10]

Happily for Rust's reputation, by the time the British Commission of the CI met in August 1930, he could report some improvement in the League's fortunes. The claimed membership was now 350, although Pollitt had his doubts about this figure. Pollitt, unlike Rust, was dubious of the League's capabilities and told the CI that members of the British YCL did not know how to talk to young people. The result was a membership figure, according to Pollitt, of 2-300 members, with the YCL exerting, in Pollitt's view, no decisive influence among the working class youth at all.[11] It was a theme he returned to a month later at the September CC meeting. He accused the leaders of the YCL as being authorities on everything except what young workers feel and want.[12] That, according to Pollitt, was the main reason why the YCL had barely 300 members. Despite Pollitt's criticisms, it was an improvement, and the YCL, not for the last time in its history, had been saved from liquidation.

While CPGB membership throughout 1930 looked very much as if it was going in the same downward direction as 1929 and 1928, there was to be a welcome, and much-needed respite at the end of the year. Idris Cox, who was now in charge of party membership could at last report to a Comintern leadership meeting in December 1930 that the spiral decline of the past four years had been halted, and a modest increase had been recorded. The low spot had been reached sometime around October 1930 when membership bottomed out at around 2350. Since then, Cox reported that the membership, in November 1930, was 2555. This was 200 more than the preceding eight weeks but 200 less than six months before. But what Cox did reveal was the long-awaited upturn. He told the ECCI Presidium that while there had been a continuous decline in the membership ever since 1926, for the first time, there had been a break in the slide and there was a minimal increase in membership.[13] The difficulty of keeping a precise track on party membership was highlighted by Pollitt who told the Comintern's Anglo-American Secretariat meeting the month before that CPGB membership stood at 2800. An inflated figure but nevertheless pointing in the same direction as Cox's more accurate assessment. The party leadership must have been jubilant, and Pollitt's prediction seemed to have come true – it was not the line but its implementation that was at fault. Only time would tell if the very modest increase noted by Cox would continue into 1931.

If the YCL was anything to go by, a further considerable increase in party membership was imminent. Although only a small upturn in membership had taken place in the CPGB, in the YCL the growth had been dramatic. From being on the point of liquidation in March 1930, with less than 100 members, Cox could now report, at the same Comintern meeting in December, that the YCL had a membership of 500. This was a considerable improvement attributable by Cox to the YCL's successful application of united front tactics.[14]

What was still apparent by the end of 1930, was that even though membership of the CPGB may have at last been on the increase, it was still predominantly a male party. Of the membership of 2555 in November 1930, 2058 were men, and only 496 were women – less than 20%. The problem of recruiting women members had been referred to by one of the few women members on the Central Committee, Nellie Usher, an upholsterer from Battersea. She had told the Central Committee in July that new women members were expected to be 100 per cent Bolshevik, but they were not. They should be given tasks equal to their capacity. She argued that the terminology used by the party was often unintelligible to working-class women.[15]

If there was a problem in recruiting and retaining women members, the CPGB was also disproportionately a party of the unemployed. Almost one-third of the membership (845 out of 2555) were on the dole. Of these, just under 60% were members of the National Unemployed Workers Movement. The average CPGB member at the start of 1931 was male and had a good chance of being unemployed, or at least have had a recent experience of unemployment.

It was not the factory-based party that the new line envisaged.

1931 was to be a momentous year for the CPGB in terms of membership. The year started with the upturn, first noted by Cox, continuing very slowly, and then accelerating at a rapid rate towards the end of the year. By the end of 1931 the CPGB had a membership higher than at any time since the immediate aftermath of the General Strike. There were reasons for this that had nothing to do with the new strategy. The failure of the Second Labour Government, and the subsequent betrayal of Ramsay MacDonald had an impact. The achievements of the Soviet Five Year Plan, which were in marked contrast to the rising levels of unemployment in Britain, were positively received Finally, a small, but a significant number of militants in the labour movement, were beginning to feel that what the communists said, both about the Labour Party, and the crisis of capitalism, had a ring of truth about it.

The turning point in the year was the Central Committee decision, at its May meeting, to organise a drive on membership. This was in part a response to the slow and inconsequential growth in the party that had taken place over the previous six months. The turnaround of November 1930 had become nothing more than a crawl. CPGB membership in June 1931 at 2780 was only 215 more than at the end of 1930. Of these two hundred odd recruits, most had come from just four Districts, Scotland, London, South Wales and Birmingham. Something had to be done, and the Central Committee decided on a well-organised recruitment campaign. All District organisers were called to a meeting, and the Organisation Department, after consultation with the Districts, set targets for recruitment. A statement giving detail of the membership campaign was sent to all Districts and locals, and was also published in *Communist Review*.

The Central Committee meeting at which these plans were drawn up was described by Gallacher, who was chairing the meeting, 'as a turning point in the life of the party.'[16] Gallacher warned the meeting that they, the party leadership, had the responsibility of turning the party outward.

Pollitt, reporting from the recent ECCI Plenum put the question of recruitment in its international context. According to the Comintern, this was the most favourable world situation for some time for revolutionary advance. Echoing the views of the ECCI, Pollitt claimed that all Communist parties, except for Germany, were failing to take advantage of this favourable situation and were failing to recruit. In Britain, faced with an economic crisis, there had been a revolutionary upsurge, but this had not resulted in a larger Communist Party. Both Pollitt and the leadership of the CI were adamant that this situation could not continue.

So far, there had been little to encourage confidence in the new strategy, but the CPGB leaders were determined that the new line was the way to advance. The May 1931 Central Committee meeting, apart from drawing up a detailed plan of recruitment, also provided an interesting insight into the ideological commitment of the party leadership to class against class. Pollitt was a fine example of this. Although later, in 1939, he was to make a principled, and almost lone stand, against those in the party leadership who saw no distinction between bourgeois democracy and fascism, in 1931 there was no indication of his later change of mind. Pollitt, like most of those on the Central Committee, was unswerving in his support of the 'social democrat equals social fascist' analysis.

He told the Central Committee meeting that fascism and social fascism could not be set against each other, saying "fascism suppresses the revolutionary organisations of the workers, with the support and assistance of social democracy." For Pollitt there was no difference between fascism and capitalist democracy: "if we say that the chief enemy is Fascism we put ourselves in the position of lending support to the social fascists, that bourgeois democracy is the lesser evil as compared with an open fascist dictatorship."[17]

Rust was in complete agreement with Pollitt's analysis. He was particularly scathing about those in the British party, and particularly the party leadership, who viewed the Labour Government as a 'lesser evil' than the Tories.

> "I do not think that anybody will dispute the statement that the idea that the Labour Government is a lesser evil, can also be found in the ranks of our party. If you consider the traditions of the party, and the fact that it was not quite two years ago that there were five leading members who voted that in a General Election we should support Labour candidates, this is proof enough that one of the reasons why our party does not react to the political events is because of these traditions and the feeling which still exists in our ranks that the Labour Party is a lesser evil." [18]

Despite the poor showing so far, there was no hint amongst the leadership that the new line was anything but a recruitment aid. As ideologically committed to the new strategy as they were eighteen months before, when they were elected at the special Party Congress, the Central Committee was convinced that the policy of class against class would invigorate the party and lead to an expansion of its membership. Armed with the membership targets set by the leadership, each party local and district was determined that over the next three months, the period of the recruitment campaign, they would respond to the Central Committee's call and play their part in the recruitment drive.

The recruitment drive was to be the first severe test of the new policy. Would it be possible to recruit? Could the CPGB gain members with its new strategy? The next three months would be critical in determining if the new policy was a liability, or, as the communists maintained, their new ideas would strike a resonance amongst some sections of the militant working class.

The first hint that the drive for membership was having a positive response was a report in the *Daily Worker* from the London party organiser. London was the largest of the CPGB's districts and stretched from the South Midlands to the South coast. In June 1931, with a membership of just under a thousand, it constituted around a third of the entire party membership. Robson, the London organiser, could happily report that with the recruitment drive still not completed the London party had made 243 recruits over the past two months.[19] Official confirmation that things were improving came a week later with a statement from the Party secretariat published in the *Daily Worker*.[20] According to the leadership, with reports in from just four districts (Sheffield, London, Bradford and Tyneside) 332 recruits had been made over the past two months. London proportionately had done exceedingly well. In all, with partial reports in from the rest of the districts, the leadership estimated that so far over 500 recruits had been made. Not an astronomical figure but it did represent a twenty per cent growth in membership in a little over two months.

The Young Communist League too benefited from the CPGB's efforts, though not immediately. Like its parent organisation, the YCL suffered booms and slumps in membership, and if anything its triumphs and disasters were more marked than in the main party. The upturn to five hundred or so members at the end of 1930 had soon lost its momentum, and by June the Politbureau was dismayed to hear that the organisation was again in a critical state. The secretary, Alex Massey, was ill, and the YCL's Central Committee had not met for a year.[21] Readers of the *Daily Worker* however were given a slightly different story. Two days before the Politbureau received the bad tidings about its youth wing, readers of the party paper were told that the League had made 'progress' and there was to be a forthcoming plenary session of the YCL National Committee.[22] Clearly, there were two somewhat conflicting views on the state of the communist youth organisation.

An enlarged Central Committee meeting of the YCL did take place the following month, at which Pollitt and Rust were in attendance from the Party leadership. Some harsh words were said, and some drastic measures were taken. It was confirmed that the League was once again in a critical state despite the favourable conditions that now existed for recruitment amongst working-class youth. There was criticism of the YCL's use of jargon and the sense of superiority which prevailed in the League over the mass of young workers. Some YCL members were accused of being 'armchair philosophers', and the League itself was reprimanded for not taking up the 'day to day issues in factories and pits'. The outcome of the discussion was a pruning of the YCL's Central Committee. Some members were removed because of their 'passivity', or 'incorrect way of working', while newer members who had shown themselves capable of carrying out 'real youth activity' were included in the leadership.[23]

So difficult was the situation in the YCL that it was also discussed at a July meeting of the Politbureau where a three-month recruitment plan, similar to that being pursued in the party, was put in place. The results were remarkable. The London district of the Young Communist League reported that two months after the 'shock plan' had been started it had already achieved its target quota of 120 recruits. This had doubled the membership of the London YCL, which in June 1931 had been 120.[24] The London membership of the YCL by the end of 1931 was 600, more than the entire national membership of the organisation at the start of the year.[25] It was not just London but every district of the YCL which benefited from the recruitment drive. Sales of the Young Communist League's paper the *Young Worker* had increased to 4500 a month. By November 1931 at the end of their very successful campaign for recruits, membership of the communists' youth organisation had risen by over 300% from 471 in June to 1355.

This success was emulated in the adult party. The twenty per cent increase in party membership first noted in August 1931, before the recruitment drive had finished, continued. Idris Cox reported to the September CC that in the last two months there had been 870 recruits, more than in all the previous twelve months.[26] CPGB membership in September 1931 was 3927 – this represented an almost 50% increase from the beginning of the year. The three-month campaign to increase the membership had been an unmitigated success. The aim had been 931 new members to bring the membership up to 3532. This figure had been surpassed and in all 1311 recruits were made, which represented almost 50% more than the target set. The CPGB and its leadership had much to be pleased about: not only had the decline in membership been stopped but significant increases had been recorded. This upward trend was to continue.

Two months later the *Daily Worker*, in an editorial, told its readers that, "everywhere thousands are joining the Communist Party". This was in November a few weeks after the 1931 General Election at which the Labour Party was routed, and a National Government returned. It was not the election itself, but its immediate aftermath that resulted in even more recruits for the rapidly expanding party.[27] The paper's excited editorial reported that in the last few weeks, 2000 had joined the CPGB. Such was the influx of new members that in Scotland, London and South Wales, membership had doubled, while in Birmingham it had trebled. Idris Cox, who had been confirmed in his position in charge of the organisation department, at a November meeting of the

Politbureau, reported that so large had the Birmingham district become that it had been decided to split it into two sub-districts, Crewe and North Staffordshire. In the two months of October and November 1931 CPGB membership soared to 6263 – a rise of over 60% on the September figure – and more was to come. By the end of the year Cox could report a party membership of 7478. Although this represented a 300% increase in the year, Cox was not satisfied. He told the Politbureau that although the paper membership was almost 7500, financial membership, those who had actually paid their dues, was only 1866 which was a thousand less than the year before. Cox reported that the Organisation Department had not been paid for half the stamps that had been sent out. The reason for this, he concluded, was that much of the membership was not organised in cells and groups and did not meet regularly. It was this lack of an organisational structure that was in part responsible for the large fluctuations in party membership that were a hallmark of the period. The other factor, according to Cox, was the way recruits were made. Mass meetings were the principal means, and recruits made this way, experience showed, did not stay long.

Throughout the first few months of 1932, recruitment continued at a rapid rate and CPGB membership peaked at around 9000. Apart from the exceptional period of the General Strike, this represented the highest figure yet attained in the party's twelve-year history. However, this did not satisfy Pollitt who through the pages of the *Daily Worker* told the membership that they must increase their efforts. He claimed that three thousand new members were not good enough given the capitalist offensive.[28] He had adopted a somewhat different stance a month earlier when addressing the CI's Anglo-American Secretariat. There Pollitt had defended the efforts of the British party and argued that because of the difficulties and the profound traditions against which the party had to fight, doubling of the Party membership was no mean achievement.[29] Whatever his true feelings, what Pollitt did reveal to the secretariat was his uneasiness about the type of recruit that was coming into the CPGB. Pollitt was unhappy that so many were unemployed.[30] Pollitt wanted a party with its roots firmly in the organised working class; he was not satisfied with the current state of the membership, which was 54% employed and 46% unemployed. To increase the percentage of employed members in the party, Pollitt stated that the party leadership was drawing up a plan to recruit from specific industries. Also, he stressed the difficulty of retaining members once they had decided to join the party. Both these points, the complexion of the CPGB and the massive fluctuation in membership were to be problems that were frequently referred to by the leadership in the coming few months.

The first meeting of the Central Committee in 1932 paid particular attention to the issue of recruitment and the type of recruit that needed to be made. Gallacher, in his opening remarks, stressed the importance of increasing party membership amongst factory workers and trade unionists. Pollitt, speaking in support of Gallacher again expressed his concern that recruitment was mainly amongst the unemployed. This was to be welcomed but if the party was to grow it was necessary to get recruits mostly from factories and organised workers.[31] Pollitt wanted the party to re-orientate itself and to take up issues concerning factory workers. He was adamant that to break out of its isolation the CPGB must establish itself in the factories:

> "this Party has suffered for the last two or three years from a very heavy dose of communist conceit. Unless our party is firmly rooted in the factories there can be no possibility of winning the leadership of the working class."[32]

At Pollitt's behest, the leadership drew up a six-month plan to concentrate on the four most important party districts – these were London, South Wales, Lancashire and Glasgow. Detailed plans were laid for mobilising in these four districts in the most important factories and trade unions. The district leaderships would have the responsibility for drafting in party members into the selected factories. The entire party was to be involved, everyone 'from top to bottom was to be attached to a factory cell or party local.' Pollitt was particularly critical of those 'leading members' who were unknown in their party local. At the end of six months, he told them if they were unequal to the job they must move on.[33]

The rather disdainful view of the mass of party recruits expressed by Cox, Pollitt and others, was taken to extreme limits by Dave Springhall, another member of the Central Committee. Springhall, speaking about the situation in Tyneside, claimed that of the 200 or so members in the North East only a handful were employed. Because of this, little work was being done amongst trade unionists, there was no Minority Movement and Springhall claimed that when the Jarrow branch was asked to mobilise for a forthcoming strike they declined because they were committed to selling the *Daily Worker* and could do nothing else. In all, the situation was most unsatisfactory, and Springhall castigated the party membership on Tyneside which in his view consisted of "a decidedly disproportionate number of 100% bums and stiffs."[34]

During the class against class period the CPGB was predominantly a party of the unemployed, and this was primarily because of its method of recruitment. It relied almost entirely on the mass meeting as the main way of winning recruits. It was a method that was criticised on numerous occasions by Idris Cox. Cox had little time for this method, which in his view led to large fluctuations in party membership. When assessing the progress of the implementation of the January resolution, at the 1932 June meeting of the Central Committee, Cox highlighted many of the problems faced by the CPGB during its quest to become a mass party in the new line period. He was critical of one of the party's leading orators, Shapurji Saklatvala. Saklatvala, he claimed, could recruit thousands through mass meetings, but many did not know what they were joining. There were many examples of Saklatvala's recruiting triumphs, and they littered the pages of the *Daily Worker* throughout late 1931 and early 1932. Two examples from Scotland illustrate the ease with which the CPGB was able to win over those prepared to listen to the communist case. At a public meeting in Dundee, addressed by Saklatvala, in December 1931, out of an audience of close on a thousand, one hundred applied to join the party.[35] Two days later in the Vale of Leven, two hundred out of an estimated crowd of one thousand signified their willingness to join the CPGB. So successful was Saklatvala that he returned to Scotland a month later, and the ability of the communists to win over new members had, if anything, increased. The *Daily Worker*, on its front page proudly proclaimed, "Scotland's 765 New Communists – Sak's successful campaign". The Indian communist's charisma had not diminished since his last visit, and the high spot of the tour was a packed rally at the city hall in Glasgow. Two thousand six hundred were present and of these four hundred and twenty asked to become members of the party.

While this prodigious rate of recruitment may have been good news to many in the CPGB, and particularly in its leadership, a rather sceptical Idris Cox had his own ideas. Cox told the Central Committee that he was unconvinced by this method of winning new members. In a survey of the ups and downs of party membership over the recent period, Cox articulated the drawbacks of this method of recruitment. Cox's experience was that while many may have applied to join the CPGB at mass meetings, in his experience, they did not stay long. He gave Scotland as an example. Of the large number of recruits made in the early part of 1932, seven hundred had already been lost. The same was true in London where over six hundred of the new recruits had left. For Cox, mass meetings with prominent speakers were not the way forward. He wanted the continuation of this method of recruitment, but he wanted it drastically altered. He had some harsh words to say about Saklatvala's recruiting techniques:

> "A good example of these (losses) are from the mass meetings of Saklatvala. For instance we had experiences in London where hundreds of workers had signed application forms, were approached personally by comrades, and it was found out that they did not know it meant joining the party......in Mid-Rhondda, where 16 signed an application form at one of Saklatvala's meetings, every one promises to turn up, only one did. This is the general experience from mass recruiting meetings in London."[36]

Cox, in charge of the Organisation Department, was in an ideal position to assess the effect of the new line on party membership. For him, the problem was not recruitment, but the ability to retain the recruits once they had been won. There was a massive turnover in membership in 1931 and the early part of 1932. Cox, whose membership figures were always precise, was honest in his assessment of the problems facing the party as it sought to grow. He did not seek to inflate the figures to impress the CI or the rest of the party leadership. Midway through 1932 he compared the figures for the first part of the year and openly admitted that there had been a drop. In January 1932 there were supposed to be 8000 members of the party, but by June 1932, Cox concluded there were only 6000,[37] despite 1500 recruits being made in the recent period. Cox compared the first six months of 1932 with the period of the 1926 General Strike in terms of fluctuation of party membership. He claimed there was a more significant change in the membership of the party during the past six months than since the 1926 lockout.[38] For Cox, the blame for this rapid turnover lay firmly on the shoulders of the mass meeting, which was regarded as the recognised form of recruiting members into the party.[39]

It was a problem that Cox was still coming to terms with some six months later when trying to gather together statistics for presentation to the party's forthcoming 12th Congress. An impatient Cox informed the Central Committee that despite his best efforts the Party Districts were less than open with information about membership figures – this was despite his having asked the District organisers for the figures some two months previously. Once again, Cox was critical of mass meetings and attributed this method of recruitment to the massive turnover in party membership. He elaborated on his earlier theme and questioned whether the unemployed workers that this type of event brought in could ever become real communists.[40] According to Cox, some 2500 'workers who could never become real communists' had joined the CPGB in 1932, while 2000 had left. In the membership organiser's view, there had never been such a high level of membership fluctuation in the party as during 1932.

Despite the new line strategy of building communist strongholds in the factories, 90% of all recruits made in 1932 were unemployed. The lack of a trade union base was a worrying feature and was continually being commented upon by the party leadership. The position was getting worse rather than better, and by the latter end of 1932, only about one in three CPGB members were members of a trade union. This figure had declined since the commencement of the new line. The low percentage of party members involved in trade union work is indicated by the following statistics for some of the most important industrial districts.

Scotland: 1200 CPGB members with 226 in trade unions
Liverpool: 200 CPGB members with 48 in trade unions
Tyneside: 174 CPGB members with 63 in trade unions
Bradford: 108 CPGB members with 31 in trade unions
Birmingham: 230 CPGB members with 57 in trade unions

If the type of recruit being made, coupled with the rapid turnover in membership were problems for the growing CPGB, so too was the lack of a functioning party apparatus. During the new line years, the CPGB singularly failed to place many of its recruits into an organised party cell or local. Joining the party should have meant being able to collaborate with other party members but this did not happen. Most communists, particularly the new arrivals, did not belong to a party unit. At the time of the Twelfth Party Congress in November 1932, of the total membership of 5400, only about 2000 were organised in a factory or street cell. The rest, almost two-thirds of the membership, only came together at local aggregate meetings which discussed general questions, primarily the selling of the *Daily Worker*. This lack of a structure led to acute problems of finance. Dues were unable to be collected, and often party organisers went unpaid. Of the 5400 members at the time of the twelfth Congress, party dues had only been received from 3200.

Although ideally, class against class aimed to have a party based on industry with a flourishing network of factory cells, this did not happen. The Eleventh Congress in

1929, had set the aim of one hundred factory cells by the time of the Twelfth Congress, and this had been achieved, but it meant that just ten per cent of the party membership were organised that way (about 550 members). By far the most significant majority of those located in a unit, 1500, were organised in street cells, of which there were about 100. The aim by the end of 1932 was to develop this form of party unit, not as an alternative to the factory cell but as a supplement. One successful example of this form of organisation that was widely publicised in the party press was the South Hammersmith local in West London. The experiences of the local in building a street cell were reported in the party organisational journal *Party Organiser* and reproduced in *Communist Review*. The activities of this local exemplified both the dedication and grassroots organisation of communists during this period.

To establish a street cell, the local decided to concentrate on half a dozen streets in South Hammersmith, where about three hundred people lived. A meeting was called at a party member's house who lived in the area but only three people turned up – not a very promising start. The group decided to hold 'interesting meetings' in future, with 'political discussions', to which all friends and contacts in the area would be invited. The article implies that previous meetings of the local may not have been that stimulating. A decision was also taken to organise a cell library, where books could be passed around for cell members to read. The initiative met with success. Membership of the street cell grew to twenty-four with an average attendance at meetings of fourteen. There was a marked improvement of dues collection, which must have been a relief to Idris Cox, and dues collectors either collected party subscriptions at the street cell meetings or visited the members at home. The cell organised an open-air street meeting. It was discovered that the local school did not provide food for the children. The cell issued a leaflet attacking the practice, and from this developed a street paper. The first edition sold sixty copies. Issue number two, which concentrated on unemployment relief in the area, did even better, and one hundred and eighty copies were sold. It was so successful that it had to be reprinted, and an additional one hundred copies were sold. All street cell members were encouraged to write something for the paper which concentrated exclusively on local issues. The cell met regularly, and there was always a discussion led by a cell member. [41] By 1933 the London district of the CPGB could boast that from being an area where street cells were little developed, now over 80% of the membership in the area were organised in street or factory cells.

The good example set by Hammersmith was being emulated to a greater or lesser extent in every party district. The aim, which had been set by the Twelfth Congress, was to get the 3500 party members who were not members of any party unit into either a factory or a street cell. For a party which saw Bolshevik organisation as primarily factory-based, the factory cell was the preferred option, but where this was not possible the street cell would have to do. The important thing was to make sure that the membership was involved in some kind of party organisation, rather than being left to their own devices and only meeting other party members at some occasional aggregate meeting. It was hoped that a tighter structure would improve both the party's finances and its ability to retain its many recruits.

The Party's Twelfth Congress took place in November 1932. It was the first congress since the one in November 1929 that had purged the leadership and installed a new one wholly committed to the new strategy. Party membership at the time of the Congress, according to Idris Cox, was 5400. As always membership figures were subject to fluctuation and interpretation and Pollitt later challenged this figure. In his report to the Anglo American Secretariat in May 1933 he felt the figure was too high. In the intervening period, between the Twelfth Congress and the meeting of the Secretariat, Robson, on behalf of the Central Committee, had investigated CPGB membership. He visited the party districts, and he estimated that in November 1932 party membership was 4700.[42] Whichever set of figures are to be believed they were a marked improvement on the previous Congress. On the negative side, the CPGB was still almost exclusively a male party. Only one in seven party members was a woman, and it was still a party of the unemployed: 60% of the membership were without work.

In the three years since the Eleventh Congress membership had increased very substantially. If we take the higher figure, as reported by Idris Cox to the Congress, membership had increased by 2200. At the Eleventh Congress, CPGB membership was 3200. Even if we take Robson's lower estimate, there had still been a membership increase of 1500. In the core period of the new line, from December 1929 to November 1932, the CPGB had grown by either 69% or 47%. In either event, not a bad performance. Even if we date the commencement of class against class from the beginning of 1929, when party membership was 3500, it was still a very credible achievement. The membership decline evident since 1927 had been halted, and a marked turnaround had been made.

Critics of the new line would have us believe that as soon as Hitler came to power, and the CI made its appeal for a united front in March 1933, there was an immediate increase in CPGB membership. This was not the case. The CPGB did make overtures to the Labour Party, but this had no immediate effect on party membership. Neither is it a simple matter to delineate the precise period of the class against class strategy. Just as it took almost two years and two congresses before the new line became acceptable to British communists, so its demise was also gradual. The idea that the British party immediately took up the CI's call for united work with social democrats is not the case. Just as the new line had been a slow process for the British party, so too was the acceptance of the popular front. It was to be almost two years after the first CI directive in favour of a united anti-fascist front before the CPGB would again give even critical support to the Labour party. It was not until the local elections in November 1934, that British communists urged their supporters, reluctantly, to vote Labour. This, more than anything else, marked the end of the class against class period.

CPGB membership from the time of the Twelfth Congress in November 1932, to the CI's call for a united front on March 3, 1933, continued its upward trend. Although membership increased only slightly, it was still going in the right direction. Reports from the party districts in these four months show some variation. Sheffield did very well with a membership increase of over a third – from 333 in January 1933 to 446 in July 1933. Alternatively, of course, it could be argued that the increase was a direct result of the CI's change of heart after Hitler came to power. However, membership figures were, at best, usually a month or two behind, so it is likely that they do correspond to the four months in question. South Wales too showed an increase, with membership up by 13%. London, the jewel in the crown of the party districts, made two hundred and eighty-nine recruits between January and June 1933, and district membership at 1800 was up by 16%. Although complete figures are not available, other districts did not do so well. The volatile Lancashire district, where membership had fluctuated enormously during the textile strikes showed a marked decline. The YCL too, whose membership had reached its peak of 1355 in November 1931 suffered a slight decrease during the last months of 1932 and the beginning of 1933. At the time of the Twelfth Congress, it was less than a thousand, but by December 1932 there had been a slight increase. This had been reversed in the early part of 1933, and by the time of the YCL's Congress in July 1933, the youth organisation had a membership of 850 – a loss of between 100-150 since 1932. But still, the YCL was now firmly established and with a regular newspaper. It had come a long way since the commencement of the new line when it had been 'close to liquidation.'

Despite this marginal decline in its youth organisation and some districts, Cox could still report at the end of 1932 that party membership at 5600 was a small improvement on the Congress figure. This figure stayed stationary throughout much of 1933. What is remarkable is that the CI appeal for a united front, issued on March 3, 1933, did not affect whatsoever CPGB membership, certainly in the short term. on When reviewing the membership situation in September 1933, six months after the appeal had been made, the Central Committee of the CPGB noted that since February of that year, the party membership of 5500 had remained stable and there had been no membership increase.[43] This stability of membership at five and a half thousand did not alter until 1935, almost two years after the CI's change of policy.

The years from 1930-33 were productive ones for the CPGB as far as membership was concerned. Thousands had passed through the party, and in response to the rapid turnover in membership there had now been put in place a structure that ensured that members were attached to a cell – this, in turn, had a beneficial effect on party finances. Most importantly, despite the fact that during the class against class years, there was tremendous fluctuation in party membership overall, the trend was definitely upwards. By 1934, the last year of the new line, membership had stabilised at a figure well in excess of that at the start of the period in 1929. It seems that the proponents of the strategy had got it right, certainly as far as the party's size was concerned. The new line did precisely what its supporters said it would. It halted the downward spiral apparent since the end of 1926 and set the CPGB on an upward path that continued throughout the popular front years and was not finally stopped until the onset of the cold war.

Notes

1. Tom Bell, *Pioneering Days*, p194-95
2. *Report of the Eighth Congress of the Communist Party of Great Britain* October 16-17, 1926 CPGB 1927, p13).
3. See James Klugmann's notes on membership, contained in CPGB Archive
4. James Klugmann, *History of the Communist Party of Great Britain*, Vol 2, The General Strike 1925-26, p354
5. CPGB Politbureau meeting, November 27 1928. 6 Presidium of ECCI, December 12 1930
7. British Commission of the ECCI, August 1930
8. *Daily Worker*, September 1, 1930
9. *Daily Worker* January 24 1930)
10. CPGB Central Committee Meeting May 31, 1930)
11. ECCI Presidium, September 1930
12. CPGB Central Committee meeting, September 13, 1930
13. Presidium Meeting ECCI December 12, 1930
14. *Ibid*
15. CPGB Central Committee July 19-20, 1930
16. CPGB Central Committee May 30, 1931
17. *Ibid*.
18. *Ibid*
19. *Daily Worker*, August 21, 1931
20. *Daily Worker*, August 27, 1931
21. CPGB Politbureau, June 18, 1931
22. *Daily Worker* June 16, 1931
23. *Daily Worker*, July 13, 1931
24. James Klugmann's notes on Quarterly Return on membership and organisation London, June 15, 1931, Contained in CPGB Archive
25. *Daily Worker* September 8, 1931
26. CC September 19-20 1931
27. See James Klugmann's notes on membership, page 11).
28. *Daily Worker* January 20, 1932
29. CIs Anglo American Secretariat December 2 1931 30 *Ibid*
31. Central Committee, CPGB January 16 1932
32. *Ibid*.
33. *Ibid*
34. *Ibid*
37. *Ibid*
38. *Ibid*
39. *Ibid*
40. CC November 9 1932)
35. *Daily Worker* Dec 17, and 19, 1931 36 CC CPGB June 4 1932
41. *Communist Review* January 1933
42. Anglo American Secretariat May 31 1933 P28
43. CC September 8-10th 1933

Left: Saklatvala and Walton Newbold
Above: William Gallacher

Above: British delegates to the Second Congress of the Communist International 1920 Seated left to right: JT Murphy, William Gallacher, Jack Tanner, interpreter, W McLaine, Sylvia Pankhurst, US delegate. Standing second from right, John Reed

5 Fighting 'social fascism' at election time

ALTHOUGH THE Communist Party began recruitment on a much wider scale during the class against class period, can this be construed as an indication of the party's increasing popularity? One test of this would be their progress in the electoral field. However this poses a problem in making a full assessment because, during much of the period preceding the new line, from August 1922 until the 9th Congress in October 1927, the party did not contest elections where it would be in opposition to a Labour candidate. It is, therefore, difficult to draw comparisons. In the earlier period where communists did win seats at either local or national elections, they did so usually, as Labour candidates. This was the case with Saklatvala in Battersea in 1922. Walton Newbold in Motherwell, elected at the same time, although elected as a communist, was the candidate of the local Trades and Labour Council. There were also many communists who sat as Labour councillors. In Battersea and Bethnal Green for example, in the early 1920s, both boroughs had Labour mayors who were also members of the CPGB.

It was during the class against class years that the communists made their first wholesale independent intervention in the electoral field. In pursuit of their strategy of superseding the Labour Party as the party of the working class, they contested on a broad scale, both at the local and national level. They also fought several important by-elections. Their overall objective was to gain the leadership of the labour movement and to do this they had to start to win the support of Labour voters. If they could not do this, then there was little hope of them defeating the Labour Party politically.

The election campaigns in the period highlight the depths of hatred felt by communists for their former allies. During these campaigns the communists spelt out in typical new line phraseology their assessment of the Labour Party, and how it was a greater danger for the working class than the Tories. In electoral terms, during the first phase of the new line from 1929-31, the communists appear to have made very little headway. Their vote was small, and they suffered some lost deposits in parliamentary elections. In most cases, they did not even make a dent in Labour's solid electoral base. If they were to replace the Labour Party as the workers' party, then the election of a group of communist MPs was vital. It was an essential part of the new line strategy and had been communist policy since October 1927. Yet for all these negative features, by 1931 the communists had achieved some positive results. The communist vote, although small, was on the increase, and in two constituencies, Rhondda East and West Fife, they posed a serious challenge to the Labour candidate. It was in the Rhondda in 1945 that Harry Pollitt, although unsuccessful, achieved the highest ever communist vote. In West Fife, Willie Gallacher won the seat in 1935 and held on to it for the next fifteen years. Much of the credit for these, albeit limited, successes can be attributed to the new line strategy, of which the need to build the communist vote was an intrinsic part.

From the Ninth Congress until 1929 the CPGB remained in a state of disarray over its electoral policy. There was agreement over the need to stand communist candidates, but where there was no communist standing a question mark remained over whether the electors should be urged to vote Labour. Over this issue, there was some wavering, and even the most committed of supporters of the new line could not, in the early stages, bring themselves to the point of urging communist supporters not to vote Labour. William Rust was a prime example. At the relatively young age of 28, he was one of the inner core of CPGB leaders, and in the two years of inner-party struggle around class against class, he made constant swipes at the leadership for being hesitant about the new strategy. He continuously chided them for being too right-wing.

Nevertheless, at the first EC meeting in 1928, after the ECCI had made known its intention that a change of policy towards the Labour Party was desirable, Rust was dubious even about CPGB candidates. He thought that they would split the working-class vote and might even lead to a Tory government.[1] Even three months later, after the discussion at the 9th Plenum in February 1928, he advocated as a general rule that workers should be urged to vote Labour.[2] Rust's vacillations were a reflection of the misgivings felt by many of the leadership over rejecting the old policy in its entirety.

Throughout 1928, neither the CI nor the CPGB leadership was clear about what to recommend to the voters in the absence of a communist candidate. The Ninth Plenum effectively sidestepped the issue and Gallacher had some difficulty in explaining the new tactic when writing in *Workers Life*. He stated "from now on we give no active support whatever to Labour Party candidates, except those who accept a real fighting programme of working class demands which we shall propose."[3]

However, at this stage neither Gallacher nor the ECCI could take the final step of urging workers not to vote Labour. "At the same time the Party will not advise the workers to abstain from voting for Labour Party candidates where, for one reason or another, a revolutionary workers candidate is not in the field".

Fortunately for the CPGB, saddled with such disjointed advice for the voters, there was no General Election in 1928, and the first opportunity to test the popularity of the new policy in a parliamentary contest came with the Aberdeen North by-election in August 1928. Writing in *Workers Life* under the title 'Why we are Standing?', JR Wilson explained that it was because of the liberalising process in the Labour Party and because of the anti-communism of the Liverpool Labour Party Conference. A similar line was pursued in a CPGB statement on the by-election. Communists were fighting Labour because of their expulsion from the Labour Party and Trade unions. There was no mention of any global change of policy; all the reasons given for the new line were domestic.

Aitkin Ferguson was selected as the CPGB's standard-bearer in the by-election, and in a relatively short campaign, he did rather well. Ferguson polled 2,618 to the Labour victor's 10,646.[4] The activity of the communists during the by-election campaign was phenomenal. There was an average of 20 meetings a day with an array of national speakers including such luminaries as Harry Pollitt, Shapurji Saklatvala, Willie Gallacher, Isobel Brown, Helen Crawfurd, JR Campbell, and many more. There was a drive to win over women voters, and during the campaign, there were 17 indoor and outdoor meetings, especially for women. It was estimated that about 1000 women attended these meetings. In a party dominated by men, the new strategy emphasised the importance of attracting women members. In addition, there were 19 street corner meetings with a total attendance of over 2000. The party organised ten factory gate meetings, each with an average attendance of between 75 and 100 workers. There were three meetings, especially for the unemployed with 200-300 at each meeting. There were two massive indoor meetings, one with 2000 people present, the other with 3000. In all the party estimated that it had organised upwards of 60 meetings in the area and that during the election campaign about 16-18,000 people had listened to the communist case.[5] During the by-election period, 49 recruits were made for the Aberdeen local. The CPGB were pleased with the result in their first contest with Labour for six years. The ECCI too was elated, and it prompted Tom Bell to send a telegram from Moscow congratulating the party on its first independent contest against the three parties of imperialism.[6]

So ecstatic was JR Campbell with the result that he wanted the CP to fight every constituency 'against a Labour Party that has abandoned socialism'. Writing some months after the by-election and by now an enthusiastic convert to communist electoral intervention, Rust claimed that Aberdeen showed the tremendous support which the CPGB was capable of rallying throughout the country.

The Aberdeen North by-election highlighted some of the dilemmas of communist electoral contests during the period. Now that a sustained effort was necessary to build the communist vote, there needed to be some consistency- but this proved not to be the case. Aitken Fergusen was not a local candidate. His activity had been centred on Glasgow where, with the support of the local labour movement, he had twice contested the Kelvingrove constituency, coming close to being elected on both occasions. There were a variety of reasons that motivated communist intervention in elections during the period, and communist activity in a locality had a very low priority. Communist candidates were shifted from one constituency to another irrespective of local knowledge or commitment. The aim was to increase party membership by such contests, and the campaigns would often be conducted in areas where there was not even a party branch. There were political considerations, too, whether to focus attention on a specific issue of importance or to attack those who were considered the main enemy, the Labour left.

Several leading party members were critical of the CPGB's whole approach to elections. JT Murphy, who for a time was in charge of the party's parliamentary department, outlined some of the problems in his autobiography. He claimed that:

"he made repeated efforts to persuade my colleagues that elections could never be won by running into constituencies at the last moment. But I was always met with the demands of this or that campaign which were all important for the revolutionary struggle ...immediately after the election the candidate was rushed off for other party work to catch up with the revolution, which was just around the corner. If he was lucky he came back to the same constituency in the next election, but the chances are that he would not"

The party's one success, according to Murphy, was Gallacher's election in West Fife, although he wrongly claims it was East Fife. The reason for this was consistency:

"in the whole course of its existence the Communist party has had but one success in elections – the election of Gallacher in East Fife. And there is a special reason. He has been forced continually to go there by the long struggle in the East Fife coalfield. Ten years of struggle in the Fife coalfield gave Gallacher the seat."[7]

Harry Pollitt, addressing a meeting of the CI's Anglo American Secretariat in 1931, some ten years before Murphy's autobiography was published, expressed very similar views. Discussing the party's vote at the recent General Election, Pollitt concluded that Arthur Horner in the Rhondda, and Bob Stewart in Dundee, had made the most significant impact because they had been brought up in the places that they fought and were associated in every struggle that had taken place. In contrast, the majority of party candidates were dumped in places without local connections, and without local records of involvement in struggle. During its class against class phase the CPGB seems to have gone out of its way to adopt a piecemeal approach to elections. Apart from a few cases, there was little coherence of either candidates or constituencies.

The communists' first local electoral challenge with the new policy came in the early part of 1928. In a rather half-hearted effort in South Wales, they contested seats for the local Boards of Guardians. In most cases, despite spending very little money and not issuing any election material, the party was pleased with the result. In some areas of militancy, the communist vote was very respectable. In elections for the Rhondda Urban District Council, they received 1689 votes to Labour's 2738. This was not a bad showing given their apparent lack of finance, resources, and electoral experience. In all, where communists contested seats against the Labour Party in South Wales, they received about 50% of the Labour vote.[8]

By the time of the municipal elections in November 1928, the CPGB seems to have adopted a far more professional approach than in its local Welsh contests earlier in the year. This time it published an election programme, which was particularly good on social issues and facilities for women. It included demands for free midwifery services, free milk and special foods at reduced prices for mothers and children, improved maternity and Welfare Centres, more municipal laundries and Wash Houses. There was a call for the stabilisation of rents and the democratic control of the police and public officials by local authorities. In all, it was a very moderate programme. It may have been tempered by the importance the party placed on these elections, coming as they did in the wake of the Annual Labour Party Conference. The significance of this conference, according to the communists, was that it had completed the process of turning the Labour Party into a Social Democratic Party of the continental type. For this reason, the CPGB needed to make a significant impact on the Labour vote, and the coming local elections offered an ideal opportunity to do just that.

The main aim in the November local elections was to secure where possible communist candidates as candidates of disaffiliated Labour Parties and Trade Councils. The Party weekly gave much prominence to this and publicised those party members who had been so adopted. By October, 200 CPGB and Left-Wing candidates had secured nomination – of these 100 were standing as CPGB candidates, and the rest were candidates of disaffiliated Labour and Trades Councils.

The party was pleased with the election results, although they were varied. In England and Wales candidates polled 10.5 % of the Labour vote. In Scotland, the figures were much better, with 19.5% of the Labour vote, and in the Scottish Parish Council elections better still with 42% of the Labour vote. The party leadership attributed these last results to work amongst the Scottish unemployed. Overall, where the CPGB contested it obtained 18% of the Labour vote. However, there were weaknesses, and the leadership was not slow to point these out. Chief among them was the lack of any real contact with the electorate, which was attributed to the party's isolation. Locals were castigated for not taking up local issues and not linking these with the party's overall strategy. The party leadership was also concerned that there was no consistent campaigning in those areas chosen to contest. There was a lack of any canvassing and public meetings. What was fascinating was the accusation by the party leadership that wards were often contested not because of any consistent work by the party local but because of local hostility to the Labour candidate. It shows once again the popularity of the new line and the widespread dissatisfaction with the Labour Party amongst the communist rank and file.

The local elections in Scotland resulted in a small number of communist gains. The party, in this, the early stages of the new line, still sought to champion left-wing candidates, candidates of local disaffiliated labour party's and trades councils. In this, they were incredibly successful in Scotland. The CPGB in its own right gained seats in Dumbarton, West Lothian, Lanarkshire and Fifeshire. At the same time, left-wing candidates made gains in the same areas. Overall, in the County Council elections in Scotland, the CPGB gained two seats, held on to two others and lost one seat. Their left-wing allies made two gains and retained three other seats. In the Parish Council elections for Scotland, the CPGB made two gains and the Left Wing Movement one gain.

Although the 1928 local elections were something of a success for the CPGB the party's overall electoral strategy, apart from favouring the maximum number of communist parliamentary candidates, did not become apparent until after the 10th Congress in January 1929. Although throughout 1928 the Central Committee regularly discussed all aspects of the New Line (including Labour Party affiliation, the political levy, and the left-wing movement) what advice should be given to voters in an election where there was no communist candidate was effectively sidestepped. Even the party's 10th Congress came to no concrete conclusions over the issue. The Congress resolution was clear only about the need for a number of communist candidates and the election of a Revolutionary Workers Government. There were no instructions to voters as to what to do in the vast majority of constituencies where there would be no communist candidate. It was not until the General Election some months later in 1929 that the

CPGB finally and unequivocally made its position clear.

Preparations for the election had been made as early as May 1928. The CPGB had adopted candidates in 15 constituencies, which were held by what were considered the most right-wing of the Labour leaders. But even at this stage the communists were prepared for a united front and wished only to promote the candidature of 'real working class fighters'. The electoral aim seemed still to be to defeat the Labour Party right-wing. At an aggregate meeting of London communists in June 1928 called to discuss the coming General Election, many questions were asked about what to advise voters in the event of there being no communist candidate. No answer was forthcoming. [9]

As we have seen (see Chapter 3), the 1929 General Election was a disaster for the CPGB. Campbell made this clear when addressing the CI Political Secretariat soon after the event. He assessed that even though the party had made eight hundred new members during the election campaign, it had still not performed well.[10] The poor showing of the communist candidates was a shock to the leadership and further erosion of their credibility by an increasingly incensed rank and file. Its most direct result was not to undermine confidence in the new strategy but to strengthen the resolve of the party faithful that the successful implementation of class against class could only come about by the removal of the old guard. This was achieved, as we have seen, and the new leadership soon changed its approach towards elections. The class against class period was marked by an obsession towards parliamentary contests with the CPGB seeking to contest whenever and wherever it could.

1930 saw the beginning of a much more measured approach to parliamentary contests than had previously been the case. The party's financial ability to contest elections may have been questionable, but their commitment to such contests was total. Throughout 1930, they threw down the challenge at a number of important by-elections. They were unsuccessful, but it showed that, whatever the party leadership may have said, the winning of votes was an essential gauge of the correctness of the new strategy.

J T Murphy was the first to contest a by-election in 1930 in his old stamping ground of Sheffield. His candidature was supported by the Amalgamated Engineering Union District Committee, a tribute to Murphy's popularity in his home town, and his work on behalf of the Sheffield engineers over many years. Surprisingly neither the *Daily Worker* nor the party leadership made much of this union support which was a serious challenge to Labour Party/trade union relations. The campaign itself featured little in the pages of the party paper: there were no reports and no exhortations to the membership to rally behind Murphy's campaign, and only one short article the day after the election gave the result. Murphy had polled less than ten per cent of the Labour vote. The Labour candidate Marshall, with 11,543 votes had won the seat and Murphy with 1,084 votes was a distant fourth. The party leadership attributed the poor result to the workers' failure to be convinced by the CPGB's programme.[11]

Two months later, a lesser known party member, Jack McLaughlan, attempted to contest the Fulham East by-election. However, because of lack of finance and the inability to raise the one hundred and fifty pounds deposit, he was forced to withdraw.[12] No such fate awaited one of the best-known communists and certainly one of the party's finest orators, Shapurji Saklatvala. Sak as he was affectionately known was selected in May to fight the Shettleston, Glasgow, by-election the following month. It was a significant contest for a number of reasons. Primarily it was a stronghold of the Independent Labour Party and Labour Party left; the Labour candidate, John McGovern, was an ILP left-winger; and the previous MP, John Wheatley, whose untimely death had led to the by-election was a veteran of left causes. Wheatley's demise was not lamented in the party paper. In harsh tones that resonated with new line rhetoric the *Daily Worker* reported under the headline "John Wheatley – A Sham 'Left' dies", that, "the passing of Wheatley will not be regretted by the revolutionary workers. It serves to remind us of the pressing necessity of a relentless struggle against these 'left' leaders, who are the most dangerous enemies of the working class."[13]

In Saklatvala, the CPGB had a candidate who as an early supporter of class against class, would not mince his words when referring to Social Democracy. At the beginning of the campaign, he made his position clear. In an appeal to *Daily Worker* readers in Shettleston, he told them that not only was the Labour Party worse than the Tories but that the present Labour Government was fascist.[14] McGovern too did not escape Saklatvala's sweeping condemnation of all those associated with his old party. He was described in the by now familiar term as a 'sham left' who was posing as a left-winger. Ironically it was McGovern who three years later was one of the first to respond positively to the CPGB's call for a united front against fascism – but that was in the future.

One of the interesting features of the by-election campaign was that the CPGB was not afraid to air any disagreements publicly. There was all the usual hype about the communist candidate's certain triumph which included the over the top statement that 'the Labour Party, which expected a walkover is now panic stricken in the face of almost certain defeat'.[15] However, at the same time, in a lengthy article for the *Daily Worker*, prominent Scottish communist, Peter Kerrigan, was critical of the Shettleston campaign. He deplored the poor response of the Glasgow party and attacked the Glasgow YCL for being away at camp rather than participating in the by-election. For Kerrigan, it was all attributable to the 'right danger in an aggravated form'. Whatever the reason, Kerrigan criticisms showed that the CPGB in this period, in some ways the most insular in its history, was not the unified, secret organisation, so often portrayed by its critics.

Kerrigan's more objective analysis of the situation in Shettleston proved correct when the result was declared. In an effort to put a brave face on things, the *Daily Worker* announced, 'Labour scrapes in at Shettleston. Majority down by 6000'. Saklatvala, far from defeating the Labour candidate, had obtained a mere 1500 votes. But that was no mean achievement. Willie Gallacher, in a review of the Shettleston campaign, disclosed that at the outset there was not even a party branch in the area. In Glasgow itself, the CPGB had been inactive for a considerable time.[16] The purpose of the campaign had been to revitalise the party and increase the membership. In this, the communists achieved a modest success. According to Gallacher, a good party local was established in Shettleston after the campaign, and Glasgow comrades had been invigorated. Saklatvala reinforced this message by stating that a party local of 37 members had been established as well as a group of the Young Communist League.

It was evident that the Communist Party wished to repeat its success at Shettleston at other by-elections. Gallacher, like Saklatvala, was whisked away from his roots and presented as the communist candidate in the forthcoming Shipley by-election in Yorkshire. His candidature was announced in September, but then there were no reports of the campaign until the election result itself in November 1930. Gallacher had polled 701 votes compared to Labour's 13,573 and the successful Tory's 15,238. There was no mention in the party press of recruitment or how successful had been any attempt to build a communist base in the area. It was a poor showing compared with the Shettleston result.

On the same day that the communists electoral hopes received a setback in Shipley, Pollitt proclaimed his intention to stand as a communist candidate in the forthcoming Whitechapel by-election. Unlike other CP parliamentary candidates, Pollitt seemed to have no problem with finance. £365 was raised in the course of the by-election campaign which was more than enough to cover his election expenses. There were no appeals for money for the deposit and no question of Pollitt withdrawing because of lack of finance.[17] His nomination was endorsed by a Workers Conference, which took place at the headquarters of the Workers Circle in nearby Aldgate. Unlike Gallacher in Shipley, Pollitt did have some connection with the area through his previous work in the docks. This may have been one of the reasons for his good showing in the election. Pollitt received almost ten per cent of the vote and twenty-five per cent of the Labour poll. The result warranted an editorial in the *Daily Worker*, which applauded Pollitt's success. The paper went on to assert that even this good vote was no indication of communist strength in the area, which had seen many mass meetings and demonstrations in the course of the campaign.[18]

Once again, the emphasis on contesting was not just about votes, vital though they were: there was also the question of party recruitment. The CPGB had been successful in Whitechapel with many recruits for the local Party branch and YCL.

1930 finished on a high note for the CPGB with the party's limited success in Whitechapel. However, things would have to improve significantly electorally if the communists were to supersede the Labour Party as the workers' party. 1931, which ushered in the first upturn in party membership for years, also saw renewed efforts to win votes. The party at local elections became more serious in its approach and was conscious of its failings in this area in the past. In parliamentary elections too during 1931 there was no wavering and every effort was made to contest any by-election that was considered suitable. These were more costly than municipal elections, and although the will may have been there, there was not always the way. The year closed with the party's credible intervention in the General Election. The communists did not receive the vote they expected, but it proved to be a good deal better showing than their previous General Election foray.

The London district of the party emphasised the importance of local interventions and the need for a detailed municipal strategy in a statement in the *Daily Worker* during the first month of 1931. In good time for the London County Council elections, which were to take place in March, the District party committee announced that the number of communist candidates would be more significant than ever before. In another change of tack, there was an admission that previous contests had been too abstract and had not dealt with the issues affecting workers in the locality. To avoid this, the London District Committee was to prepare suitable materials that would convince workers of the practicality of communist solutions to their problems.[19]

Sixteen communist candidates were adopted to contest the 124 vacant London seats. There was good coverage of the campaign and an editorial in the party paper on the day of the election spelt out the importance of a big communist vote to London workers – but all to no avail. The total communist vote in the capital was 2,845.

In an attempt to salvage something from the wreckage of its campaign, the CPGB resorted to the usual gloating over the Labour Party's drop in support. It reported that Labour's vote was down and that the Municipal Reformers had gained seven seats at the expense of Labour. This setback in the party's largest district was somewhat overcome by a good result in the local elections in Wales a few weeks later. The paper reported that the CPGB vote in the area for the Urban and Rural District Councils was up dramatically on the County Council elections of a month before. In the elections for the Welsh County Councils at the beginning of March, the CPGB in those areas contested had averaged 13% of the Labour vote. Yet four weeks later CPGB candidates on average achieved one-third of the Labour vote. In some areas, the Communist vote was particularly impressive. In the elections to the Urban District Councils in Monmouthshire, for example, the CP's four candidates polled almost as well as the Labour Party, with almost 80% of the Labour vote.[20]

While local elections, because of the lack of a deposit required, were relatively easy to contest, the same was not the case with parliamentary elections. These demanded financial commitment. The CPGB was not averse to contesting by-elections, particularly those it saw as significant, but it was not always in a position to raise the money required. This was particularly true in the early part of 1931. Pontypridd in South Wales was the first casualty of the CPGB's lack of finance. On the same day as the London County Council elections, March 5 1931, the *Daily Worker* announced the importance of having a communist candidate in the forthcoming Pontypridd by-election. On that day and virtually every day until nomination day, the paper carried an appeal for money to provide the necessary £150 deposit. However, by the closing day for nominations, almost a week later, the money was not forthcoming, and so the paper sadly announced that there would be no communist candidate.[21]

However, that was not to be the end of the campaign, and Pontypridd voters were asked to write 'communism' on their ballot papers. As recompense, and to bolster up the spirits of the faithful, Saklatvala was despatched to South Wales to weave his magic. His oratory attracted over 600 people to an afternoon meeting in the constituency, and over 1000 were in attendance at a public event in the evening. In a unique appeal, Harry Pollitt urged that the campaign in Pontypridd be carried on even though there was no party candidate. By the lack of any comment in the *Daily Worker* about the Pontypridd result, it must be construed that not many had heeded the party's advice and that there were few spoilt ballot papers. The only hint that things had not gone according to plan in Pontypridd was contained in an article in the paper about the importance of contesting three more by-elections. The *Daily Worker* emphasised once again the importance of such contests – how it "would be a crime" not to contest, but also "don't repeat Pontypridd and limit these fights to propaganda meetings" (*DW* March 23 1931). Whatever the drawbacks, the CPGB, throughout the first half of 1931, continued with the tactic of urging its supporters to write 'communism' on the voting paper in a constituency where there was a by-election, and the lack of finance meant that there was no communist candidate.

In the battle to make inroads into the Labour vote, it was the wish of the party leadership to contest the forthcoming 1931 by-elections in Woolwich in London, St Rollex in Glasgow, and Ogmore in South Wales. In the first two of these contests, finance was again to prove an obstacle, and despite repeated appeals for money, it was not possible to raise the £150 deposit. In Woolwich, the party local even hired committee rooms in anticipation of the campaign. In St Rollex Peter Kerrigan was adopted as the candidate, and unlike Woolwich, there was a sustained effort to raise the money. The Glasgow party organisation was in favour of the contest, and although the money could not be found, once again communist voters were asked to write 'communism' on their ballot papers. Even William Allen, the leader of the United Mineworkers of Scotland, in a late attempt to contest Rutherglen in Scotland in May 1931 could not raise the money for the by-election deposit. It had been hoped that the money would be forthcoming by the organisation of a workers' sports tournament including football and boxing. Sales from tickets would have contributed to the election expenses – but it was not enough. Allen, in an attempt to show up the iniquity of the election deposit system, presented his nomination papers with three hundred signatures supporting his candidature. It was rejected, and the CPGB complained at the financial 'capitalist barrier to working class candidates'. [22]. Other communist candidates unable to raise the money in by-elections included Jim Ancrum in Gateshead and Edmund Frow in Manchester, both in June 1931.

The party's one big success story in by-elections during 1931 was in Ogmore in South Wales. Once again, the drive to raise the deposit was all-important, and only a last-minute loan of £50 from a well-wisher made the contest possible. J R Campbell was the candidate, and an early indication that he might do well came with the news of the increased communist vote in the Wales local elections mentioned above. One of the wards contested lay within the Ogmore parliamentary constituency, and the CPGB candidate received 668 votes compared to the Labour candidate's 1114.

The Ogmore campaign contained some innovations by the CPGB. Even before the deposit was secured, communists organised a pithead ballot amongst the miners who formed a substantial part of the electorate. The ballot asked whether the miners wanted Campbell or a Labourite as their candidate. Campbell did very well and in this unofficial ballot 2719 voted for him and 2234 against. At the same time, there was an official South

Wales Miners Federation ballot taking place over who should be the Labour candidate.

There were just two candidates in this by-election, Labour and Communist. Campbell attracted large numbers to his meetings. At one meeting in Maesteg Town Hall, there were over 1500 people in attendance. At another in Caeran, there were over a thousand. Sakltavala was once again sent on a speaking tour of the constituency and in a piece for the *Daily Worker* reporting on the campaign even he went a little over the top in his enthusiasm for the new line. He claimed that not only were social democrats social fascists but that, "the Labour Government will come out with their machine guns and Fascist supporters to openly fight the British working class."[23] Saklatvala was never one for mincing his words.

The campaign in Ogmore, conducted mid-way through the class against class period, with a Labour Government in power and when anti-Labour feeling and rhetoric amongst the communist rank and file was at its height, yielded very tangible results for the CPGB. Campbell received 5219 votes. It was an outstanding result for a party whose membership, even though on the increase was still less than four thousand. Campbell had increased the communist vote by over 350%. At the 1929 General Election, he had obtained 1525 votes, less than 4% of the poll. This time he polled over 20%. The winning Labour candidate Edward Williams still won very easily, with 19,536 votes, but it was a very credible performance and was by far the party's best by-election result to date. It would remain to be seen if the *Daily Worker*'s prediction was correct, that workers are, 'falling away from the Labour Party'.[24]

The prevailing feeling in the Communist Party that workers had been betrayed by social democracy and that this sense of betrayal would soon spread and find expression amongst the Labour rank and file was undoubtedly not discouraged by the Ogmore result. Another factor that was also important was that the Labour candidate, Edward Williams, had been selected because of his record as a militant. That a communist candidate had made substantial inroads into this support showed, just as the party had maintained with its new line policy, that it was even more important to defeat the Labour left. Ogmore was a very satisfactory result from both class against class perspectives. Not only had the communist vote increased, but it had grown at the expense of a Labour left-winger. Many in the party must have been convinced by the *Daily Worker*'s assessment that 'to get such a big increase in the vote was a fine achievement.'[25]

Not only did Ogmore raise the spirits of those in the CPGB who may have been wondering about the possibility of a communist electoral breakthrough, but in a practical way it also helped build the party organisation. Over the two-month period of the by-election, between its first announcement and the result, the campaign in the constituency had yielded fifty-eight new members of the party, and the Ogmore branch of the Young Communist League had recruited a further forty new members.[26] Electoral intervention not only increased party membership – which was the main reason for standing a communist candidate – but it also now looked like the communists were on the brink of a historical breakthrough in their class against class battle with the Labour Party for the hearts and minds of the working class.

The test of the CPGB's ability to win over Labour voters in any significant number was to come with the General Election of November 1931. It was the disastrous performance of the previous election in 1929 that had led to the changes of party leadership and the election of a Central Committee that was fully committed to the new line. Between the Ogmore by-election in June 1931 and the announcement of the general election later in the year, there were no local or by-elections for the communists to contest.

When the news was first announced towards the end of August 1931, that the Labour Government had split, and that Ramsay MacDonald, J H Thomas and Philip Snowden had formed a National Government with the Tories and Liberals, it must have seemed to the communists that their constant warnings about the inadequacy of social democracy had at last proved correct. With a General Election announced for November 1931, the CPGB, with its limited resources, set about making as great an impact as possible. It was undoubtedly an election that would be fought in the most favourable of circumstances for the party. The Labour Government, even to its staunchest of supporters, was perceived as a betrayer of their hopes for a better Britain. That the most right-wing members of that Government had lined up with the Tories and Liberals to bring about cuts in benefit for the unemployed, only underlined what the CPGB had been saying for some time. If the communists were to try to become the party of the working class, then they could have wished for no more favourable circumstances than those that prevailed in the latter part of 1931.

The major obstacle was still one of finance. By October, the party had managed to adopt eighteen candidates, but it had still not yet raised the money necessary for the election deposits.[27] A week later there was better news: 25 communist candidates had been adopted and their deposits raised. In addition, there were to be a further 15 'demonstrative' party candidates in constituencies that were unable to raise the £150 deposit. There were to be eight candidates in London, seven in Scotland, six in the English Boroughs and Counties and three in Wales. The *Daily Worker* carried the announcement under the headline, "Class Against Class Vote Communist".[28]

Not only was the CPGB hampered by lack of money in the general election campaign, but the party also complained about harassment of its candidates and supporters.

RW Robson, the party's London organiser, was arrested at the start of the campaign, as was Bert Williams, another party worker. the *Daily Worker* commented that the CP faced tremendous difficulties. Candidates were in prison, and agents, organisers and leading comrades had been arrested.[29] Six of the party's candidates were in prison. Shaukat Usmani, one of the Meerut Prisoners, was the candidate in South East St Pancras. He was in jail in India, and his candidature was an expression of the solidarity that the communists were trying to build between Indian and British workers. Wal Hannington, the communist leader of the Unemployed Workers Movement and the candidate for Bermondsey in London, was also behind bars. So too were Bob Stewart (Dundee) and Chris Flanagan (Gorton). Two other communist candidates, George Allison and W G Shepherd were in jail awaiting trial on charges of incitement to mutiny.[30]

The communist vote at the 1931 General Election was 75,017. This was a fifty per cent increase on the previous election with the same number of candidates. The actual number of communist candidates in 1931 is the subject of some minor disagreement. The *Daily Worker*, in its coverage of the result, says there were 26 CP candidates.[31] This figure is also the one accepted by *Communist Review* in an article appraising the General Election result.[32] It is not, however, the figure that Pollitt gave in a report to the Political Bureau: he claimed there were 25 candidates.[33] Be that as it may, 25 or 26 candidates, the CPGB still polled much better at this election than the previous one. However, Pollitt was not pleased. He told the British Commission of the Communist International that the expectations had been that between 150,000 and 200,000 would vote communist. The result had come as an "incredible surprise", especially considering the favourable circumstances. Pollitt expressed dismay that after two Labour Governments and the betrayal of the General Strike, the Labour Party still managed to retain the voting allegiances of six and a half million voters.[34] Pollitt was expressing the gut reactions of many communists during the new line years. They could not understand why social democracy, after all that it had done, could still exert such an influence on the British working class. It was the rationale of class against class that eventually the lesson would be learned, and the labour movement would accept communist leadership. It did not happen at the election, and Pollitt's answer seemed to be that although the masses were disillusioned with the Labour Party, they had still not accepted the communist's way out of the crisis. The reason for this was pretty much the same as before _ 'the isolation of the Party from the broad masses.'"[35]

Pollitt and the party leadership may have been perplexed as to why the CPGB had not done better, but their recipe of more of the same was a good deal better solution than the one offered by Gerhardt of the CI. In his report to the Anglo-American Secretariat just after the election, Gerhardt's analysis as to why the election was called was that it was all part of a 'left manoeuvre.' The resignation of the Labour Ministers from the Government was a 'left manoeuvre'. The expulsion of MacDonald and co was also a 'left manoeuvre'. In all, 'the left manoeuvres of the Labour Party were a part of the class manoeuvres of the British reactionary camp.' For Gerhardt, these so-called 'left manoeuvres' by the Labour leadership were responsible for the CPGB's failure to mobilise more support. The Labour Party had lost two million votes since the last election, and these voters had instead voted for reactionary candidates. What was particularly worrying for Gerhardt was that the Labour Party, despite its social fascist policy, still managed to poll seven million votes. It showed that 'the Labour Party had succeeded in preventing in a decisive measure – the transfer of large masses of workers to the revolutionary camp with the help of its 'left manoeuvres'.[36]

Pollitt, who was also in attendance at the same meeting as Gerhardt, gave short shrift to this analysis. According to Pollitt, Gerhardt was wrong. Disillusioned Labour voters had stayed at home and had not voted for the Tories. If the two million lost Labour voters had voted for the Tories, how did that square with the new line notion of the radicalisation of the masses? As Pollitt rightly pointed out, if Gerhardt was correct, what became of the CI's overview that during the third period of class against class the working class would reject social democracy and side with the communists, "if the Tories won those two million votes that were lost by the Labour Party what becomes of the theory of the radicalisation of the working class ?"[37]

Gerhardt had no answer to Pollitt's question.

One of the more exciting features of the General Election was not so much why so many Labour voters abstained but rather the impact of the Communist campaign and vote on that small number of constituencies where there were CPGB candidates.

The *Daily Worker* gave the full election results of all 26 Communist candidates. What was remarkable was that in 5 of the 26 constituencies, the communist candidate obtained enough votes to deny victory to the Labour candidate. In four constituencies communist votes allowed a Conservative to win and in one constituency they were sufficient to allow a National Liberal to claim victory. Most of these areas had traditionally returned Labour MPs. The five constituencies were:

Stepney (Whitechapel)	Harry Pollitt	(Com)	2,658
	B Janner	(Nat Lib)	11,013
	J Hall	(Labour)	9,864
	Kid Lewis	(Fascist)	154*
	Kid Lewis was a Jewish boxer who later broke with Mosley.		
Sheffield (Attercliffe)	G H Fletcher	(Com)	2,790
	C Pike	(Con)	15,185
	C H Wilson	(Lab)	15,020
Glasgow (Springburn)	A Haimes	(Com)	1,997
	C Emmott	(Con)	16,092
	G Hardie	(Lab)	16,058
Bothwell	B McCourt	(Com)	2,163
	Mrs H Shaw	(Con)	16,571
	J Sullivan	(Lab)	14,423
West Fife	W Gallacher	(Com)	6,829
	C Milne	(Con)	12,977
	W Adamson	(Lab)	11,163

At the 1931 General Election, the Communist Party had not made a major electoral breakthrough, but it had improved on its 1929 performance. In electoral terms, since the beginning of class against class, the party's aim had been to win the allegiance of large numbers of Labour voters: "the victory of revolution in this country is not possible without the destruction of the mass influence of the Labour Party, and without winning the greater part of their supporters for Communism."[38]

Clearly, this had not been achieved, but there were some positive features of the election that the party welcomed. An assessment of the election results in *Communist Review* gave comfort to those who may have been disheartened by the party's poor showing – the "incredible surprise" as Pollitt described it.

In those constituencies where the party had candidates, there was an increase of almost 60% in the communist vote. In turn, the Labour Party vote in these 26 constituencies had declined by almost 24 %. It allowed the party to draw the favourable conclusion that the relation between the votes for the CPGB and the Labour Party had, since the General Election of 1929, been changed in favour of the Communist Party.

Besides, at the 1929 election, the total votes recorded for the communist candidates was 9.2% of that obtained by the Labour candidates. In 1931, the total communist vote constituted 19.2% of the Labour Party votes, in the twenty-six constituencies.

However, the communist vote was uneven. The party did better in Scotland and South Wales compared with London, and other English constituencies. In Scotland, the CPGB obtained nearly 30% of the Labour vote in the eight constituencies contested. In South Wales, three communist candidates polled nearly 18000 votes, which was 26 % of the Labour vote. In some areas, the CPGB was a serious challenge to the Labour Party. In West Fife, for example, Willie Gallacher's vote steadily increased from 20.5% in 1929 to 22.1% in 1931. His persistence was rewarded when in 1935 he won the seat and became the first Communist MP since Saklatvala was defeated in 1929. In Rhondda East, the popular miners' leader Arthur Horner also increased his vote during the new line years. It went from 15.2% at the 1929 election to 31.9% in 1931 and then to 33.8% at a by-election in 1933. It was in Rhondda East that Harry Pollitt, although unsuccessful, got the highest ever-communist vote at the 1945 General Election.

The CPGB had undoubtedly made progress in this the first and only General Election that had been fought with a leadership and a strategy that was in harmony with the new line. It will be remembered that the 1929 election was controversial because many of the party rank and file complained that the Central Committee was not committed to the new strategy. The party had made some limited progress since then. What is undeniable is that the class against class strategy was not a hindrance, at least in electoral terms. In most areas contested the popularity of communists, as attested by the votes recorded for party candidates, had increased. The party's rationale for its failure to do even better at the 1931 election, was not the class against class policy itself, but an inadequate explanation of this strategy to the voters. This it considered a major weakness. Many of the workers who were sympathetic to the party voted for the Labour Party, only because they wanted to prevent a Tory victory. They still believed that the Labour Party was a lesser evil in comparison with the Tories.[39]

The extent of the hatred felt for the Labour Party by many communists and inexplicable other than in domestic terms was seen in the lengths that ordinary party members would go to vent their anger on anything connected with social democracy. Such was the animosity generated by what was perceived as class betrayal that many communists would have little to do with Labour Party members even at the local level.

An article in *Communist Review* showed the depth of this hostility:

"Often our comrades satisfied themselves with the breaking up of Labour Party meetings, with hostile interruptions, without concentrating themselves upon the difficult task of finally convincing the Labour Party supporters. There has been very little personal discussion, canvassing and so on."[40]

It is yet a further example of how the distrust sown in the middle and late twenties between the communists and their former allies bore such bitter fruit in the new line years.

Not only did the 1931 General Election increase votes, but it also ushered in the significant increase in party membership. There were nearly nine hundred recruits in the immediate aftermath of the election.[41] By the end of the year, the recruits were still coming in, and the CPGB had grown to over six thousand members. It had doubled in size in less than six months, thanks in part to a successful general election campaign.

It was not just in parliamentary elections that the popularity of the communists was beginning to take an upward turn. In municipal elections as well, which took place around the same time as the 1931 General Election, there were some notable communist gains. In Scotland, 11,600 people voted communist at the local elections in November.[42] In some areas, the communist vote almost trebled. A few months later, in the local elections in Wales, the communist vote also increased. It went from 32% of the Labour Party's in those seats contested in 1931 to 41% in April 1932.[43]

By 1932, the CPGB took elections, particularly local elections, much more seriously than at any previous time in the party's short history. So important had they become that it was decided to postpone the forthcoming party congress until November 12-14 in order not to detract from the municipal elections on November 1. The Central Committee took this decision after representations from the party districts.[44] A fortnight before the elections the *Daily Worker* carried the communists' election manifesto. The CPGB argued for the following reforms:

- Abolition of the Means Test
- Increase in Poor Law Relief to all destitute families
- Confiscation of empty houses
- 25% reduction in council rents
- Free fares, gas, light and water for the unemployed
- Free medical services
- Free maternity and children's clinics in working-class areas
- Free meals and clothing to working-class children
- Free milk to working-class children of five years and under [45]

It was an interesting document for two reasons. One, it concentrated on a set of demands that would have struck a resonance with that section of the working class that were unemployed and living in poverty – a not inconsiderable number.,. Two, the demands were not unreasonable. In fact, so realisable were they, that thirteen years later, with the election of a reforming Labour government, many of them, in one form or another, were put into practice.

Although the *Daily Worker* gave comprehensive coverage to these municipal elections, reporting on the issues and the campaigns, there were only 150 CP candidates in all, a disappointingly small number. Of these, almost half were contesting in Scotland where there were 63 communist candidates. On the day of the elections once again the *Daily Worker* told its readership to vote communist. This advice was adhered to by an increasing number, particularly of Scots. Two days later, the paper reported that the party candidates in Scotland had received 29,000 votes. There had been a four-fold increase in Glasgow where over ten and a half thousand had voted communist. The entire communist vote in Scotland had gone up by over 250% since the local elections of the year before.

It was in Scotland too, in the earlier part of the year, that the communists did rather well in a parliamentary by-election in Dumbarton. Harry Pollitt used the occasion to remind the party membership of the importance of elections. He told them through the party paper that elections were a barometer of the state of mind of the working class. It was vital that they be contested.[46] However, it was not the enthusiasm of the membership that was the problem with fighting elections, as Pollitt well knew, but the lack of money. On this occasion, with the help of a loan the £150 was raised, and Hugh McIntyre was the party candidate. He was a local activist in a traditionally militant area, and the vote was a reflection of the Communists' popularity. McIntyre polled 2,870 votes compared to Labour's 13,704 and the winning Tory's 16,749. The communists not only fought an excellent local campaign, but they also managed to strengthen the party organisation in the area. Because of the by-election, new party groups were established in several villages in the constituency, and a post-election meeting in Dumbarton resulted in 69 recruits. The two prime reasons for standing CP candidates, the winning away of Labour voters and the building of the party, seem to have been fulfilled at Dumbarton.

For those who view the CPGB only in terms of an addendum to the CI, a British party only in name, whose every policy turn was determined and dictated by Moscow, the year 1933 presents something of a conundrum. Hitler came to power in March 1933, and the CI immediately issued an appeal for working-class unity to confront fascism. This change of policy had a minimal effect on the British party, which continued with its class against class strategy until the tail end of 1934. Nowhere was this more apparent than in the field of electoral struggle. There was no jumping to attention at the CI dictate, and the new line continued to be the bedrock of CPGB policy.

During 1933, the CPGB made even greater efforts to build their electoral support at Labour's expense. The Communists still believed that if the new strategy was to make headway, then they must achieve Parliamentary representation. Despite all their reservations about the importance of elections, for the Communists these remained the 'acid test' for the achievements of the new line. In 1933, they contested three by-elections, a significant number considering the party's small size. It is worth looking at two of these, one at the beginning, and one at the end of the year, for they were an excellent example of how the Communists' strategy was slowly, very slowly, beginning to change. They also show how support for the Communists varied tremendously.

Rhondda East was the first of such contests and took place in March 1933. It was an ideal constituency for the communists to contest – it was a mining area that incorporated the notoriously militant pit village of Maerdy. In Arthur Horner, the Communists had an ideal candidate; he was a long-standing party member with a good record of activity in the South Wales Miners Federation. To help in the campaign, the party sent its leading orator, Saklatvala, to work in the constituency virtually full-time. A report of one of his first meetings indicated the enthusiasm there was for Horner's candidature. At a meeting in Maerdy in support of Horner, Saklatvala gave a rousing speech, and 65 members of the audience enrolled to work in the election campaign.[47]

The CPGB held a large number of such meetings in the constituency. At one of these, Saklatvala made clear that despite Hitler's accession to power, the communists' attitude towards the Labour Party, and particularly the previous Labour Government, remained unchanged. At Porth, Saklatvala told a large audience that the Labour Government had robbed workers in order to pay the war lords and law lords. He accused the Labour Government of colossal expenditure on the slaughter of colonial peoples. At the same time, it was unable to meet the demands of the unemployed for proper maintenance.[48]

Although the campaign only lasted for two weeks, the result when it was announced was very impressive. Horner received 11,228 votes to the successful Labour Candidate's 14,127. It was an improvement on Horner's General Election figure, and it helped reinforce the view in the party that in some areas the communists could supersede the Labour Party as the party of the working class.

Horner's performance was not an isolated example: in the local elections contested by the party in Wales in 1933 the CPGB scored on average 61% of the Labour vote. The communist vote at local elections in Wales had more than doubled in two years.

Despite the CI's call for a united front, the Rhondda East by-election campaign saw no substantial change in Communist Party strategy. The Labour Party, and particularly Labour Left Wingers, were still regarded as the enemy. Nevertheless, by August 1933, there were signs that the communists were slowly beginning to rethink their new line policy, and this was graphically illustrated in their campaign in the Clay Cross by-election. There was a Labour Candidate at Clay Cross, Arthur Henderson, and the communists, during the campaign, continued with their class against class phraseology. The difference was that they recognised for the first time since the new line strategy began, that it was essential to unite with the Labour left, and where possible to win their support.

It was ironic that during the campaign the ILP left winger who had responded to the communists' appeal for unity should be none other than John McGovern, the MP for Shettleston, who had been so roundly condemned by Saklatvala only three years before in the Shettleston by-election. The *Daily Worker* gave a good deal of publicity to McGovern's plea to the Clay Cross electors to vote for the communist candidate, Harry Pollitt. McGovern spoke on Pollitt's behalf at many meetings and urged support for the communist candidate through the *Daily Worker*. He said that Pollitt was conducting 'the working-class offensive against the two Tory candidates and I stand with him in that struggle.'[49]

This was an unequivocal attack on Henderson, the Labour Party General Secretary, which also laid McGovern open to disciplinary action for not supporting a Labour candidate. McGovern was unrepentant and the *Daily Worker*, as further publicity, published a photograph of McGovern standing alongside Pollitt, Horner and Gallacher, outside the CPGB headquarters in Clay Cross.[50]

McGovern's intervention had come about as a direct result of the CPGB's softening attitude towards the ILP. Only a year before the Executive Committee of the CPGB had proclaimed that the ILP, with the support of the bourgeoisie, was the most dangerous barrier between the party and the masses. Yet it was the ILP who had made the most positive response to the communists' appeal for unity. The CI's call for a United Front in March 1933, motivated the British party to approach the Labour Party and TUC for joint action against fascism. This had been rejected by both those organisations but had been sympathetically received by the ILP. Negotiations took place between the two parties about the necessity of organising joint action. These negotiations and their outcome were well publicised in the *Daily Worker*, and it was in response to these discussions that McGovern made his public declaration of support for Pollitt at Clay Cross.

Unlike Rhondda East, Clay Cross was not a constituency where the communists had been involved in mass work over a period of time, and neither was Pollitt, in contrast to Horner, a local labour movement figure. The election result showed that these factors were the important ones when it came to the communists winning votes. Pollitt received 3,404 votes compared to Henderson's 21,931. Considering that Pollitt was a well known national CPGB leader, the result was disappointing and compared very unfavourably with Rhondda. It proved once again that the communists fared much better when they fielded a candidate with strong links with the constituency and the local labour movement.

However, throughout 1933, so keen were the communists to win parliamentary representation that these considerations were discarded in the struggle for votes. The communists were prepared to contest virtually anywhere, with any candidate, at any expense, in order to prove the viability of their new line strategy in the critical arena of electoral politics.

Although the first signs of a crack in the class against class strategy had become apparent with the CPGB's softening approach towards the ILP, there was no sudden break by the communists with their old policy. Some eighteen months after Hitler had come to power, and the CI had urged tentative steps towards unity, the CPGB's class against class policy remained, towards the end of 1934, very much intact. It was in the field of electoral struggle that the first policy breakthrough was to occur.

At the London County Council Elections in March 1934, the communists decided to contest widely and put up candidates in eight boroughs. The Communist Party issued a list of demands for London that were both practical and well thought out. They had been costed and were a realisable set of reforms that could be implemented without revolutionary change. They showed that the communists were keen to make a breakthrough at the local level, an opportunity that had so far been denied them in parliamentary contests. Their proposals included: the reduction of council rents by 25%; the taking over of empty dwellings; the destruction of slum areas and basement dwellings and the building of 250,000 houses at the cost of 86 million which would in turn give employment to 125,000 men and 25,000 indirectly. The rebuilding and repair of London bridges, roads and traffic crossings was another proposal, costed at £10 Million and employing upwards of 20,000 workers. The strengthening of river banks to prevent flooding at a cost of 30 million pounds would give work to 60,000 unemployed. Other proposals included building an electric railway and transport system, equipping every working-class home with gas and electricity, and building new schools, playgrounds, playing fields, hospitals etc., which would employ thousands more.

The communists at this election were much more even-handed in their attacks on the two main parties. Previously, much of their venom had been reserved for the Labour Party, but now they were equally scathing of the Tories. These were both small but significant changes in CPGB tactics.

On the day of the election, *Daily Worker* readers were urged, in a front-page article to, 'Vote Communist in London Today'. Then, as if to dispel any possible illusions that may have been gathering about the imminent demise of the new line, the article went on to reaffirm the Party's class against class strategy. London electors were told that the Communist candidates were challenging the 'anti-working class policy of the Labour Party'.

The Labour Party was still referred to as anti-working class and as a party of capitalism, and there was no call to vote Labour where no Communist candidate was standing. In the final analysis, very little seemed to have altered – but by the way the election was conducted, it was apparent that there was some change of thinking taking place in the CPGB.

By November 1934, this change of thinking had gathered momentum. However, despite numerous Party statements that the Labour Party were the allies of fascism, in the Borough Council Elections that month the communists decided, for the first time in six years, to give grudging support to Labour. The news must have come as something of a shock to Party members, who had only three months before been told in a Central Committee Statement that the whole policy of reformism in practice prepared the way for fascism.

The news of the change in the electoral line was first publicly revealed to the membership through the *Daily Worker*. The communists were contesting sixty seats in London and agreement had been reached with the ILP to support each other's candidates. If no Communist or ILP candidate was standing, the voters were told to vote for those Labour Candidates who pledged themselves to build up the united front of struggle. The New Line in the electoral field had been effectively broken. Although the communists were not yet prepared to give unequivocal support to Labour candidates, the fact that they recognised differences within the Labour Party was itself a dramatic turn away from the old strategy.

Once the breach had been made, the trickle soon became a flood. Less than a month later, in a discussion in the *Daily Worker*, entitled, 'Should We Support Labour Candidates?', Gallacher told the readership that only in constituencies where there is a chance of breaking through will the party stand candidates. In all others, the message must be to get rid of representatives of the National Government and support Labour candidates. It was not yet Party policy, but when someone of Gallacher's standing on the Central Committee was making such statements, it would certainly not be long before there was a full discussion about a change of line. Even then there was still considerable opposition to any change.

The discussion continued until the Communist Party's Thirteenth Congress in February 1935. At this Congress, the communists decided to work for unity to defeat the National Government. They dropped their slogan calling for a 'Revolutionary Workers Government' and returned to their pre-New Line strategy of maximum support for Labour. The party pledged itself to develop;

> "...... the militant mass movement of the workers to the stage at the General election, where it can sweep away the National Government, returning a majority of Labour members and thus provide the conditions, despite the character of the Labour Party programme and the consequent character of the Labour Government, for powerfully pressing forward the united working class front and its demands – and united working class action against fascism and war ......"[51]

However, the communists did not revert entirely to their previous electoral policy: in future the party would contest against Labour candidates. At the general election in November 1935 Willie Gallacher beat the Labour candidate in West Fife, and Harry Pollitt gained nearly 14000 votes in East Rhondda. These were the only two seats contested by the CPGB.

This was one of the lasting effects of the new line. From 1935 until the CPGB's dissolution in 199, the party never again returned to its pre-class against class position of not competing against Labour candidates. This was despite the renewal of its campaign to gain Labour Party affiliation. Despite the short-lived duration of class against class, its ramifications were still felt some years afterwards, and nowhere was this more true than with the party's electoral policy.

It was during this period, which is often referred to as the CPGB's most sectarian, or revolutionary phase, that electoral intervention gained a prominence never experienced before or since. It is one of those interesting contradictions of British communism that at a time when the CPGB was at its most scathing of capitalism and all its institutions, and when there was real feel amongst the communist rank and file that fascism was imminent that the CPGB decided to launch a full-scale attack on every election front. It was during the three years that class against class was at its most strident, from 1931 until the end of 1933, that the CPGB made a tremendous effect to gain communist representation at local and parliamentary level. The party, with fewer than five thousand members, most of whom were unemployed and hindered by a lack of money, attempted to fight virtually every parliamentary by-election that took place. Its intervention in local politics became more professional, and local, as the period progressed. It was ironic that a party who deplored those who thought that socialism could be achieved through parliament and whose main campaigning slogan was the call for a 'revolutionary workers government' should be so obsessed by the number of working-class votes it polled.

The involvement in electoral politics during the class against class years, the contests fought, and the experience gained particularly by three of the party's heavyweights on the Central Committee, Pollitt, Gallacher and Campbell, had an effect. Gallacher represented West Fife for fifteen years, Pollitt tried to win in the Rhondda, Whitechapel and Seaham. Campbell had a good campaign in Ogmore in South Wales. This constant contact with working-class voters, particularly Labour voters, cannot have left untarnished the thinking of these three communist, working-class leaders. It seems no accident that after the conclusion of the anti-fascist war in 1945 and the subsequent growth of communist influence that the CPGB began its first tentative steps towards a strategy of peaceful advance towards socialism, a strategy that was finally encapsulated its 1951 programme the *British Road to Socialism*. By the late 1940s the party proclaimed that the balance of world forces had shifted so that the British working class could take power by a combination of parliamentary and extra-parliamentary struggle.

It would be impossible to prove that the CPGB's first sustained and widespread electoral intervention between 1928 and 1934 had the effect of persuading the party leadership that there ought to be a shift away from the policy of a revolutionary seizure of power. This was certainly not the case. Nevertheless, the need to win the working-class vote, which was intrinsic to the new line, meant that communists had to face up to the realities of winning over those whose traditional support went to the Labour Party. They needed policies, particularly at the local level, that touched the realities of working-class life. Also, the communists were confronted continuously on the doorstep by the hegemonic social democratic argument that elections could change things. Once again, it was not all a one-way process. Some sections of the working class were won over by the communists and a small, but increasing number, particularly in Scotland and Wales, given the opportunity for the first time to vote communist did so. For their part, the communists confronted continuously by Labour voters who saw the importance of the ballot box for bringing about social change, also began to rethink their ideas. The seeds planted during the new line finally came to bloom less than twenty years later when the party admitted that it was possible to change capitalism by peaceful means – the working class had been right all along. The importance of elections, first proclaimed during class against class, became, a few years later, a major component of communist strategy and was to remain so until the party itself disappeared.

Notes
1   James Klugmann Folder CC Jan 7-9 1928

2	James Klugmann Folder CC April 28-30 1928
3	*Workers Life* March 9, 1928
4	*The Communist* Sept 1928
5	*Workers Life* August 17, 1928
6	*Workers Life* August 24, 1928.
7	J T Murphy, *New Horizons*.
8	*Workers Life* April 13, 1928, and April 20 1928
9	*Workers Life*, June 8, 1928
10	ECCI Political Secretariat July 1, 1929
11	*Daily Worker*, February 8, 1930)
12	*0....*, April 26, 1930
13	*Daily Worker*, May 14, 1930
14	*Daily Worker*, June 14, 1930
15	*Daily Worker*, June 25, 1930)
16	*Impreccorr* Vol. 10, No 32, July 10, 1930,
17	London District Party Committee Materials and Reports 1931-Report to the LDP Congress March 1931 JK material Blue Folder 12 1931 material.
18	*Daily Worker*, December 5, 1930
19	*Daily Worker*, January 20, 1931
20	*Daily Worker*, April 4, 1931
21	*Daily Worker*, March 11, 1931
22	*Daily Worker*, May 14, 1931
23	*Daily Worker*, May 18, 1931
24	*Daily Worker*, May 21, 1931
25	*Daily Worker*, May 21, 1931
26	*Daily Worker*, May 30, 1931
28	*Daily Worker*, October 17, 1931)
29	*Daily Worker*, October 20, 1931
30	*Daily Worker*, October 23, 1931
31	*Daily Worker*, October 29, 1931
32	*Communist Review*, December 1931).
33	Polit Bureau, November 5, 1931
34	*Ibid*
35	*Ibid*
36	*The General Election in England*, Gerhardt, Report at the Anglo-American Secretariat of the CI, November 16, 1931
37	*Ibid*
38	*Communist Review*, December 1931
39	*Ibid*
40	*Ibid*
41	Polit Bureau, November 5, 1931
42	Scottish District Circular. *Lessons of the Elections*, November 24 1931)
43	*Daily Worker*, April 11, 1932)
44	*Daily Worker*, October 7, 1932
45	*Daily Worker*, October 13, 1932
46	*Daily Worker*, March 3, 1932
47	*Daily Worker*, March 20, 1933
48	*Daily Worker*, March 28, 1933)
49	*Daily Worker*, August 28, 1933
50	*Daily Worker*, August 31, 1933
51	Draft Resolution on 'The Communist Party and the United Front', submitted to the Thirteenth Party Congress, Manchester, February 2nd-5th, 1935. CPGB,1935,p 9

Workers of the World Unite!

DAILY WORKER

No. 1   WEDNESDAY, JANUARY 1, 1930   One Penny

WOOLLEN WORKERS TAKE THE FIELD

MASS STRIKES AGAINST WAGE REDUCTIONS
Police Attack Pickets
ALL WORKERS SOLID AND DETERMINED TO WIN FIGHT

OVER two thousand woollen textile workers are on strike. The attempt to cut wages is meeting with real mass resistance. The workers are in a militant mood and maintain the utmost solidarity against employers, Labour Government, trade union bureaucrats and police.

The young workers are especially active and are giving increasing support to the Communist Party Campaign for rank and file Committees of Action.

BONDFIELD, SCAB;
Labour Prepares to Smash Wool Strike
(From Our Own Correspondent.)

BRADFORD.—The council of the wool textile employers has not yet commented on the letter of the Minister of Labour proposing to set up a court of enquiry into the situation in the woollen industry under Part 2 of the Industrial Courts Act, 1919.

Before availing themselves of the offer to improve the wage reductions by means of arbitration the woollen bosses are assiduously watching the strikes which are repeatedly breaking out and bring carried on with remarkable determination.

I understand that Margaret Bondfield is going ahead with the setting up of the Court and that the constitution and terms of reference will be announced shortly.

DYE WORKERS STRIKE
Lightning Strike follows Dismissals

There was a lightning strike of 250 dye workers at the Kirk Lane Dye Works on Monday. The strike was due to the dismissal on the Saturday of 100 men.

Pickets were placed on the gates in the early morning and only the office staff and the key men on the mechanical side remained at work.

So far there is no news of a settlement and the works remain closed.

VOTE AGAINST WAGE CUTS

The strike at the Prospect Mills, Pudsey, continues. In answer to the opening of the mills in an attempt to impose a reduction of 1s. 6d. in the pound, a well-attended meeting of strikers held at the Town Hall decided unanimously to resist any cut in wages for any section of the workers. A strike committee was elected and pickets appointed.

All operatives, union and non-union, are out.

DEPIANT SPIRIT
Determined to Resist Lower Wages
(From Our Own Correspondent.)

SADDLEWORTH.—The attempt of the Saddleworth millowners to break the strike in nine mills against a wage cut of two shillings in the pound has completely failed. Although the mills were opened on Monday morning not one of the thirteen hundred strikers, mostly women and girls, returned.

The police have repeatedly attacked the pickets and some arrests have been made. The defiant attitude of Lily Hutton, a young women worker, who "on trial" for assaulting a burly police inspector, typifies the spirit of the workers.

A long period of short time and low wages has made them determined to resist to the utmost.

Tom Thurlbeck, who was fined £10 or two months on a charge of assaulting the police at the strike, has now been released, the workers having collected sufficient money to pay his fine.

GREENFIELD STRIKE
Employers appeal to Labour Govt.

The operatives of the Kinders Mill, Greenfield, Yorks, are on strike and pickets are operating at the mills. The employers' secretary has sent the following telegram to the Home Secretary:—

"Operatives of Messrs Buckley Co. (Greenfield), Ltd., Kinders Mill, Greenfield, Yorkshire, are being prevented by pickets from entering the mill, and are being otherwise intimidated at their homes. I am to ask that you will take such steps as well to render intimidation of the workers and afford them adequate protection."

REVOLUTION IN INDIA GROWS
Congress Chiefs Feel Mass Pressure

The All-India National Congress, which opened at Lahore yesterday, adopted by 942 votes, against 75, the resolution moved by Gandhi, deploring the throwing of a bomb at the Viceroy and congratulating him on his escape. The minority, waving Red Flags, raised angry protests. Ghandhi's second motion is to deal with the new manoeuvre of withdrawal of "Dominion status" in favour of independence.

The reports of meetings of the Congress Committee in Session since Christmas Day, shows that the continous rising tide of the Indian masses, led by the heroic Indian proletariat whose determined fight, marked by mass political strikes, is the enormous motive force which has compelled the leaders of the Indian bourgeoisie, who have in the past two years gone over to the side of British Imperialism, to make a desperate attempt to retain their hold on the masses by a show of opposition.

The resolution of the bourgeois nationalist leaders in favour of independence and boycott of legislature significantly leaves the campaign for civil disobedience and non-payment of taxes to the discretion of the Congress Committee, "as and when necessary."

At the 24th Conference morning yesterday, also in Lahore, Khazal. Singh, the president, stated that out of thirty-one recent death sentences on revolutionary Indian nationalists, twenty-seven were Sikhs.

When Sir Frederick Sykes, Governor of Bengal, visited Ahmedabad two days ago he was met by a demonstration outside the station waving flags and with shouts of "Frederick Sykes, go back."

SIXTY DEATHS IN CINEMA FIRE
Many Children Amongst The Victims

A fire which broke out at the Glen Cinema, Paisley, near Glasgow, during a children's matinee yesterday afternoon, capsed a panic, resulting, it is feared, in about sixty deaths.

As soon as news of the fire spread frantic mothers ran to the Cinema, and began searching for their children.

One hundred and fifty people were taken to hospital.

It is certain that at least six children are in it.

FASCISTS WOUND WORKERS

MONCEUR, Tuesday.—On Sunday night sixteen armed Fascists attacked a group of workers who were kissing their brats out in a thoroughly workers' quarter.

The Fascists fired on the unarmed workers and wounded four of them seriously. As usual, the police arrested two workers.

PRINCE'S JAUNT
To Travel Into Impenetrable Jungle—By Train
WITH HIS VALET!

On Friday the Prince of Wales will again start a jaunt that will cost thousands of pounds of the money the workers have earned for him.

He is going to Capetown, and from there will journey into the jungle—by train!

There he will display his intrepidity against the wild beasts of Africa. His valet is to accompany him; probably to hold the rifle.

An official of the "Keniiworth Castle," on which he is to travel, states that he is expected to play a prominent part in the "strenuous" deck games which are to be played on board.

"Otherwise, he will use an ordinary first-class cabin with the usual dressing-room."

SHOOTING THE UNEMPLOYED
Social Democrat Police Chief Orders Massacre in Cologne

BERLIN, Tuesday.—Yesterday evening 10,000 unemployed workers demonstrated in front of the Cologne Town Hall in order to support the proposal of the Communist faction for winter assistance for the unemployed.

The social democratic Police President was in charge of large forces of police, who tried to prevent the demonstrators from reaching the Town Hall. At first the police used their batons, but when their efforts proved ineffective the Social Democrat gave the order to fire.

Many workers were wounded by the police bullets and over 100 arrested, including the Communist, W. Deputy Kolwen. The Communist proposals in the Town Council were rejected.—Inpreéor.

CLOSING THE RANKS
Woollen Workers Consolidate Against Wage Cuts
From Our Own Correspondent.

SHIPLEY, Tuesday.—Rank and file conferences are to be called in the textile area to consolidate the workers' resistance to the threatened wage cuts.

To counter the proposed woollen wages' enquiry, the Bradford district committee of the Communist Party issued today a statement to all wool workers.

The statement compares the statement with the Lancashire arbitration, which served the same purpose of breaking the workers' resistance.

The woollen textile workers are advised not to return to work, but to extend the struggle, and to build up all committees of action to both the strike-breaking court of enquiry proposed by the Labour Government.

"DAILY WORKER" PRIZE DRAW 1st 15585, 2nd 7036; 3rd 5569, 4th 7094, 5th 15465, 6th 8776

Left: The first editorial and business address of the *Daily Worker*. 41 Tabernacle Streeet, London EC2
Above: First issue of the *Daily Worker*

6 The *Daily Worker*: weapon of the New Line

THE *DAILY WORKER*, which first appeared on January 1, 1930, came about as a direct result of the new line. The need for a daily communist paper had been constantly stressed, both by the party rank and file and the CI, almost since the birth of the party. The adoption of the policy of class against class, and the perspective of the independent communist leadership of the working class, made the appearance of such a paper of the utmost importance. So it was that on New Year's Day 1930, a little less than a decade after the party's creation, that the *Daily Worker* was launched.

The paper was an achievement of the new line and if the new line did nothing else, it at least ensured the foundation of what is now the only surviving English language communist daily paper. That in itself would be achievement enough, but during the few years in which the policy was in force not only did the paper survive, but it established itself as a voice on the left with a growing circulation. This was no mean achievement at a time when newspapers were closing and the one lone, and by now muted voice, of the Labour movement, the *Daily Herald*, had been taken over by Odhams Press. That the *Daily Worker* survived at all is almost entirely due to the dedication of the party members who backed it financially, wrote for it, and became responsible for its distribution. They rallied to its support after attempts by the police, the courts and the newspaper wholesalers to block its publication. Almost since its beginning, there was a sustained attack on the paper's right to publish. There were police raids on the newspaper's premises, harassment of staff, censorship, fines, imprisonment of its printers and publishers, and the closing off of the normal channels of distribution. All these methods, and more, were tried in attempts to close the paper down, and failed. By the end of class against class, the *Daily Worker* had been established on a firm foundation with a regular readership that was on the increase and exceeded by manifold the membership of the CPGB.

The need for a daily communist paper had been recognised long before the advent of the new line, but with the adoption of the new strategy, the party needed to have its own daily voice. The paper would act like an organiser and disseminate the Party line in the day-to-day struggles of the workers. Most important of all it would help to recruit to the CPGB, which would need to be a great deal larger if it was replace the Labour Party and become the vanguard of the working class.

The CI had first urged the creation of a communist daily in 1923, as a means of expanding the small and struggling British party. A report on the work of the British section of the International argued that the absence of a daily paper was making itself felt and that one of the immediate tasks of the party was to prepare for the establishment of a daily newspaper.[1] The CPGB leadership took little notice of the advice, and in the immediate aftermath of the General Strike in May 1926 the ECCI again urged the party's central committee to consider starting a communist daily. This time there was a recognition of the difficulties that this might entail for such a small party and the ECCI recommended that it might be better to establish regional communist daily papers, first in London and then in other urban centres.[2]

Once again the international body's instruction went unheeded, and the leadership of the CI returned to the issue the following year when Petrovsky, the CI's representative in Britain, again called for the establishment of a daily party paper during a meeting of the Anglo American Secretariat.[3] The lack of such a paper and the unwillingness to even discuss its possibilities was one of the criticisms levelled at the British Party at the important Ninth Plenum of the CI in 1928.

It was not just the CI that was sceptical about the party leadership's apparent reluctance to act quickly over the issue; there was also dissatisfaction amongst the party rank and file. Saklatvala, an early advocate of the new line and a member of the Sunday Worker Campaign Committee, was one of those who recognised the importance of the Communist press. In an article in *Workers Life* in 1928, he not only stressed the significance of newspapers in the class struggle, but also urged party members to pressurise the party leadership into bringing out a communist daily,

> "where would the capitalist movement have been without a capitalist press-now come up you lads and lasses, work for your solution. To work for it you have first to have a good fighting press of your own, there is your *Workers Life*. Buy it and see that everyone buys it and then ask for a daily copy."[4]

He returned to the theme eighteen months later. He told delegates at a Minority Movement Conference that he had stopped buying the *Daily Herald* and was instead purchasing six copies of *Workers Life* which he distributed to sympathisers. He urged the delegates to follow his example as a step towards creating a 'Workers Daily'. It was yet another attempt by Saklatvala to popularise his view amongst the party activists that the leadership should do more to establish a daily paper.

Saklatvala was not alone in his criticisms. At the all-important 10th Congress of the CPGB, which ushered in the new line, important rank and file delegates were critical of the party leadership for not implementing CI instructions and starting production of a communist daily. Tom Wintringham, a delegate from Camberwell branch in London, accused the Central Committee of procrastination over the establishment of a daily paper, which he asserted was due to the "right-wing danger". The future Scottish miners' leader Abe Moffat also attacked the leadership for not fighting hard enough to start a communist daily voice. JR Campbell in an attempt to justify the leadership's alleged inactivity over the issue explained to the delegates that the Central Committee's original intention was to raise the circulation of *Workers Life* in order to create the basis for a daily paper.[5] This was an interesting perspective given that Pollitt was highly critical of *Workers Life* and saw the weekly as the leading cause of the party's loss of membership. At an ECCI Presidium in the February following the Congress, he expressed the view that it was too much concentrated on high political questions, and neglected to give leadership on the day-to-day struggles of the workers. In Pollitt's estimation, recruits for the party would be made when the weekly paper gave a clear courageous lead that would gain the confidence of the best elements in the working class.

Between the 10th and 11th Congresses in 1929, the party leadership increasingly focused its attention on the need for a daily paper. Recognising their own dithering over the issue, the Central Committee at its March meeting endorsed a closed letter from the ECCI, which, among other things, criticised the CC for not campaigning amongst the membership for a communist daily. Neither was it just the leadership that was concerned at the lack of any drive for a paper: the party membership in their criticisms of the Central Committee's timidity in adopting the new line also cited their unwillingness to establish a daily paper. The delegates at the Young Communist League's Sixth Congress in August 1929 also joined in the attack, and they argued that one of the failings of the Party's Central Committee had been that there was no campaign for a daily paper.[6] Similar criticisms were echoed at important party aggregate meetings in July in Tyneside and London.[7] Spurred on by this grassroots revolt the party leadership responded, and a few weeks later *Workers Life* carried a front-page article devoted to the need for a daily paper. Through its weekly, the party leadership admitted that 'our Party is the only section of the CI that has not got a daily paper' The membership was told that the new paper would appear on January 1 1930. If it was to be a success, then it required finance, so there was the inevitable appeal for money. The Central Committee was under no illusions as to the formidable task that they had taken on and the venture was described as, 'the biggest political task ˑr party has had'.[8]

The 'big po ' task' was not helped by the spiralling decline of readership of *Workers Life*. Less than ɔnths before the proposed launch of its daily successor an article in the weekly d ɩt the readership was decreasing by 150 a week. The leadership had aimed to ɩ ɩles to at least 50,000 a week, but this now looked like an unrealisable ob sides, the prospects for a new communist daily, indeed for any daily newspape good. Newspaper production was expensive, and the lack of any revenue frɩ ɩt advertising made the long-term prospects for the venture bleak. Just hov publication of a daily paper could be was highlighted by the experience of tl ald. Exactly two months before the communists proposed launch of their ɩ ɩily Herald ceased to be a newspaper owned by the Labour movement. On Ν 1929, it was taken over by Odhams Press, who would control the majority of shɑ compared to the Trade Union Congress's 49%). The change of ownership empɩ ɩ difficulties involved in the production of a daily paper. If the *Daily Herald* cɩ survive with the financial backing of the TUC, what chance was there for a comrɩ ɩaily?

At the same time, ɩ ɩcquisition by Odhams Press did open up a niche in the market. Former readers of the *Dɩily Herald*, which had started life as a radical strike sheet before the First World War, could be appealed to as readers of a the new communist daily, rather than get their news from a capitalist owned paper. As it transpired, for the most part, this did not happen, and no special effect was made to recruit former *Daily Herald* readers to readership of the paper. The communists' newfound hatred of all things connected with the Labour Party, in any case, made this an unrealisable option.

The 'big political task' also faced problems in another area: who was to be the editor?

Arthur Horner, for one, had no doubts that it ought to be J R Campbell. At the August Central Committee meeting preceding the paper's launch, Horner disclosed that Campbell was the only person considered for the job. However, Campbell was one of the five members of the CC accused by Rust of urging support for Labour candidates during the debate about the new line. Campbell was considered at best to be lukewarm towards the class against class policy. To make him the editor of what was to be the spearhead of the new strategy would not go down well, either with the rank and file, the CI, or the party leadership. Lilly Webb, at the CC meeting following Horner's suggestion, was quick to criticise any attempt to put Campbell in charge at the paper. In a two-pronged attack, she accused the leadership of being wrong in considering Campbell for the editorship and in allowing Horner to stay in a position of authority in the Minority Movement. Both individuals were, according to Webb, on the party's 'right-wing'. Campbell did not become the editor of the paper. At this stage, that role was assumed by Rust. Horner did leave the as soon as the paper began production and started work on the paper's industrial side. This was done for purely political reasons so that Horner 'would be politically controlled in his work on the '*Daily*'.[9]

Rust was a strange choice as the first editor or the new paper. By his own admission his experience of journalism was practically nil.[10] His only experience on the publishing side of party work had been to edit the Young Communist League's *Young Worker*. But Rust was not chosen for the task because of his journalistic talent, or experience, he was chosen because of his commitment, both to the new strategy, and for his enthusiasm for the role that the paper might play in implementing the new line. He made this clear some years later, in the months before his early death in 1949, when writing a history of the paper. He described how the launching of the *Daily Worker* 'was a political decision and the result of a political fight within the ranks of the Communist Party, a long, drawn-out conflict on whether the establishment of a communist daily paper under British conditions was possible.' In the end, according to Rust, in his retrospective view, "the doubters and pessimists were routed'. The new editor considered himself neither a doubter nor a pessimist and his ideas for the paper were within the Leninist model. That is, that the paper was to be both an agitator and an organiser, and was to be intrinsic in helping to expand the party from a small sect into a mass organisation. For Rust, the launching of the *Daily Worker* was fundamental in re-orientating the party towards mass work, "the Communist Party was now able to advance from the stage of general propaganda to the handling of daily political events as they occurred, to give a daily and direct answer to the problems before the people as they arose, and to organise action in support of its policy."[11]

Rust's ambitious project had still to overcome some teething problems. At the August 1929 meeting of the Central Committee the CPGB leadership responded to the pressure from the rank and file and agreed on a date for a special Congress in November. In preparation for that event, there were to be a series of District Conferences at which one of the main items for discussion was to be the urgent need for a daily paper.[12] The anticipated date of the paper's publication, January 1, 1930, was not soon enough for the ECCI. This was made clear on the second day of the special Congress, November 30, when the ECCI representative criticised the Congress discussion and claimed that the projected date for the paper was too late.

The CI representative argued that the delay in producing the paper was not due to technical reasons but, 'because the mass of the membership is not politically convinced of the necessity of using the paper for the mobilisation of the masses'.[13] The importance of a daily paper had again been reinforced with a letter to Congress from the ECCI. The international leadership told the delegates that the CPGB would not advance unless it established its own daily voice.

The party delegates were encouraged to emulate their Russian comrades, who hadpublished their own daily voice, under much more adverse conditions,[14]

Despite the international pressure, Pollitt, the new party leader, was apprehensive about January 1 as a starting date for the paper, and he expressed these concerns at the first CC meeting after the Congress. He thought it was too soon, but the rest of the leadership overcame his doubts, and the starting date was reaffirmed. News of the January 1 deadline had already been conveyed to the membership as early as November 1 through an article in *Workers Life*, entitled, 'Defects in the Daily Campaign'.[15] There was at this stage even some disagreement over a name for the paper. The choice of *Daily Worker*, which had been floated by the leadership, came in for some criticism, and this was expressed in letters to the party weekly. *Workers Life* responded by asking for suggestions for an alternative title. None appeared to be forthcoming and the *Daily Worker* was the accepted, and popular title, for the new publication.[16]

If Pollitt was concerned about the apparent lack of preparation for the publication date of January 1, his close comrade in arms, R Palme Dutt, had no such doubts. Dutt, in an important article in *Communist Review*, published on the eve of the paper's appearance, outlined his vision for the new publication. It was remarkably perceptive, and many of the problems foreseen by Dutt were to beset the paper during the first years of its publication. In the article Dutt also alluded to the contradictions between what he called the paper's technicians and its political overseers, who, at all times, must maintain a firm control. Their respective roles were to become a source of disagreement during the paper's early days. Dutt, in his assessment, was clear about why a daily communist paper had not appeared before. It was entirely due to 'the lack of confidence in the independent leadership of the party'. Dutt argued that now that the class against class strategy had been adopted, a communist daily became possible. It had not been an option before because of the 'right errors' of the leadership who had not implemented an ECCI decision made seven years before that the CPGB should have a daily voice.[17]

Dutt used the party's theoretical journal to outline his ideas about what the paper should be. He argued it should be a mass organiser and collective agitator. To do this, it must place a heavy reliance on party members, particularly those who were involved in industrial action, who must relay to the paper news of their struggles. The party's rank and file militants must write for the paper; they must become 'worker correspondents' and continuously feed the paper information about all aspects of the class struggle. Dutt's vision was one of a group of journalists employed by the paper, but relying for much of their input on 'a chain of worker correspondents.'[18] During the new line years, the *Daily Worker* tried very much to follow Dutt's advice, although there were times when shop floor information was not forthcoming, due to the high percentage of unemployed party members, which made the reporting of industrial disputes difficult. Also, the lack of finance during the early days made the employment of an adequate number of reporters something of a luxury.

The influence of these worker correspondents over the paper's journalists cloaked another potential problem for Dutt – the possible dominance at the paper of what Dutt called the 'paper's technicians'. He was particularly worried that these technicians might have brought with them some of Fleet Street's capitalist habits and mentality.

Dutt, who at this stage was rather puritanical over the issue, was even averse to having any of the techniques learnt on other newspapers being transferred to the *Daily Worker*. He called into question the reliability of those journalists, even if they were communists, who had been trained on other, capitalist, papers.[19]

It was an approach that, later on, was to bring him into conflict with other party members involved in the newspaper industry.

Dutt was at his most penetrating when dealing with the possible problems that might arise with the paper's distribution. His predictions were uncanny. He foretold the distributors' boycott, which began soon after the paper started, and the continued attempts to censor the *Daily Worker*, both of which were features of the new line period. The answer to the first of these problems, according to Dutt, was a reliance by the party on its own distribution network, which must have at its heart sales of the paper in the factories.

Dutt was convinced, and rightly so as it turned out, that the wholesalers would boycott the paper and that party members must rally to its defence and organise their own distribution. Even down to the resistance by the newsagents and the wholesalers' boycott, Dutt was correct in his assessment of what might happen. The newsagents did protest, and Dutt argued some months before it happened that the onus was on the CPGB to give every encouragement to the newspaper sellers in their conflict with the big wholesalers.

Dutt's article, almost like a map of the future, outlined in detail what was likely to happen once the *Daily Worker* began publication, and what ought to be the party's response.[20]

The new paper, as planned, was launched on January 1, 1930. It was printed in Worship Street in London by the Utopia Press, which was owned by Robert Blatchford's *Clarion*. The paper's editorial offices were a few streets away in Tabernacle Street. The first issue of the paper was produced by eight people which included William Rust, the editor, and William Gallacher. It consisted of twelve small pages, with no photographs, and very few advertisements. The conditions under which the paper was written were primitive. There were no telephones, or tape machines, and on the first night not even any heat or light. Added to these technical problems was the failure by the paper's staff to ensure that the paper was loaded onto trains for distribution around the country. During the first few days, these train deadlines were missed, and this harmed sales. The first print run had been an optimistic 70,000, but ten days later this was down to 46,000.

According to Rust, in his first report on the new paper to the party's January Central Committee, not only were the paper's staff untrained for the task of producing a newspaper, but their political level needed to be improved.[21] Rust, echoing Dutt's commitment to worker correspondents, claimed that these were the "life and soul of a revolutionary paper", and that it was necessary to build up a network of such correspondents in every locality around the paper. This had not happened, and as a consequence, a weakness of the paper was its lack of contact with the masses. Rust, in a swipe at the party's leadership, argued that this failure came from the top. No member of the Politbureau was connected to a factory cell, and this situation should be remedied immediately. Otherwise, there was a danger of right-wing mistakes.

During the paper's first month, the most significant controversy seemed to be over what to do about the coverage of sport. The party-controlled British Workers Sports Federation was the favoured organisation, but what to do in the interim, while the BWSF was without mass support? Should the party daily give coverage to capitalist sport? This was undoubtedly the view of David Ainley; he wanted the paper to cover sporting events as a means of developing the BWSF.[22]

This view seemed to win majority support amongst the paper readers, who had been asked for their views about sports coverage, in the wake of a letter published on January 4, attacking the reporting of horse racing. The letters in response had broadly supported Ainley's idea that capitalist sport should be reported because the BWSF was not yet a mass organisation. Where there was hostility towards the paper's position over sport, it was not about its coverage, but the paper's willingness to give racing tips. The editor opposed this practice and it was soon withdrawn, but not without an explanation which appeared in an article entitled 'Why Sporting Tips Are To Be Discontinued'.[23] The readers were told that racing tips and results were to be stopped because 'the *Daily Worker* can't possibly assist the capitalists in the carrying out of a gigantic swindle and money-making concern'. However, the article did concede that many readers wanted the practice to continue. The paper pledged that it would carry on covering sporting events and urged its readers to join the BWSF. The differences over sport were still being aired in the paper the following month, even though the *Daily Worker* had stopped giving racing news. More letters appeared in early February attacking horse racing and betting in particular.[24] After that, the controversy subsided, as more pressing matters, in the shape of a wholesale distributors boycott, came to threaten the paper's very existence. Before dealing with this genuine threat to the *Daily Worker's* survival, one other issue is worth looking at, and that is the paper's treatment of women.

At the same time as the discussion over the coverage or non-coverage of sport was being aired, the paper announced that there was to be a page devoted to women. In an article entitled, 'To Our Women Readers', the *Daily Worker* declared that in the future page nine of the paper would be concerned with women's issues, although it would not be called a 'Women's Page'. The arguments in favour of this innovation were interesting and were outlined in the article. Firstly, page nine would have nothing in common with the women's pages in capitalist papers, which, according to the *Daily Worker*, 'are about nothing but clothes and housework'.[25] Secondly, page nine would not just be for women, but for men as well: 'we want men to read it too, because there can be no division between the struggles of men and women in the working class fight'. It was symptomatic of the approach adopted by the party during its new line phase: there were no separate 'women's issues' as all issues were class issues. What transpired, however, particularly in the early days of the paper, was that the 'page devoted to women', did become nothing more than a mixture of class politics, and the very worst aspects of all that the *Daily Worker* had condemned in the treatment of women in the capitalist press.

There were numerous examples of the paper's portrayal of a traditional view of women, and it is hard to believe that the CPGB leadership did not notice this inconsistency in the coverage of gender issues in the pages of its new paper. It has to be said, although it is no defence, that the CPGB was overwhelmingly male, with less than twenty per cent of its membership being made up of women, and there were few women in either the leadership or in full-time positions. However, just how the following example got by the editorial staff, given the stated commitment, 'not to treat women like they were treated by capitalist newspapers', it is difficult to say. One of the first pages devoted to women carried a picture of Madge Brown's baby and an article on babies' clothes. Women readers may have found some consolation in a letter about the Sheffield National Unemployed Workers Movement, which they were told had a Women's Section of four hundred members. More stereotyping of women was to follow and the next day the 'page devoted to women' consisted of a recipe for orange marmalade and a ' How to make your own dress ' pattern. By early February the paper had established some sort of routine and only occasionally did the Women's page lapse into total sexism. Often the emphasis was on building the National Unemployed Workers Movement Women's Section and the paper did contain much good advice about how to involve working women in the labour movement. Suggestions raised included opening party offices at stated times for use by unemployed women, organising socials particularly for women, and trying to establish 'women's action groups'.[26] Nevertheless, for every appeal to women as workers, there was the inevitable recipe (one for Russian toffee was particularly interesting).[27] So too was an article on, 'What you should and should not do during pregnancy', which was followed, a few months later, by a piece on 'How to make baby clothes'. What was particularly striking was the number of adverts for birth control, which was a consistent feature of the new paper. It contrasted starkly with the lack of advertising for other products.

The dilemmas involved in the portrayal of women in the early *Daily Worker*, as with the reporting of sport, soon faded into insignificance when the paper was confronted with its first major obstacle barely three weeks after it had first appeared. This was a wholesaler's boycott, so accurately foretold by Dutt in his article for *Communist Review*. News of the impending attempt to destroy the *Daily Worker* in its infancy was conveyed to the readership in a news item on January 22 1930. The Lancashire wholesalers struck the first blow. Lancashire was the scene of much industrial militancy over the attempted speed up in the mills. The local boycott was reported on, as was the response by Communist Party members in the area to distribute the paper themselves. The action started in Lancashire soon spread, and two days later the paper announced that the Provincial Wholesalers Association had decided that all its members would cease to distribute the *Daily Worker*. Over the next few months, other wholesalers followed suit. London wholesalers decided to cease distribution of the paper in May 1930, and Scottish wholesalers followed their example in July 1930. Two of the CPGB's largest and most important districts were now left without a means of conveying to members and supporters the party's new daily voice.

The wholesalers' boycott lasted for twelve years and was only finally lifted in 1942 when the wartime alliance with the USSR provided the communists with a popularity boost. It was all part of a sustained attempt to destroy the communists' attempts at maintaining a daily communist paper.

The party was quick to respond to the boycott, and a mass meeting of party members in London decided on a plan of action to beat the ban. This included pressurising newsagents to take the paper, sales of the paper by readers and supporters, and regular sales at factories at least once a week.[28] Just how successful the communists were in some parts of London in overcoming the wholesalers' action can be gleaned from a small news item a few months later. The Stepney local reported that since the boycott began it had regularly supplied ninety newsagents in the area with copies of the paper.[29] Given the small size of the Communist Party and the level and commitment of organising such a task, it is an indication of the dedication felt by the communists towards their new daily voice. It was, however, not always a success story, as news from the other side of London, in Tooting in South West London showed. There the distribution network broke down, and readers of the paper in the area were told that henceforth they would have to obtain their paper by post.[30]

The communists made all kinds of efforts to ensure their paper's circulation. In Hackney in East London, the comrades were commended for their use of motorbikes and sidecars in distributing the *Daily Worker*; the use of this form of cheap transport in helping to overcome the boycott was urged by the paper on other party branches.[31] In the long term, however, such reliance on spontaneity and local innovation could not be relied upon, and by the middle of 1930, the effect of the boycott was beginning to tell.

At the end of August 1930, the paper was reduced in size from six pages to four. A front-page editorial informed the readership that the smaller paper was a defeat but appealed to them to 'Win Back the Six Pages.'[32] By October of that year, there were signs that the resumption of a larger paper was a possibility, and that as a first step every Friday would see the appearance of a six-page paper. There was further encouragement in the news that if all went well, as from November 7 the *Daily Worker* would be six pages every day. This announcement at the beginning of October admitted that the reason the paper could not expand immediately was due to the lack of finance brought on, in part, by the wholesalers' boycott and the added expense that entailed.[33] In addition to the news of the paper's poor financial situation, the announcement also made apparent that a more systematic approach was being adopted to beat the wholesalers' boycott. This involved the *Daily Worker* itself being responsible for the direct distribution of copies to the newsagents. It was already being undertaken in Inner London and would be extended to other areas where practicable.

The paper's long-term strategy was to establish its own distribution machinery using the railway network. Workers at the paper were responsible for its conveyancing to London railway stations, after which it was transported by train to railway stations in all parts of the country, and from there it was picked up by local party members and taken to newsagents in the locality.[34]

Throughout the sustained boycott newsagents and their organisation remained friendly towards the new arrival's distribution. The Retailers Federation, which represented all newsagents, was opposed to the wholesalers' boycott. However, even with support from the newsagents' organisation, it was still difficult without the wholesalers' co-operation to place the paper at any large number of retail outlets. Even in a particularly militant city like Sheffield, the paper's distribution relied almost entirely on the machinery of the party. In March 1931, when sales nationally had picked up to just over twelve thousand, a large advert in the paper, placed there by the Sheffield party organisation, revealed the total reliance on the CPGB for the paper's distribution. The advert, which was entitled, 'Where To Get Your *Daily Worker* in Sheffield' listed all outlets in the city where the paper could be obtained. These comprised in the main party members houses, the party rooms, and significantly, just one newsagent. If this was mirrored in the rest of the country, the paper must have been available at only a minimal number of retailers. Sales must have been almost entirely dependent on the party membership, which was then still under three thousand.

Apart from the blatant attempt by the newspaper wholesalers to crush the *Daily Worker* before it had become established, the paper also faced other pressing problems, the most onerous of which was finance. The paper, throughout its early period, limped from one financial crisis to another. If the communists were totally bankrolled by their Soviet masters, an allegation that has now become an accepted part of British communist historiography, then a willingness to help the struggling paper should have been a priority. The finances that did come from Moscow were insignificant compared with the money raised in Britain for the paper's survival, and, as so often happened in the first year or so, these were not enough to ensure that the paper size was not curtailed. The threat to the paper's independence came not from Moscow, but from within Britain, where there were powerful forces that wished to see the *Daily Worker* eliminated. During its first few years, the paper was constantly threatened with libel actions. There was censorship, almost *daily*, and the paper's publishers and printers faced fines and imprisonment. Such was the onslaught on the paper that its continuation was always in doubt. That it did survive owes more to the dedication of its supporters than to any handouts from abroad. Not that the communists were ashamed, or secretive, about receiving money from other sources: in 1928 the *Daily Worker*'s predecessor *Workers Life*, had even published the CI's balance sheet on its front page, which showed that almost seven hundred thousand roubles had been spent on subsidies to party papers, publications and educational work in seventeen of the International's sections.[35]

The CPGB's financial arrangements, particularly concerning its paper, were, of course, a matter of concern to the ECCI and there seemed to be an undue reliance on gaining the CI's approval before even minor matters of reorganisation could be undertaken, as the following example concerning the *Daily Worker* shows. In order to cut down on the printing costs of the paper the party had decided to sell Dorritt Press, which it owned, and with the money made available by the sale, purchase a machine capable of printing the *Daily Worker*. This relatively minor operational change needed the approval of the CI, which was not always that easy to obtain quickly. At the CPGB's April 1930 Central Committee meeting, it was reported that authorisation for the sale of Dorritt Press had been sought from the ECCI and that JR Campbell, one of the CPGB's two representatives at the ECCI, had been sent to Moscow to obtain the necessary permission. Pollitt, in his report, stated that 'we are not in a position to carry out decisions of this character unless wunduee have the sanction of the ECCI'[36] Pollitt, at the same meeting, also relayed to the party leadership some of the difficulties that could be involved with belonging to an international organisation with a hierarchical structure. Campbell had telegraphed the Central Committee from Moscow explaining that there was general agreement with the proposals but that the matter would have to be agreed to at the highest level before a final decision could be made. Campbell was still sojourned in the Soviet Union awaiting the ECCI's final pronouncement, at the time that his own party Central Committee was meeting to discuss the issue.

Because of the *Daily Worker*'s inability to increase its sales, it sustained continuing criticism from the ECCI. At the British Commission meeting in August 1930 the paper's low circulation, just eleven thousand, was deplored, and the whole position was described as 'unsatisfactory'. Pollitt was clear that the reason for the lack of readers was due to the paper – it was its own worst enemy. It was "full of stuff that the working class does not want". In a critique that must have left Rust wincing Pollitt told the international leadership that the *Daily Worker* was a piece of sectarianism and was not getting across the party message as it should. Pollitt stressed that it was because of the paper's narrow character that it was not forging ahead – rather unfair attack on the paper's editor. It could be argued that neither the paper under Rust nor the CPGB under Pollitt, was growing much throughout 1930.[37] Things were so bad during the early part of the year, with the communists being attacked in every direction by their political opponents both inside and outside the Labour movement, that there was even talk amongst the leadership about the possibility of the CPGB and its paper being declared illegal. A discussion amongst the Politbureau at the end of May 1930 decided that it would be almost impossible to produce the *Daily Worker* in conditions of illegality.

Internal criticisms of the paper coupled with a boycott by the wholesalers were not the only challenges that the struggling *Daily Worker* had to contend with. There was also, particularly during its first year, a concerted effect by the paper's enemies to sue and imprison its proprietors at every available opportunity in what can now be recognised as one of the most sustained attacks on press freedom ever witnessed. If that were not enough, the paper was censored, particularly over its handling of news about discontent in the armed forces. It regularly appeared with blank spaces where a news item had fallen foul of the censor. The police, who were frequent visitors to the building where the paper was produced, carried out censorship. It was left to the police commander to determine what was permissible to print and what was not. The publishing of their daily paper during the new line years was for the communists a risky business. It was often carried out under police surveillance, and those responsible for its printing and publication faced threats of imprisonment and its sellers were continually harassed. In addition, there was the threat of massive fines.

As Pollitt had pointed out, the *Daily Herald*, with a readership of over a quarter of a million, had, in the end, succumbed to a takeover by a 'capitalist combine', Odhams Press. The party paper, without the subscription base of the *Daily Herald*, and with no influential financial supporters, could only rely on the self-sacrifice of its readers and supporters to keep it going.[38] This was often a mixed blessing. Finance appeared to be the easier of the sacrifices to make. In July 1930, the paper announced that every employed member of the party and Young Communist League was to set aside a day's wages for the *Daily Worker* Fighting Fund.[39] This presented no problem. However, when the paper wished to carry reports on the activity of the CPGB, this proved more difficult. The directive had come from the CI, which was critical of the *Daily Worker* for not carrying enough reports of CPGB activity.[40] The paper responded that they would be only too willing to publicise the communists' public work, but despite numerous appeals for information about party activity little was forthcoming.[41] Finally, in exasperation, the editorial board of the paper issued a directive to all units of the party that they must send in reports about their activities. The paper again emphasised the political importance of carrying details about the work of the CPGB.

The threat seemed to work. There were more reports of party activity, and the editorial board made no further exhortations for information to the party rank and file.[42]

The first in a string of prosecutions against the paper took place in July 1930. The *Daily Worker* sought to capitalise on the event with a typical class against class headline, '*Daily Worker* Prosecuted by Labour Government'.[43] The paper was being taken to court for a story and comments it had published the previous week, about the sentencing to eighteen months hard labour of a party member, E J Thomas, for distributing revolutionary leaflets to soldiers. The paper had been scathing of the judge in the case, Justice Rigby Swift. It was the first of many actions brought against the *Daily Worker* concerning its reporting of matters concerning the armed forces. Writs had been issued against the paper's publisher, Workers Press, which was owned and controlled by the CPGB. Three of the partners in the company, Frank Priestley, Frank Patterson, and F Brennan Ward were found guilty and sentenced to nine months, six months, and five months imprisonment respectively. Another collaborator, and party member, R McIlhone, was sentenced later to six months imprisonment. In addition to the prison sentences passed on the publishers, the printer was also fined two hundred and fifty pounds. In the wake of the prosecution, the paper announced on its front page, 'Our Worst Financial Crisis.'[44] The readers were told that not only did the paper have to find the money for the libel costs, but there was also an outstanding loan to be repaid. The usual appeals for finance were pepped up with a strongly worded statement that the paper was indeed facing a grave shortage of money that jeopardised its very existence.

Having been severely financially curtailed by its intervention into matters concerning the army, the paper faced a further threat the following year when it sought to intervene in the running of the senior service, the navy. During the first month of 1931, the paper paid undue attention to what it described as a 'mutiny 'aboard a depot ship, the *Lucia*, which serviced the second submarine flotilla. The issue was over leave, with the *Lucia* crew claiming that they received two days less than the rest of the Atlantic Fleet. The discontent was such that the men refused to take part in fatigue duty. In retaliation, thirty of them were arrested and marched to Devonport Naval Barracks where a court of enquiry took place. While the enquiry was taking place, the *Daily Worker* tempted fate by proclaiming in a front-page article that the affair was of the utmost importance because it 'revealed widespread discontent throughout the pride of British capitalism – the Royal Navy.'[45] The paper also gave wide publicity to the solidarity that was building up in the labour movement with the *Lucia* crew. The paper's readers were told that the Stratford Three branch of the Amalgamated Engineering Union in London had 'passed a resolution demanding the release of the thirty sailors, and urging that all members of the armed forces be given the right to join a trade union. In South Wales, Arthur Horner called for solidarity with the 'Lucia' men, when he addressed striking South Wales miners. The paper also advertised other trade union branches that had expressed support for the 'mutiny'. A few days later in response to the Court of Enquiry's report that four of the thirty should be court marshalled, the paper called for continued pressure on the Admiralty to drop the case.

When the sentences on the four accused were announced, towards the end of January, the communists were unequivocal in their condemnation of the whole procedure. One of the prisoners was sentenced to three months hard labour, after which he was to be dismissed from the service, and the other three were to be sent for trial. The *Daily Worker* argued that it was alone amongst the press in claiming that the whole affair was due to the harsh conditions suffered by the men, coupled with bullying by some of the officers on the ship. For the paper, the outcome was never in doubt given that the court-martial was conducted by what it described as, 'boss-class disciplinarians of an approved type'.[46] Such accusations put the paper once again under the threat of court action, but surprisingly none was taken, and the *Daily Worker* carried on covering the story. The communists continued to call for solidarity with the *Lucia* crew and publicised all messages of support from the Labour movement. The paper even exposed the secrecy surrounding the case. *Daily Worker* readers were told that twenty-seven members of the Lucia's crew had been marched under armed guard to a light cruiser, *Canterbury*. Sentences had been passed on the men but no one outside 'naval circles', not even the men's relatives, knew what these sentences were.

It was with no small measure of self-satisfaction that on January 29 1931, after more than three weeks devotion to the case, that the *Daily Worker* told its readers in a front-page spread that '*Lucia* Officers to be put on half pay'. The paper's agitation over the issue seems to have met with some success. The First Lord of the Admiralty had announced to the House of Commons that the sentences passed on the crew were to be reduced and that some officers were to have their appointments terminated.[47] The Admiralty conceded that the behaviour of individual officers on the *Lucia* had contributed to the discontent. In triumphalist tone, the *Daily Worker* declared:

> "the tremendous indignation and sympathy for the 'Lucia' men that existed throughout the lower decks and amongst industrial workers has had its effect, and the Government hopes to stave off further manifestations of anger by this half-hearted concession. On the other hand, it should encourage the working-class movement to press forward with its demands for the immediate and unconditional release of the *Lucia* prisoners and the fight for the demands contained in the Sailors' and Marines' Programme of the Communist Party." [48]

Such an uncompromising stance, with its veiled incitement to mutiny, made it almost sure that the *Daily Worker* would again be taken to court. It did not happen. For some reason, the paper escaped prosecution over the 'Lucia' affair, and it was to be a further nine months before its coverage of a similar outbreak of discontent in the Royal Navy came under scrutiny. This time there was to be no such leniency, and the paper's support for the Invergordon mutineers of September 1931, brought down upon the paper the full force of the courts, and the wrath of the censors.

Before the events at Invergordon took place, the *Daily Worker*, like the CPGB, saw an upturn in its fortunes. The turnaround in party membership first noted by Idris Cox in December 1930 (see Chapter 4) was also reflected in a growth in sales of the paper, which by June 1931 were up to 12,346. Cox reported to the ECCI that sales of the paper had increased and that there was an additional sale of six thousand extra copies on a Saturday. Cox attributed this to 'a more efficient method of distribution which is carried on on business lines, thus enabling the Party membership to carry on the campaign for increased readers for the daily'. [49] The growth in the paper's circulation continued throughout 1931, and toward the end of the year, sales had increased by over fifty per cent, rising from 12,068 in January to 18,252 by October. What was particularly encouraging was the upsurge in weekend sales. These were first reported on in April 1931when the paper announced that weekend sales had 'surpassed all previous records with an additional 11,250 copies being sold'. The readers were told that if just one in four of these new supporters would take the paper on a daily basis then the *Daily Worker*'s weekend six pages, which was under threat, could be saved.[50] Despite the record weekend sales, it was not to be, and as from May 1931, the Saturday six pager ceased.

Despite the curtailment in the paper's Saturday size, the weekend sales continued to grow, and there were almost monthly announcements of the paper's good fortune. At the end of June, records were again broken with extra weekend sales up to 13,379.[51]

In July, as part of the campaign against war, the paper decided on a special six-page Saturday edition with two pages devoted to the party's anti-war campaign. The following month the paper reported yet another record increase with an extra 16,283 copies of the paper being sold at the weekend. The paper was now sufficiently established to produce, as a one-off, the first-ever eight-page edition, which came out on August 1 1931. By the beginning of September, weekend records had again been broken with extra sales now at 18,454. Such was the confidence of the communists in their new venture that the readership was told that with just a little extra push the *Daily Worker* could expand to become six pages every day. There was some substance in the claim. The paper had increased its daily circulation, as opposed to weekend sales, by two thousand copies over the past two weeks. This represented more than a twenty-five per cent increase in sales and took the paper's circulation from 10,209 copies in August to 12,838 copies in September 1931.[52]

By the end of the summer of 1931, prospects for the *Daily Worker* looked good. Despite the wholesalers' boycott, sales were on the increase, thanks to the dedication and adaptability of the party members who had instituted their own distribution network, and weekend sales could more than double the circulation achieved during the week. The expansion in size of the paper was a distinct possibility, and most important of all, it was mainly due to the success of the paper that the CPGB was beginning to grow. Of the recruits made during the latter part of 1931, it was estimated that about forty a week were achieved through the *Daily Worker*.[53] All these achievements were put in jeopardy when the paper voiced its admiration for the naval mutineers at Invergordon in Scotland, whose grievances it had first brought to the attention of its readers in September 1931. The papers continued support for the naval ratings earned its publishers and printers fines and jail sentences and its journalists and workers the undivided attention of the police with their draconian powers of censorship.

News of the unrest amongst the sailors of the Atlantic Fleet was first conveyed to the paper's readers in a front-page article published on September 17 1931. The announcement that some of the men had gone on strike and were not prepared to accept pay cuts prompted the paper to pursue a similar tack to that employed during the 'Lucia' affair, focussing onthe working-class backgrounds of those involved in the dispute. This was in accord with the CPGB's demand for trade union rights for all service personnel. The paper gave extensive coverage to the stoppage and claimed that, 'the action of the men of the Atlantic Fleet afforded still further proof that the working class lads who joined the navy did not thereby lose their class feeling.'[54] Such was the militancy of the men that the paper even reported that the 'Red Flag' had been sung in the canteen. The next day the *Daily Worker* continued with its news of Invergordon and carried parts of the manifesto issued by the striking sailors which stated that they would accept cuts in their wages but that the cuts would have to be reasonable. George Hardy, a prominent communist seamen's leader, followed up news of the men's demands a few days later with an article.

Whether it was the paper's coverage of Invergordon or the interest aroused by the impending General Election, it is difficult to say, but what is certain is that the popularity of the *Daily Worker* continued to grow. In the immediate aftermath of the mutiny the paper announced that in future it would be six pages on a Saturday, and that weekend sales had now exceeded over 23,000 extra copies. [55] It was at precisely this moment of its greatest triumph since its creation that the paper faced its biggest test. On September 28, 1931, the paper appeared, but with many blank spaces. The surprised readership was told that the previous day there had been a raid by the police, who had entered the building, without a search warrant, and had taken away documents and files belonging to the paper, and seized all cheque books. Names and addresses of all those working at the *Daily Worker* had been taken, and so too were those of anyone visiting the paper. An article by Saklatvala on Gandhi, which was to have been published, was confiscated. In addition, the paper's staff were informed that henceforth they could publish nothing that related to the armed forces – a ban that was extended two days later to the Minority Movement's publication, *The Worker*. Clearly, the tolerant approach by the authorities, which had been in vogue at the time of the 'Lucia' affair, was now a thing of the past, and the *Daily Worker* was to be on the receiving end of an assault by all those who viewed any incursion into what went on in the armed services, particularly by a communist newspaper, as little short of treason.

The paper replied to what it viewed as an attack on press freedom, with an announcement that it was to double its print run. It was a brave response, and over the next months, supporters of the *Daily Worker* rallied to its defence. The censorship continued for some time, and in a most unusual step, what was to be considered libellous was to be determined, not by the courts, but by the police. According to the paper's editor, he had to pass on all material that was to appear in the *Daily Worker* to a senior policeman, who would then decide what could be included. [56] Even parts of the cartoon character Micky Mongrel, a militant dog, did not escape the censor's axe, and parts of the cartoon series, when they appeared, had blank spaces. Throughout the General Election campaign of October 1931, the *Daily Worker* was faced with a continuing attempt to censor its news. Despite that, the paper announced that two thousand extra *daily* readers had been won.[57] Within a week of the commencement of the censorship, one of the paper's printers was taken to court and charged with, "seducing persons serving in His Majesty's Forces from their duty". He was committed for trial and three weeks later was found guilty and sentenced to nine months imprisonment.[58] The following month another party member, and, on paper, one of the owners of the *Daily Worker*, Frank Paterson, was found guilty on a similar charge of incitement to mutiny and sentenced to two years hard labour. The day after Paterson's sentence two other leading communists involved with the paper, George Allison and Bill Shepherd were put on trial over Invergordon. They too were found guilty and sentenced to three years and twenty months hard labour respectively.

The sustained attack on the paper's very existence continued into 1932. Barely a week after the start of the New Year, the paper's business manager, Frank Priestly, was arrested, once again on the charge of incitement to mutiny. The communists claimed that this latest threat 'carried the attack on the *Daily Worker* still further'.[59] Priestley, at his trial, fared no better than any of the others, and two weeks later, he too was found guilty of incitement and sentenced to three years in jail. Yet another of the paper's employees, one of the newly named proprietors, Clarence Mason, was found guilty of publishing inflammatory material and received a jail sentence of six months, and the paper was fined £1500. The new managing director of Utopia Press, which was controlled by the CPGB, Kay Beauchamp, was also fined. Unable to pay the amount, she went to prison, where she was detained for five months. Such was the persecution of the paper during 1932 that at the end of the year the *Daily Worker* carried a full-page spread documenting the actions that had been taken against it since its foundation.

It was not just the threat of imprisonment or fines that the paper faced. The building where the paper was produced was under constant surveillance, and the *Daily Worker* even published a photograph on its front page, which somehow got by the police censorship, that showed two policemen on duty watching the premises.[60] Apart from attempts to intimidate the staff, the police also took measures to prevent the sale of the paper, particularly during industrial disputes. This is certainly what happened during a strike of London dockers in early 1932 when attempts were made to prevent the sale of the paper outside the dock gates.[61]

The assault on the *Daily Worker* was beginning to tell, particularly the financial constraints posed by the fines. In May 1932 came the warning that without one thousand new *daily* readers, and five thousand new weekend readers, the paper would once again have to be reduced in size to four pages. So urgent was the need for more money that a statement appeared on June 2, 1932, from the Editorial Board, appealing for nine hundred and fifty pounds by June 14; otherwise the paper would have to revert to four pages. June 14 came and went, and still, the paper remained at six pages. Some of the nine hundred and fifty pounds must have been collected because by September, well past the June closing date, there were still exhortations to 'save the six pager' and to fulfil the by now four hundred pounds appeal.

Despite the ups and downs in the paper's size, and the regular crises of finance, the *Daily Worker* was for the communists a success story of the new line. It survived the wholesalers' boycott, the police harassment, the censorship, the fines, the intimidation of those trying to sell the paper, and the imprisonment of its owners and printers. Not only did the paper overcome all these obstacles, but it also managed to increase its circulation, and by the end of the class against class period its survival, at least in the immediate future, was not in doubt.

The establishment of the paper, as we have seen, was a vital prerequisite of the new strategy. If the communists were to become the undisputed leaders and organisers of the working class, then they needed a daily paper that would popularise their tactics and ensure that their vanguard role was understood by the class they sought to represent. The circulation of their new paper was an essential factor in this fight.

The *Daily Worker*'s predecessor, the weekly *Workers Life*, had a circulation, at its demise, of about 45000, and there were expectations that the daily sales of the new paper would be in the region of that figure. It suggests that the party leadership had an optimistic assessment of how many copies the new paper would sell. By the middle of the year realism had settled in and by June 1930 circulation was around 10000-12000 daily.

Sales of the paper, like the party, reached a low point towards the end of 1930.

Circulation dropped from about 11000 in July 1930 to 10,614 in February of the following year.[62] It will be remembered that Party membership made a rapid increase during the first part of 1931 and this was reflected in increased sales of the paper, which by June 1931 had increased to 12,346.[63]

The significant increase in *Daily Worker* sales came with the General Election of October 1931. In the one month period of the party's campaign around its election candidates, sales increased by almost fifty per cent, going from 12,838 in September 1931 to 18,252 by the end of October. What was particularly pleasing for Pollitt was that he was able to report to the CI's Anglo-American Secretariat meeting at the end of 1931 that the figure of 18000 plus was for papers actually paid for and not just for the numbers printed.[64]

Enthused by the success of their new venture, at their first Central Committee meeting of 1932 the Party leadership, recommended some changes for the *Daily Worker*. In what Rust must have considered a slight on his editorship, the paper was criticised for not carrying out 'a more offensive struggle against reformism'.[65] In order to more effectively hone its new weapon, the Central Committee decided on several measures that in its view, would draw the paper closer to the working class and its struggles. The party's political committee would develop its contacts in the factories, and make the workers' criticism of the paper known to the editorial board. The board itself would be expanded to include those comrades who were involved in mass work. There would also be established a Press Commission consisting of twenty to thirty workers who would meet the editorial board regularly.

These changes, particularly the novel idea of a press commission, sparked some controversy about the future direction of the paper and its organisation. The two protagonists in the dispute were the Chairman of the London Communist Print Cell and RP Dutt. The differences were aired in the May 1932 edition of *Communist Review*. An article appeared entitled 'A Popular Workers Newspaper', which was critical of certain aspects of the *Daily Worker*'s presentation. Both Rust and the newly arrived Allen Hutt were castigated for their poor sub-editing skills and lack of imaginative headlines. The paper was described as 'dull and heavy' and worst of all, it 'uses many formulations which deviate from the line of the Party'. It was accused of pursuing a 'leftist line' on sport which was, 'sport is a capitalist institution'; therefore let us ignore it". Although critical, the article made several suggestions about ways of improving the paper. It welcomed the idea of a firm reliance on 'worker correspondents' for news. However, it argued that these volunteer reporters needed training, which could be done at classes organised by the communists in the *Daily Worker* Print Cell. The idea was to, 'build a corps of working-class journalists who could fight as they write and fight the better because they can write'. The tone of the message was that the paper needed to learn from capitalist technology, just as the USSR had learnt from advances in American technology. Besides, to get away from its amateurism, the paper should consider employing communists who had already been trained as professional journalists but were currently employed by other newspapers.[66]

This reliance on aspects of capitalist technique by a communist daily was too much for R P Dutt who swiftly penned a reply which appeared in *Communist Review* two months later. Dutt attacked the whole idea of being able to learn anything from what he described as 'bourgeois journalism'. For him, journalists working for capitalist papers were, 'spiritual, ideological agents of capitalism, in the same sense as clergymen.' [67] Dutt rejected the suggestions made by the communist print workers, almost in their entirety, and the controversy petered out. As there was no marked alteration in the *Daily Worker*'s presentation throughout 1932, it would appear that Dutt's more orthodox views for the paper's immediate prospects prevailed. One change that did occur at the end of 1932 was that the paper's original editor, Bill Rust, was replaced by Jimmy Shields. Rust went to Moscow to represent the British party at the ECCI.

Disagreements over the paper's direction did not affect its continued rising popularity. Throughout 1932 its sales steadily increased and by the Party Congress in November stood at 21000 for weekday sales, from Monday to Thursday. A special effort by party members for the weekend ensured sales of 30,000 on a Friday, and the Saturday edition of the paper, which was six pages, sold 46,000 copies. This figure corresponded with the sales of *Workers Life* at the time that the '*Daily Worker* superseded it'. It was quite a remarkable effort given that the party membership, who were primarily responsible for the sale and distribution of the paper, numbered no more than 5,400 – admittedly double that at the start of the new line, but still very small. By the end of 1932 the sales of the paper were four times that of the party membership. This factor of four to one was reasonably constant throughout the period.

The popularity of the paper continued to grow as the class against class strategy began to wane. By May 1933, a few months after Hitler's coming to power and the CI's call for a united front against fascism, sales of the paper had crept up to 21,602, a modest three per cent increase. There was no sudden inrush of new readers because the ECCI changed line. The *Daily Worker*, like the party it represented, underwent no radical change of perspective because of the CI's policy change. It was to be another year before the British party finally jettisoned its class against class tactics and the paper, with its anti-Labour rhetoric, continued in the same vein until well into 1934. The change of editor at the end of 1932 also made no difference to the paper's commitment to the new line. Rust may have been known for his devotion to the new strategy, but his departure for Moscow brought no perceptible alteration in the paper's policy or tone.

The *Daily Worker* was very much a product of the new line. Without the Communist Party's conversion to the new strategy, it is doubtful that the paper would have made the appearance when it did. For seven years, a daily communist paper had been placed on the back burner of CPGB priorities. The party had tailored its tactics to suit its overriding objective, which was Labour Party affiliation. Once this aim became unrealisable, and the communists embarked on the course of unremitting hostility towards the larger organisation, a daily communist voice became imperative – without one, it was felt that communists would be incapable of giving leadership to the working class in their day to day struggles.

That the *Daily Worker* not only survived but also managed to increase its sales during the years of class against class says something about both the commitment and the dedication of its readers and workers. Born on the eve of the *Daily Herald's* demise as the voice of the labour movement, the *Daily Worker* with a much smaller readership base, never more than one-tenth of that of the Herald, relied on its supporters, not only to sell the paper but to initiate a distribution network when after one month the newspaper wholesalers began their concerted effort to destroy the new publication. Not only did the communists have to improvise and turn themselves into distributors of their new venture, but they also needed to finance the paper when the many fines imposed by the courts also threatened the paper's existence. Finally, workers at the paper, and those directly associated with it, sustained jail sentences and harassment during its early years and they were subjected to close police scrutiny and censorship in their endeavours to establish the paper's credibility. They were rewarded when, after many early assertions that the paper would not survive, not only did it become a regular and potent advocate of communist policy, and one that won many recruits for the party, but it also managed, during the three core years of the new line, to double its readership and emerge from the period as a formidable weapon of the party it represented.

The paper gave a focus to the embattled communists at a time when the liquidation of the party must have seemed a real possibility. It provided them with a rallying point, and sales of the paper became a priority. Party locals mobilised around the paper distribution, and the party's campaigning themes were given expression through its pages. It was a paper aimed at the militants in the movement and provided them with information on a range of national and international issues. It covered all aspects of the class struggle and managed to reach out beyond the small but growing number of party members. The message was sharp, but it was increasingly being taken up by those activists who accepted the communists' view, at least in part, that nothing could be gained by adherence to the Labour Party. For modern critics of the class against class policy, and they are numerous, it must come as something of an irony that the strategy they despised and put down solely to Moscow's intervention, should have produced one of the few lasting monuments to British communism.

Notes
1 *From the Fourth to the Fifth World Congress: Report of the Executive Committee of the CI.* CPGB,1924, p37
2 Closed Letter to the CC of the CPGB from the ECCI, May 9, 1926
3 Meeting of the Anglo American Secretariat of the CI. August 8, 1927
4 *Workers Life*, March 9, 1928
5 Report of the 10th Congress of the CPGB,
6 *Workers Life*, August 9, 1929
7 See *Workers Life*, July 26, 1929, and August 1, 1929
8 *Workers Life*, 23, August 1929
9 CPGB Central Committee Meeting, January 11-12, 1930
10 *The Story of the Daily Worker'*, Bill Rust, page11
11 *Ibid.*
12 CPGB Central Committee Meeting, August 7-11, 1929.
13 CPGB Central Committee Meeting, November 30, 1929 at Leeds after the Second day of discussion.

14 Letter to the Congress of the CPGB from the ECCI, November 28 1929
15 *Workers Life*, November 1, 1929
16 *Workers Life*, October 18, 1929
17 *Communist Review*, December 1929 18 *Ibid*
19 *Ibid*
20 *Ibid*
21 CPGB Central Committee Meeting, January 11-12, 1930)
22 *Ibid*
23 *Daily Worker*, January 22, 1930
24 See *Daily Worker*, February 6, 7, 8, 1930.
25 *Daily Worker*, January 14, 1930.
26 *Daily Worker*, February 5, 1930
27 *Daily Worker*, February 5, 1930
28 *Daily Worker*, January 27, 1930
29. *Daily Worker*, July 20, 1930
30 *Daily Worker*. August 2, 1930
31 *Daily Worker*, August 21, 1930
32. *Daily Worker*, August 25, 1930
33 *Daily Worker*, October 2, 1930
34 See, *The Story of the Daily Worker*, Bill Rust
35 *Workers Life* March 2,3 1928.
36. CPGB, Central Committee Meeting, April 5, 1930
37 ECCI Report of the British Commission, August 1930
38. *Ibid*
39 *Daily Worker*, July 8, 1930.
40 *Daily Worker*, March 6, 1930
41 *Daily Worker*, February 4, 1930
42 *Daily Worker*, March 19, 1930.
43 *Daily Worker*, July 12, 1930.
44 *Daily Worker*, October 20, 1930.
45 *Daily Worker*, January 8, 1931
46 *Daily Worker*, January 21, 1931
47 *Daily Worker*, January 29, 1931
48 *Ibid*.
49 ECCI Presidium Meeting, December 12, 1930.
50 *Daily Worker*, April 21 1931.
51 *Daily Worker*, June 30, 1931.
52 See James Klugman notes
53 See James Klugman notes, Report on Party organisation Nov 1931
54 *Daily Worker*, September 17, 1931
55 *Daily Worker*, September 25, 1931
56 See, The Story of the *Daily Worker*, Bill Rust
57 *Daily Worker*, October 3, 1931
58 *Daily Worker*, October 3, 1931
59 *Daily Worker*, January 5, 1932
60 *Daily Worker*, February 1, 1932
61 *Daily Worker*, January 9, 1932
62 See, Anglo American Secretariat of the CI, July 30, 1930
63 See, James Klugman Notes, Report on Party Organisation Nov 1931
64 See, Anglo American Secretariat of the CI, December 2, 1931
65 *Communist Review*, March 1932, 'Building a Bolshevik Party in Britain'.
66 *Communist Review*, May 1932
67. *Communist Review*, July 1932

7 The struggle against imperialism

IT WAS DURING the class against class period that the Communist Party conducted some of its most memorable battles against colonialism. Anti-imperialism, which had been crucial since the early days of the party, now became the pivot of the party's entire strategy.

Almost since the party's formation, there had been significant disagreements over this issue between British communists and the Communist International. So profoundly different were both organisations in their approach, that at the CI's Sixth World Congress in 1928, virtually the entire British delegation voted against the Comintern's manifesto on the subject. This document so incensed the British delegates that they issued an amendment to the Colonial Thesis. This amendment was overwhelmingly defeated by 515 votes to 12. The twelve dissidents consisted almost entirely of the majority of the British delegation. In the debate, the CPGB delegates did not mince their words. They recommended that the delegates vote against the CI thesis because in the words of their spokesman:

> "in an effort to reconcile false premises and wrong conclusions with actual realities and the principles of Marx and Lenin, the thesis repeatedly falls into an eclecticism unworthy of a Comintern document...This eclectic method deprives the thesis of all semblance of a militant document, such as a Comintern resolution ought to be".[1]

These were strong words and hardly fit in with the fashionable stereotype, beloved of so many historians of British communism, of a British party overawed and subservient to its international superior.

From 1920 until 1928, there was a running battle between the CPGB and the CI over how to conduct the anti-colonial fight. If proof was necessary of the CPGB's independent approach towards defining policy. nowhere was it more apparent than over this issue. For the first eight years of its existence, the CPGB pursued a line on colonialism that was at variance with that of the Comintern. Not only did the CPGB disagree over anti-colonial strategy, but one of its leading personnel in this field, Shapurji Saklatvala, was suspicious of CI functionaries, and of the leading CI spokesperson on colonial matters, the Indian communist, MN Roy. British communists, in turn, were criticised by the international body and the CI was scornful of the CPGB's efforts around anti-imperialism.

The British party was right to be critical of the CI. Colonialism as an issue did not figure prominently in the thinking of the communists' international organisation, at least until 1928. It was not until the Sixth Congress of the Comintern in that year that there was to be a full debate on the subject. At the inaugural Congress of the International, in 1919, the question of colonialism was practically ignored. At the third international gathering, it was hardly referred to at all, despite attempts by MN Roy, to raise it as an issue. There was no resolution on colonialism or imperialism, and no other delegate, apart from Roy, referred to its importance. At the Fourth Congress, there was a fuller discussion, but it revolved around the 'Eastern Question', and there was little debate about the nature of imperialism, or anti-imperialist strategy. At the Fifth Congress, in 1924, colonialism was linked to the National Question and every speaker but one, was concerned with the latter issue. Given this lack of interest, it is not surprising that the British Party, with very little guidance coming from Moscow, pursued its own course.

In the period preceding the new line, the CPGB was active on all matters concerned with imperialism. Not only did the party conduct its own independent campaigns, but communists, who were Labour Party members, repeatedly raised imperialism as a matter of concern within the larger organisation. This agitation went almost unnoticed by the leadership of the CI. At a plenary session of the ECCI in 1923, to which the entire Executive Committee of the CPGB was invited, there were complaints against the CPGB for its lack of concern with colonial matters. These complaints were repeated at the CI's Fifth Congress the following year. Maniulsky, speaking on behalf of the ECCI, even accused the CPGB of not advocating colonial freedom. This false accusation was without a shred of evidence and only emphasised how uninformed the CI was about the CPGB's contribution to anti-colonialism. At the Party's Sixth Congress, which had taken place only a few months before Maniulsky made his assertions, the resolution on colonialism recognised the need to build unity between British and colonial workers and contrary to ECCI claims called for an end to colonisation. The British Party even went so far as to claim that there could be no revolution in Britain while the colonies were subjugated.[2]

During the first few years of its existence, the British Party campaigned around some of the following critical colonial issues. Soon after the CPGBs formation, and despite internal difficulties, it agitated against the conflict of imperialist interests in Turkey. It campaigned for the release of the Kawnpore prisoners – a group of Indian communists arrested in 1924, which included MN Roy, who was tried in his absence. The party condemned the action of McDonald's 1924 Labour Government for continuing the colonial policy of the Tories. There was very little that happened within the British Empire with which the CPGB was not concerned. At the Party's Seventh Congress in 1925, it reiterated its opposition to imperialism and again highlighted the importance of colonial freedom in the fight for socialism. The CPGB recognised the failings of the Labour movement in this area of struggle and all party members were urged to make anti-imperialism a vital cornerstone of their work.[3]

During the period from 1920 until 1928 the communists made many attempts to raise anti-colonialism within the broader Labour movement. The Seventh Congress urged communist members of the Labour Party to ensure that it was taken up both locally and nationally by the larger organisation The Congress resolution instructed all party members who were members of the Labour Party to make it a priority that anti-colonialism was raised as one of the most important issues within the Labour Party. Communists were, if possible, to initiate a discussion in their local Labour Party branches, and also to try and ensure that there was a resolution on imperialism on the agenda at Labour Party National Conferences.[4]

Up until their expulsion from the Labour Party the communists were in an ideal position to push colonialism as an issue, primarily because one of their leading members, Shapurji Saklatvala, was not only Indian but was for a brief period a Labour MP. He had been a Labour Party and Independent Labour Party activist since soon after the time of his arrival in Britain in 1906. He was sufficiently well thought of in the Labour Party that had he renounced his communist views it is almost certain he would have been offered the post of Under Secretary of State for India in the 1924 Labour Government.

Saklatvala, on instructions from CPGB, raised colonial freedom at his first National Labour Party Annual Conference in 1922. He unsuccessfully moved a resolution that the conference should not support the Government of India Act. The Indian National Congress opposed the act because it enfranchised just five per cent of the people. It was Saklatvala too who was instrumental in establishing the broadly based Indian Defence Committee in response to the trial of MN Roy and the Kawnpore prisoners in 1924. The trail, which was conducted during the period of the first Labour Government, was condemned, not just by the communists, but also by others on the left. The agitation around the Kawnpore trial enlisted the support of such noted Labour left-wingers as George Lansbury and James Maxton.

The broadly based Indian Defence Committee was a forerunner of the much more successful League Against Imperialism, established three years later in 1927. This international organisation was another communist initiative that originally brought together national liberation movements in the colonies and the Communist and Workers Parties in capitalist countries. The idea was first mooted by the CI and then extremely successfully taken by the CPGB. The League was one of the first casualties of the new line and Labour Party supporters of the League, along with their counterparts in the colonies, were successfully driven out by the communists. Throughout much of the period of class against class, the League, by now totally communist-dominated, still managed to conduct campaigns against all aspects of colonialism and continuously struggled to keep colonial issues alive in the working-class movement.

Yet another anti-imperialist organisation with which the communists were closely associated was the Workers Welfare League of India. Established in 1916 by Saklatvala, the League sought to bring to the attention of the Labour movement social conditions in India. So well established was the League that until 1928 it was the All India Trade Union Congress's official mouthpiece in Britain. In that year, because of the League's open association with the CPGB, it was decided that in future that role should be delegated to the Trades Union Congress. Until then Saklatvala had spoken on the League's behalf at several Trade Unions Congresses. The WWL too continued to flourish during the class against class period, although like the LAI it was little more than a communist front.

Saklatvala too in the period preceding the new line was involved in the party's active participation in Indian affairs. Under the direction of the CPGB's Colonial Department, he was in contact with Indian students who were temporarily resident in Britain before returning home. His role was to ascertain their political reliability and to maintain contact with them after their return to India. He was thus able to help the Indian National Congress, and also assist the small number of communists living in India. This dual-task, of assisting the INC and helping to form a Communist Party in the subcontinent, was given a tremendous boost when Saklatvala, as an MP, visited India for three months at the start of 1927. The tour, undertaken at the CPGB's behest, had two purposes. The public or open side of Saklatvala's activities was a whole series of public events and meetings at which he spelt out his ideas about the future direction of the Indian national movement. This included several meetings with Gandhi and the famous Gandhi-Saklatvala dialogue, which was reproduced in the Indian papers and subsequently issued as a pamphlet in Britain. In the dialogue, both participants expounded their views about India's future development. There was also, however, another more clandestine side to Saklatvala's visit, and that was to make contact with the small and scattered groups of Indian communists. While there, he also planned to attend the convention of the newly formed Communist Party of India.

It is necessary to deal briefly with the CPGB's anti-colonial record before class against class in order to show that right from its formation the British Party was concerned with the overthrow of the British Empire. One of the major criticisms of the 1924 McDonald Government had been that it took no steps towards colonial liberation. Tom Bell, addressing the Sixth Party Congress, meeting midway through the Government's short term of office, stated that:

> "the first thing that MacDonald does is to send a letter to the struggling masses of India, warning them that if they attempt to embark upon militant or direct action in order to get the first principle of social democracy, the right of determination of their own political destination, that such actions shall be met with all the power of the Empire and state'.

Language, Bell went on, 'that Lord Curzon himself would use.'[5]

It will be remembered that it was the performance of the first Labour Government that was an essential contributory factor in pushing the membership of the CPGB towards the new line and nowhere were the communists more exasperated than over the Government's handling of colonial issues.

This negative assessment of social democracy was further hardened by the communists' second experience of Labour in power – the 1929-31 Labour Government. In the view of the CPGB, this Government also took no steps whatsoever towards granting colonial freedom and the lot of colonial workers was, if anything, worse under Labour than the Tories. The *Daily Worker* published a list of all those colonial possession of Britain's in which oppression had taken place under the Labour Government. These included India, Burma, China, Egypt, Palestine, West Africa and South Africa.[6] In the run-up to the 1931 General Election in October, the communists again exposed Labour's record in this area, and there was a significant article in their paper entitled 'The Starvation Empire'.[7]

If, in the estimation of the CPGB, the Labour Government's colonial record was terrible, what was even worse was that it tried to make matters difficult for those who were ready to fight against imperialism. McDonald's administration prevented Saklatvala from making a return trip to India in 1930. There were problems in gaining an entry visa for Mrs Wright, the mother of one of the imprisoned Scottsboro boys. Even an International Negro Conference organised by the CI was banned from meeting in Britain. It was the lack of action around colonialism by the second Labour Government that was persuasive in hardening even further communist hostility towards social democracy. The Party's Eleventh Congress meeting sometime after the General Election that brought the Labour Party to power spelt out both the communists' antagonism towards Labour over this issue and the party's commitment to improving its colonial work, "The colonial work must be changed from a sort of departmental task into a living part of the daily work and bound up with the struggle in the factories, so as to realise the united front of the British workers and the colonial masses against the Labour Government." [8]

The new line successfully harmonised the CPGB's domestic and international strategy, which became one of opposition to social democracy at home, and war on social democracy's allies in the National Liberation Movement. For the communists, the Achilles heel of social democracy was the Empire. As the first of their new line congresses made clear 'the fight against reformism and the socialist traitors in the British working class movement turns essentially on the question of the British Empire.' [9] It was a 'go it alone' approach that brooked no compromise. The CPGB during the class against class years from 1928 onwards jettisoned any attempts to seek allies amongst either the colonial national bourgeoisie or the non-communist elements in the various freedom movements in the colonies. The party's previous commitment to a broad class alliance in the colonial struggle, which had brought it into conflict with the Comintern in the period preceding 1928, was now scrapped. Henceforth the links that had been established with Gandhi, and the leadership of the Indian National Congress, were severed and it was not until 1935 that the British Party returned to its pre-new line strategy of a broad, class-based alliance to win national liberation.

To mount a campaign against colonialism, whose ideology had deep roots in the working-class movement, was a problematic task – rendered even more difficult by the CPGB's small size. For much of the new line period, the party was a minute organisation, which, even in times of membership boom, never reached, even momentarily, more than 9000 members. For most of the time, there were less than 5000 party members, and during the early part of the new line, from 1929-31, no more than 2500. As a group, British communists were poor, unemployed, often victimised for their trade union militancy, and many were in prison for their activities. Their daily paper was constantly harassed, the rights of communists in their trade unions were under threat, and some, rather than give up their party membership, relinquished their posts as full-time trade union officials. In the broader Labour movement, they were ostracised and isolated.

Nevertheless, with all these disadvantages, they still managed to conduct guerrilla warfare against colonialism, and it was during the new line that they, virtually alone, kept to the forefront these issues and brought them to the attention of the British people. It needs to be remembered that to be anti-imperialist at this time was to be very much swimming against the stream of public opinion. Even the most internationalist sections of the Labour movement never gave a high priority to colonial freedom. It was left to the communists to raise this issue and small in number though they were, they did so very effectively.

In dealing with the CPGB and its efforts against colonialism, this chapter will look at the CPGB's steady and continuing propaganda and activity around this issue. The party's contribution to the fight against racism, which was unique amongst the political party's at the time, will be dealt with in the following chapter. Invariably, however, both imperialism and racism overlap. For example, the party's demand for India's independence necessitated an explanation of why India was subjected, and how Indians were perfectly capable of governing themselves. It would be an unlikely scenario for, on the one hand, the party to campaign against colonialism, and yet on the other hand not to conduct an ideological battle against those ideas that underpinned colonialism. As we shall see, the CPGB did both. It campaigned against racial subjection abroad, and it sought to root out racism at home.

This chapter and the next draw heavily on reports and publicity published in the party press, particularly the *Daily Worker*. There are no excuses for this. It is possible to write a history of the CPGB during this period by looking at CPGB Central Committee minutes and Comintern deliberations – no credible research would be complete without referring to the proceedings of these higher bodies. The writer would, of course, need to be aware that the CI was constantly criticising all parties belonging to the international body. Nevertheless, any attempt to give a rounded view of the CPGB at any stage of its history would not be complete without resorting to what the party membership was doing in its everyday activity. For this, the party press is invaluable. It tells us what local branches were up to, what campaigns were being undertaken, what meetings were being called and how the membership was responding in a myriad of ways to the demands placed upon them by the party leadership. The *Daily Worker* was particularly useful for racism and imperialism. No amount of research in the now opened Comintern archive can substitute for the rich resources that are contained in the pages of the paper. The *Daily Worker* kept the party membership and sympathisers informed about the day-to-day activities of the CPGB. Only by trawling through the paper and its contents is it possible to get an overview of what concerned Britain's communists during the period. What stares out at us is their obsession with colonialism and their avant garde approach to fighting racism.

Until 1928, the CPGB had many commendable campaigns around imperialism to its credit. What was different with the advent of the new line was that the party integrated anti-imperialism into its overall activity, rather than regarded it as a separate entity. This meant that the fight against colonialism could no longer be seen as merely the property of the Party's Colonial Department. Delegates to the Eleventh Congress were told that 'colonial work must be changed from a sort of departmental task into a living part of the daily work and bound up with the struggle in the factories, so as to realise the united front of the British workers and the colonial masses.'[10] At its first new line conference earlier in the year there was a special resolution on 'The Colonial Tasks of the CPGB', in which the party leadership spelt out the importance of anti-imperialism in the Party's work and how it was 'to occupy a more and more important place.' [11]

From now on, the fight against colonialism was to be one of the communists' major objectives. The new approach that saw the struggle against imperialism as inseparably bound to the fight for socialism was best articulated by Pollitt, who told the delegates to the Twelfth Party Congress meeting in the midst of class against class, that:

"...... once we can begin to get a better realisation of the conviction that anti-Imperialist work is not something apart from our usual work, but is part of the *daily* work, then our work will begin to take on a much more positive character. There can be no speedy and successful building of socialism in this country if the revolution came tomorrow, unless we have in a thousand ways and by a thousand means already established contact and won the confidence and trust of the Indian, Irish, Chinese and all the colonial masses." [12]

It was a conception that lasted throughout the new line and beyond. From 1928 onwards, British communists placed greater emphasis on showing the importance of defeating imperialism as an integral part of the realisation of socialism. Even at the demise of the class against class phase, the CPGB still declared that, "....the struggle for the national liberation of the colonial and semi colonial masses is a component part of the world proletarian revolution, that the struggle for independence of the colonial toilers is indissolubly allied to the struggle of the working class for power.."[13] Unlike the CI, Pollitt drew no subtle distinctions between colonies like India that were categorised as semi-colonial by the CI – for the CPGB colonial freedom meant freedom for everyone. It was a lasting achievement of the new line that forever afterwards, the Britishparty's approach to colonialism was never the same again. From 1928 until the CPGB's demise in the 1980s anti-Imperialism was considered an inseparable component of the fight for socialism.

It was in the midst of the discussions about the new line that the League against Imperialism, established in 1927, organised a public meeting in November 1928, in Limehouse in east London, which was the constituency of Clement Attlee, a Labour MP and the future leader of the Labour Party. The aim of the meeting, at which the communist MP Saklatvala, was the principal speaker, was to pressurise Attlee and Hartshorn, another Labour MP, to withdraw from the Simon Commission of Enquiry into India. Both the CPGB and the Indian National Congress opposed the enquiry. In the event of Attlee refusing to withdraw, the workers of Limehouse were urged to relinquish their support for the MP. The CPGB welcomed the campaign, and it was reported on at its Tenth Congress a few months later. [14]

This event was of some significance, in that the Limehouse meeting was one of the last occasions before the onset of class against class, at which prominent Labour left-wingers, like Maxton, shared a platform with communists. At the same time it was also one of the first such meetings that heralded the start of the new line. The denunciation of left-wing Labour MPs and the call to withdraw support from them would have been an unlikely scenario in the popular front days. The communists would have been too nervous about sabotaging their chances of Labour/Communist cooperation and the effect this might have on their hopes for affiliation. As it transpired the meeting, although a large one, did not achieve its desired aim: despite the threats, Atlee remained a member of the Commission and the MP for Limehouse. What is important though is that the communists were keen to gather support for their aim of colonial freedom. Limehouse, situated in the east end of London, was not a promising area for their message, dependent as it was on the docks for the livelihood of many of its inhabitants. Trade with the Empire was the mainstay of work for the dockworkers in the vicinity, and that the communists tried to win over this section of the working class that would potentially be hardest hit by any disruption of that trade was to their credit. The communists saw themselves as part of an internationalist tradition, a tradition that stretched back to the previous century when cotton workers in Lancashire had been prepared to sacrifice their jobs for a nobler cause, on that occasion the support of the North during the American Civil War.

The communists, in another display of solidarity with Indian workers and the Indian National Congress, decided to stand the imprisoned Indian communist, Shaukat Usmani, as a candidate against Sir John Simon in the Spen Valley division of Yorkshire in the 1929 General Election. 's candidature came about as a direct result of the Party's Tenth Congress decision to raise colonialism as an election issue at every opportunity. [15]

's vote was derisory, just 242, against the victorious Simon's 22,039. However, in the election, which lacked 's presence, and was bereft of finance, the communists made unity between Indian and British workers the main focus of their campaigning efforts. It was a unique endeavour.

This idea of international working-class solidarity which was tested at Spen Valley was explored even further when a group and trade unionists and communists, along with three of their British comrades were arrested and imprisoned in India in 1929. The trial, which became known as the Meerut Conspiracy Trial, was not completed until 1933 and became something of a cause celebre in the history of anti-colonialism during the class against class period

The trial had become necessary because of the direct intervention of the CPGB in Indian affairs. Before the advent of the new line, a small number of active party members had been despatched to India to help the nascent Labour movement. Those arrested and tried at Meerut included two CPGB members, Ben Bradley and Phil Spratt, plus another non-party sympathiser, Phil Spratt, along with thirty of their Indian comrades. The Meerut prisoners, mainly, though not exclusively, communists, were accused of conspiring against the British crown. Their crime had been to be involved in strikes, mainly in the textile industry, for improved wages and conditions. When they were arrested, in March 1929, their plight was headlined in a front-page article in *Workers Life*. Throughout the whole period of the imprisonment and trial, which was almost three years in duration, the communists continued with the agitation for their release. This had the dual purpose of placing Indian independence firmly at the forefront of the party's campaigns. At the same time, it had the added advantage of exposing the imperialist nature of the Labour Government, which was in power for much of the time and did nothing to halt the trial.

It was to focus attention on the events at Meerut and to consolidate the CPGBs commitment to raise anti-colonialism as an election issue that was the rationale behind standing Saklatvala as a communist candidate in the Shettleston by-election in Glasgow, in 1930. (See Chapter 5) There was no other reason for the decision to stand Saklatvala in a Scottish constituency with which he had no links and one that was four hundred miles away from his tried and tested base in Battersea. That this was the rational was made clear in a *Daily Worker* editorial even before Saklatvala's nomination. Stressing the importance of a communist candidate in the by-election, the paper proclaimed:

"the Labour Government is striving to crush the Indian revolution by bloody military repression; thirty one leaders of the workers and peasants of India are still in the dock after thirteen months. The record of the Labour Government stinks in the nostrils of every class conscious worker." [16]

Throughout the Shettleston campaign, the party paper continued with the theme of building unity between British and colonial workers. Saklatvala, supported by the Workers Welfare League of India, won the endorsement of the traditionally Labour-supporting Glasgow branch of the Irish Labour League. This was a significant plus, as Ireland was still viewed as a colony by the CPGB, and others on the left, and was usually grouped with the other colonies in the demand for independence. The day before the election, the *Daily Worker* summed up in its editorial the approach of Britain's communists. It linked together the two issues of unemployment and India. It argued that they were both interconnected – the solution was a vote for Saklatvala, who was the 'embodiment of the joint struggle of Indian and British workers.' [17]

It may be that a retrospective view taken from the vantage of today will not look favourably on such actions. Our approach to international cooperation is now more sophisticated and urbane. Nevertheless, this simple call by the communists ninety years ago for workers solidarity, echoed the words of their mentors Marx and Engels and their slogan 'working men of all lands unite'. However, it did not touch a chord amongst the voters of Shettleston where only twelve hundred followed the party's advice and voted for Saklatvala. However, the fact that it was made in the first place says something about the commitment and the foresight of the communists. At the start of the campaign, there was not even a party branch in Shettleston, and what is even more pertinent is the fact that there was no community from the subcontinent living there. That the communists appealed for unity to an audience that was almost to a person white and that their chosen candidate was Indian does indicate that the CPGB was not only prepared to talk about international working-class unity, it was also ready to practice what it preached. For a party that has been castigated by the CI for neglecting anti-colonialism, it was a brave decision to take.

Neither was it just at the national level, in the spotlight of a by-election campaign, that the CPGB, with a nationally known candidate, was prepared to challenge imperialism. At a local level too the communists strove to publicise the evils of Empire. In April 1930 every district committee of the party was urged to establish a department for colonial work to win British workers to support the freedom struggle in the colonies.[18] Also, it was decided to conduct an educational campaign amongst the party members around the issue of colonialism.

When civil unrest broke out in India in April 1930, it was given extensive coverage in the party paper. Under the new line headline 'Labour Government attacks Colonial workers' the *Daily Worker* reported, not just on the repression, but also on how British workers were being mobilised in support of their Indian comrades. Publicity was given to a meeting of railway workers in Battersea, in South London, called in solidarity with striking Indian railway employees.[19] The CPGB made every effort to mobilise its less than three thousand members in support of what the *Daily Worker* called 'the Indian Revolution'. In response to the situation, which included Gandhi's arrest, the party leadership urged all party districts and locals to organise meetings and demonstrations in support of the Indian struggle. All party factory papers were asked to produce a special edition 'at once' devoted to India. This was not just the usual general call to action, but all party districts were asked to call big mass meetings immediately about India.

Throughout May 1930, the unrest continued, and the communists maintained their focus on India. Every day there were articles in the *Daily Worker* about the subcontinent, and often the situation was the subject of the main front-page story. The party issued regular calls for India's independence, and it demanded the withdrawal of British troops from the colony.[20]

With India in an uproar, the campaign for the release of the Meerut prisoners became of crucial importance. For the next three years, the communists conducted an almost single-handed campaign on their behalf. This was, it must be said, a situation almost entirely of their own making. Since the start of the new line cooperation with others on the left, particularly the 'social fascists', was discouraged. This had led to the League Against Imperialism, which was an international organisation, with a British section, becoming virtually a communist front. Prominent Labour Party supporters of the League had been forced out of any leadership role with the onset of class against class. There were even suggestions from the CI that the League be disbanded, a proposition that was successfully resisted and defeated with the help of the British Party. At the end of 1932, in the closing stages of the trial, the League organised many mass meetings calling for the prisoners' release. The speakers were invariably party members with Saklatvala as the most popular choice. At rallies in Sheffield and London, over two thousand five hundred listened to the communists demand that the prisoners be freed.

Although they may have been isolated in the Labour movement, it did not prevent the communists from conducting their own sustained campaign throughout the period on behalf of those imprisoned in Britain's foremost colony. The importance of Meerut had been stressed at the Eleventh Congress, and a detailed plan of action had been agreed. Gaining the release of the prisoners was to be the party's main anti-colonial activity. The Congress had decided that there were to be significant demonstrations in London, Glasgow and Manchester. Each party district had the task of selecting several factories where meetings should take place about Meerut and where possible there should be strikes and demonstrations in sympathy with the strikers. It was an ambitious programme that the communists struggled to achieve. There were large demonstrations as planned, but no factories took strike action in support of the detainees. Neither were the communists successful in achieving their other Meerut demand which was to, 'mobilise the workers for the revolutionary independence of India.' [21]

When the sentences on the detainees were announced, even the communists were surprised at their severity. The prisoners received sentences of anything from three years imprisonment, to life. Meerut, where the trial was conducted, was, the communists pointed out, a small isolated town and away from the major industrial centres of disturbance and militancy. It had been chosen as a venue precisely for those reasons, and it had the additional advantage of being in an area where an English judge could preside, without the unnecessary inconvenience of a jury system. That the prisoners were found guilty was not unexpected by the party, therefore, although the length of the sentences was a shock.

Throughout 1933, the communists maintained their local and national campaigns calling for the prisoners' release. The party called mass meetings specifically about Meerut in Glasgow, Stepney, Shoreditch and Hammersmith in London. The worldwide campaign, in which the CPGB played a significant part, achieved a success, when at the end of 1933, some of the prisoners were released and others had their sentences reduced. Ben Bradley was one of those freed and it was Saklatvala, who welcomed him back home at Victoria Station in London on behalf of the Communist Party. This final episode of the Meerut prisoners' saga was a striking example not only of British communists commitment to anti-colonialism but of the party's whole anti-racist approach. Saklatvala embracing Bradley on a Central London station after his return from an Indian prison exemplifies everything the party stood for – unity of purpose irrespective of race, and workers solidarity across continents. It can be said of no other organisation at the time, Labour movement or otherwise, that they had such a commitment.

India played a prominent role in the party's anti-colonial activities. This was in part due to a directive from the CI which allocated responsibility for work in the subcontinent to the British party – a decision that was not at all to the liking of M N Roy, a prominent Indian communist who was supported by the CI until his defection. There were other reasons though for India's importance that had little to do with Comintern directives. Both numerically and geographically the subcontinent constituted the largest part of the Empire. In the Indian National Congress, founded in 1888, it had a very developed national liberation movement. Communist organisation in India was far and away more advanced than in any other of the colonies, where it was practically non-existent, with the exception, perhaps, of South Africa. There was a developing proletariat, centred on the textile industry, and an infrastructure built around the railways that had spawned militant trade unionism amongst railway workers. In all, India, certainly politically if not economically, was the most developed of all Britain's colonial possessions. A revolution in India was for the new line communists a genuine possibility. The pattern for this assessment had been made at their Eleventh Congress which declared that India was 'one of the central areas of world revolution'.[22] That assessment waned with the demise of the strategy of class against class.

In addition to India's importance because of its development, other factors warranted the CPGB's exceptional attention to the subcontinent. Two of the party's leading members had extensive knowledge of India. Saklatvala had toured his homeland in 1927 and would have returned for a further visit had he not been banned by the second Labour Government. Apart from his role as founder and leading light in the Workers Welfare League of India, he was also a member of the London branch of the Indian National Congress, where during the class against class years he conducted a running battle against the supporters of Gandhi. In his view they were the Indian counterparts of the dreaded social fascists. Rajani Palme Dutt, although only half Indian, had written a great deal about the colony, including the heretical *Modern India* which did not find favour with the CI, but was, nevertheless, considered a standard Marxist text on the subject. Through his editorship of *Labour Monthly*, Dutt also helped draw the attention of his British readers to the many-faceted side of the Indian struggle.

Given India's advance economic development, the importance attached to the subcontinent by the Comintern and specific expertise on the subject by leading CPGB personnel, it would have been perfectly understandable for the British Party to have concentrated its efforts solely on freeing one of the oldest of Britain's colonies. However, that was not the case. Despite all these pressures to confine its anti-colonial efforts to just one area, the already overstretched forces of the tiny CPGB were active on a range of anti-imperialist issues that touched virtually every one of Britain's colonial possessions. Africa, the West Indies, the Far East, wherever British imperialism had left its mark, the British Party sought to advertise the horrors of colonialism. Neither were British communists just concerned with Britain's imperial role. The building of other empires too was lambasted. Even the United States and its then little publicised subjugation of the native Americans did not go unreported in the communist press. For such a small party and all the time struggling against what it had described at its Ninth Congress as 'imperialist prejudices', during the class against class years the CPGB made monumental efforts, virtually alone, in bringing home to the British working class and Labour movement the harsh realities of Empire.

In its exposure of colonialism, the *Daily Worker*, and its predecessor, *Workers Life* played a valuable role. The communist press, like the party that it represented, was under-resourced and continuously being harassed by a combination of libel suits, police surveillance, and ultimately the wholesalers' boycott. Despite all these intimidating efforts, the communists continued with their message. The Empire was evil, British workers should unite with their class brothers and sisters who were being subjugated in the colonies and any attempt to divide workers along a colour line, either at home or abroad, was playing into the hands of the bosses. The message was simple, and the communists hammered away at it throughout the new line. Virtually alone, the CPGB and its publications put the spotlight on what was happening in the colonies. Nowhere was this truer than in Africa. The goings-on in this vast continent, itself prostrate and divided between the major imperialist powers, was the subject of much of the party's propaganda. The CPGB, twenty years before it was fashionable, was telling its readers about the denial of rights to non-whites in South Africa, and the iniquities of apartheid. It may have come as something of a surprise to many in Britain, when after the Second World war, and particularly in the 1950s, what was happening in South Africa suddenly became a cause celebre. Anyone who had read the communist press in the early 1930s would not have been shocked. What was happening in Southern Africa, in its Labour movement and within the Africa National Congress, had been a constant theme of new line period CPGB propaganda.

South Africa, of all of Britain's African colonies, was economically and politically the most advanced. There was mining on a large scale and industrial production. The country could not only boost a proletariat, but there had also developed an infrastructure. The population was overwhelmingly black, but there was a substantial white minority, including a small white working-class mainly based in the extraction industries. Politically South Africa was on a par with India with which colony it shared many similarities. There was an established national liberation movement led by the African National Congress. Also, there was a small and multi-racial Communist Party, which had been created soon after the birth of the CI. During the class against class years, this party was rendered some ideological assistance by the CPGB in order to help eradicate racist practices from within the organisation. Apart from this significant contribution, the CPGB, at the beginning of the new line, also pledged itself to give more aid to the liberation movement in South Africa. These achievements were referred to at the Party's Eleventh Congress, "the aid already given to the South African Party in ideological clarification and in the fight against white chauvinism must be continued and practical help given in the organisation of the negro masses in South Africa and other colonies". [23]

Given its own small size and difficulties this assistance by the CPGB to another struggling communist party was commendable. It is worth noting that the South African Communist Party/Communist Party of South Africa was for many years the only functioning communist party on the African continent.

In its treatment of South African affairs, the CPGB sought to do several things. It frequently highlighted every effort by the South African communists to unite the often divided working class. Every strike or industrial dispute which united workers was supported by the CPGB and its press. On the national question British communists were at pains to show the gains made by the Africa National Congress in the pursuit of its goal of independence. Finally, the party was keen to expose the conditions under which workers lived in the South African colony. These aims were being pursued at a time when support for the Empire was strong, and there was very little support for the demand for independence. The communists' *Daily Worker* was unique in its coverage of not just South Africa, but colonial matters in general. No other newspaper reported on the draconian measures being taken against the people of the colonies in their subjugation, and no other paper or party was interested in how they could assist the struggle for democratic rights. It was this constant support for African liberation that led many future African leaders to be closely associated with the Communist party during the class against class period.

At the onset of the new line, the party was keen to emphasise the importance of communist leadership for the working class. What was true in Britain was equally valid in the colonies. The party's assessment of an industrial dispute by clothing workers in Johannesburg, soon after the elaboration of the new strategy, was symptomatic of its approach. The CPGB outlined to its supporters how black workers had supported a strike by European tailoresses in the city. It was, the party recalled, 'one of the first strikes in which white and black workers have fought together.' [24] What was even more pleasing for the communists was that the strike, which had been led by the Communist Party of South Africa, was successful. The theme of working-class unity was returned to again a few months later when *Workers Life* reported on the efforts of the South African communists to unite the country's laundry workers. There were in existence two unions, the white Cleaners and Dyers union, and the black Laundry Workers Union. The Communist Party of South Africa had spent many months trying to overcome the prejudices of both sets of workers. Under the heading 'Overcoming Race Antagonisms,' the CPGBs weekly paper considered that the efforts of a sister party many thousands of miles away, in trying to unite workers was worth bringing to the attention of its readers. This would have the effect of both keeping them abreast of imperial affairs and also countering any notions that might be lurking that race rather than class was the predominant factor. In case the readership had not got the message the paper followed it up a week later with another report on how black and white workers were` uniting in South Africa and how this unity was being undermined by the South African Social Democrats, who were accused by the CPGB of racism.[25]

British communists were well informed about events in South Africa. Throughout 1929, there was regular coverage of what was happening in the colony. In the same month as the disastrous General Election that took place in Britain, which resulted in the party's special congress and the installation of the new class against class leadership, a general election also took place in the colony. So keen was the CPGB to keep its membership informed of what was happening that it covered the South African election in its paper. It should be borne in mind that *Workers Life* was a weekly of just ten/twelve pages. The average reader was probably unemployed, or if not, an industrial militant, and was more concerned with trade union or unemployed workers movement events in Britain than with what was happening five thousand miles away. Despite that, the CPGB was determined that colonialism, in line with its new strategy, should occupy much more centre stage. The party's 10th Congress in January 1929, the first of the new line congresses, had placed the, 'struggle in defence of the revolutionary movement in the colonies' as second only in importance to the 'fight against the war danger'. Both these principal tasks were ahead of the 'fight for the independent leadership of the party', in importance. [26] With this aim in mind, the party's supporters were told that the results of the South African General Election were a setback for the South African blacks. The Hertzog government, which had fought the election around 'the native question', had further curtailed Negro rights, and the outcome was, to use the heading in the party paper, 'More Slavery For Negroes.'[27]

After the 1929 South African general election, the communists continued to spotlight developments in the colony. The CPGB was at pains to point out to its supporters that its predictions about the likely actions of the Hertzog government were, unfortunately, being proved correct. Every aspect of the South African struggle, whether it be the fight for black liberation or the support of South African workers in action was conveyed to the communists' small band of supporters in Britain. It was the *Daily Worker* that consistently exposed the ongoing denial of democratic and other rights to the colony's non-white population. When, in 1930, laws were passed restricting the right of assembly to blacks, and giving the Minister of Justice power to prohibit meetings or deport active nationalists to other areas, communist supporters in Britain were told how the new laws would be used against both the Africa National Congress and to suppress 'communists and Negro workers.' [28]

Even the minutia of events in South Africa was commented upon, and the paper carried regular articles and commentary on the ill-treatment of blacks by the police. In its coverage of these outrages, the communists' mouthpiece made constant reference to the racist nature of the South African state. In an article entitled 'Negroes and the Police' the paper not only commented on the brutal treatment of three black prisoners by the police, but party members and their supporters were also made aware that the jury system in South Africa, which tried the white policemen, was made up entirely of whites. [29] This kind of information was not readily available elsewhere.

In its treatment of colonial rule in Africa the CPGB tried not only to expose imperialism as a system but also endeavoured to educate their own supporters about just how colonialism had developed. They tried, through their daily paper, to educate their supporters about the history of colonialism and colonial acquisition. It was their version of what took place, and it was a truncated one, but throughout the new line years the CPGB did consistently try through its propaganda to offer a continuing critique of colonialism and all that it entailed. A striking example of this approach was early in 1931 when the *Daily Worker* in just one edition of the paper attempted both to educate the readership about colonialism, and at the same time rouse them into action against its consequences. First, the readers were told about the development of 'the slave system in South Africa' and how the 'Europeans, both Dutch and English invaded and wrenched South Africa from the hands of the native Africans after a series of bloody wars lasting for more than two centuries.' [30] This conquest, the readers were told, resulted in a system of white supremacy whose leaders:

"while they profess with such fine words to have the benefits of the Africans uppermost in their hearts, in reality, they stick at nothing to keep the African people subjected to British imperialism. They shot down and drown hundreds of African women in Nigeria; they prohibit meetings and newspapers, suppress trade unions and hold in prison African workers and peasants who try to revolt against their rule."[31]

Such was the ruthlessness of the system that in South Africa, Europeans, who amounted to only twenty per cent of the population, owned almost ninety-seven per cent of the land.

The same edition of the paper homed in on a further erosion of African rights and again attacked the South African Prime Minister, General Hertzog. The paper's readers were told in some detail about the denial of democratic rights to Africans. Readers of the *Daily Worker*, in contrast to the readership of other daily papers, were kept abreast of the finer points of what was happening in Britain's African colonies. They were told that 'no African by law is allowed to carry firearms. All Africans by law are forced to carry an identification card or 'pass. All Africans, except for a tiny minority in the Cape province, are excluded from the franchise.' [32] Party members and supporters were even told about new laws that were being introduced in the colony that would 'deprive the franchise to those living in the Cape' and, 'bind the African peasant more closely still to the service of the white farmer by compelling him to work for at least three months of the year for the farmer before he can seek other employment.' [33]

It was through their paper that communists and their supporters were kept well informed about developments in the colonies – but information for its own sake was not enough. At the same time, action was necessary, and during the new line this action could only be led by the Communist Party. So while informing party supporters about colonial developments at the same time, the party's propaganda emphasised the heroism and self-sacrifice of communists living under colonial rule and the role that these militants played in the National Liberation movement A case in point was JW Nkosi.

Nkosi, whose fate would have been unknown outside South Africa had his martyrdom not been taken up by the CPGB, was a South African communist who was killed during a demonstration. The background to the events leading up to his death was given wide publicity by the CPGB. Nkosi was a farm labourer and kitchen boy who had joined the South African Communist Party in 1926. He became the Communist Party organiser in Durban in 1929. He was one of the organisers of a demonstration which took place on Dingaan's day (December 16) This celebration of the Zulu's defeat of the British was to be used as a protest against the hated pass laws.

The *Daily Worker* reported that:

> "over 2000 African workers assembled under a red banner and flung their passes and tax receipts into a huge bonfire. This was an act of defiance to the white exploiters who compel the Africans to carry passes so that they cannot escape from the farms where they are forced to work on yearly contracts at starvation wages."[34]

After the bonfire, the police then started to beat up the demonstrators, and Nkosi and four others were killed. To show up the brutality of the system, the *Daily Worker* reported just what happened to Nkosi. He was, 'first stabbed with an assegai and then beaten with knobkerries by the police'. He died the next day and there over a thousand people at his funeral. [35]

Having roused the indignation of its readers, the paper concluded the article with an appeal to join the League Against Imperialism.

The coverage of Nkosi's death also had another purpose. In keeping with the CPGB's class against class strategy, national liberation movements to be successful must of necessity be communist-led. The CPGB was keen to show that by their sacrifice communists were the best leaders of the national liberation movement. The paper had jubilantly reported just the previous year that the ANC, at its annual conference, had disclosed that 25% of the delegates were members of the Communist Party of South Africa. [36]

Whilst because of its economic and political development the communists focused much of their attention on South Africa, other parts of the continent were not ignored. Slavery within Britain's African colonies became a campaigning theme. The party highlighted the case in Bechuanaland of a runaway slave being flogged to death, [37] and exposed the system of forced labour, which was widespread in the colonies. Party members were told how forced labour for public works was legal in India, East Africa, Nigeria, Sierra Leone, Cyprus, the Cameroons, the West Indies, Australasia and Oceania and details of how the system worked in different colonies was conveyed to the membership. Even information about what would now be described as institutional racism and should have caused concern to the British public was made readily available by the communists. The *Daily Worker*, which was close to extinction due to a distributors' ban could still find room to report that the South African Athletics Association had decided to bar athletes from India and the West Indies from the Empire Games in South Africa in 1934. [38]

In its coverage of African affairs during the period the *Daily Worker* consistently hammered away at one of the communists main themes – the unity and common purpose of British and colonial workers. In its portrayal of the class struggle in the colonies, the CPGB adopted an approach that was remarkably similar in tone to the one that it pursued in Britain. The conflict between the working class and the employers was covered in much the same way. Greedy bosses, whether they are at home or abroad, were, according to the communists, always trying to make more money at the workers' expense. Whether it be the British South Africa Company's efforts to steal land in Bechuanaland, [39] or the reporting of labour conditions in Nyasaland,[40] the communists were keen to expose one thing – it was all part of an international fight against imperialism. As far as Africa was concerned, the considered view of the CPGB was that, 'African independence from imperialism is not merely the way out for Africans, but also for British workers too.' [401] It was a line the party adhered to throughout its class against class phase.

To rouse British workers against the indignities of colonialism, the CPGB attacked not just British imperialism but all other colonising powers. The Portuguese colonialists who operated near their British counterparts in Africa were castigated for their part in the subjugation of blacks in their territories. The enslavement of black workers in Africa by an alliance of Portuguese and British colonialism was exposed by the CPGB early in 1930. Black workers in Portugal's African colonies who went to South Africa, where wages and conditions were marginally better, were to be treated as clandestine immigrants – unless they agreed to work in the mines. In that case, they could stay in South Africa; otherwise, they were to be repatriated. This understanding between the two colonising powers was denounced by the CPGB who described the agreement as, 'part of the whole process of enslaving the Portuguese Negroes. They are forced off their own land by 'economic development' and try to get jobs in South Africa. The South African capitalists force them to work in the mines from which millions of pounds come every year to British parasite capitalists.' [42]

It is ironic that Britain's communists, who have been accused by some historians of ignoring Africa during the twenties and thirties, should have opened their new line period with extensive coverage of land grabbing and murder in Africa, particularly in Kenya. Within a month of the first appearance of the *Daily Worker*, the paper carried an article by the then little known Jomo Kenyatta. This Kenyan nationalist, who some thirty years later became the leader of the independent state, by which time he had severed any remaining links with the Communist party, was during the class against class period sympathetic to the communists. Three-quarters of a page of the ten-page paper was given over to Kenyatta and his account of the massacre of Kenyans by the British occupying forces, and the subsequent stealing of Kenyan land. [43] When further land grabbing by white settlers took place, the communists focused attention on the injustices this created. They publicised how white settlers owned 5 million acres of land in the colony, and how the Masai tribe were being turned off their land. The communists were also sensitive to African tribal customs and decried the and grabbers for completely ignoring the ancient rites of the indigenous population. [44]

The communists were continuing with their attacks on this practice three years later as the class against class period was ending. This time though they were happy to report that due mainly to their efforts (although this they never said) there was an organised attempt at solidarity between Africans and British workers. In response to the land grabbing in Kenya that was taking place after the discovery of gold on Kenyan owned property, there was a meeting in Britain organised by the communist supported Negro Welfare Association. The Kenyans had been offered alternative land after the discovery of gold, but that was no longer available. The NWA had pointed out that the Kenyan Government aimed to create a 'force of workers who from sheer starvation will be only too willing to work for the gold mine owners – at any miserable wage.' [45] To further develop the protest movement, there was to be a joint public meeting of the NWA and the LAI at the end of the month. In addition, there was a call by the communists for protests by all working-class organisations against the denial of land rights to Kenyans. Once again, solidarity between African and British workers was very much the order of the day. In their treatment of the African colonies the communists had been consistent throughout the new line. They had exposed colonial rule and with scant resources had attempted to inject the British labour movement with anti-colonial sentiments.

The CPGB, using its weekly, and then daily paper, actively campaigned to expose the colonial system. It was incredibly successful in highlighting events in Africa and the Indian subcontinent. Nevertheless, Britain's Empire was massive, multi racial and complex and Britain's communists, in line with what they saw as their internationalist duties, were not slow to point out any injustices that were taking place in this vast expanse. In Western Samoa, on the other side of the world, the party drew attention to the actions of the New Zealand Government in sending in a force of military police to quell disturbances. [46] It returned its attention to this little known part of the world the following month with an exposé of how Britain was attempting to install in Western Samoa chiefs who were friendly to imperialism – the old British imperialist trick, the communists claimed, of divide and rule. [47]

The West Indies too was focused upon by the CPGB. The islands, which had been divided up between Britain, France and Spain, with Britain taking the lion's share, was the scene of much unrest during 1930. In Guadeloupe, in the French West Indies, there was a strike by sugar workers, who were fired upon by the police – an action condemned by the CPGB. [48] The party tried to stimulate interest in the Labour movement in these islands and their claim for independence. To this end, the Negro Welfare Association organised a public meeting in London around the issue of self-government for the West Indies. The Barbadian communist Arnold Ward, a member of the CPGB, took the chair and the main speaker was Captain A A Citriani from Trinidad. That a multi-racial meeting of this nature should have been organised around a topic that was of no great interest to the Labour movement says something about the CPGB's commitment to anti-colonialism. It also shows the endeavours that the small party would make to try and build a following among Britain' tiny black community. Political meetings where black and white speakers shared the same platform were not commonplace in early 1930s Britain. [49]

At the Party's Ninth Congress in 1927 a decision was made to take action against the annual 'Empire Day' celebrations. The Young Comrades League had taken the initiative for this action and were supported by the Young Communist League in turning Empire Day into a day of protest against colonialism. This was welcomed by the party. Successful protests against Empire Day celebrations had been made in many areas, and party members were encouraged to support and continue these actions in future years. Not only were the demonstrations to be ones in support of colonial workers demanding their freedom, but the party was also keen to use Empire Day for an ideological assault upon the ideas of colonialism – particularly the indoctrination of children. Schools were to be specially targeted by the party and the school curriculum subject to attack because it was being used to instil 'imperialist doctrines into the children.' [50]

The disruption of Empire Day celebrations was so crucial for the CPGB that anti-Empire Day campaign notes were included in a 1930 pre-Empire Day edition of the *'Daily Worker.'* [51] Neither was this kind of activity a one-off. Throughout the new line, the CPGB used Empire Day to put forward its case for colonial freedom and local initiatives were especially welcome. One action undertaken by the Tottenham Young Pioneers Group put the members at some risk. In 1930, as part of the anti-Empire campaign, they distributed leaflets to schoolchildren explaining the hardships under which colonial workers lived in the British Empire. Their actions were considered such a serious threat by the local authority that they placed the matter in the hands of the Town Clerk, who could if he/she saw fit refer the issue to the police.

Will Paynter, a future mineworkers' leader, shows in his autobiography just how dangerous it could be to be anti Empire in the 1930s:

"the Glamorganshire police were taking on the role of storm-troopers in the mining valleys of South Wales. Take, for example, the incident that led to my imprisonment. On May 24 1930, celebrated then as Empire Day, we held a meeting in the evening in a side street off the main shopping street in Porth, for the purpose of exposing the colonial exploitation and brutal repression that the Empire really represented. The` police came in numbers and tried to break up the meeting. We resisted by linking arms in a circle around the speaker, which they tried to but failed to break. As soon as the meeting closed, however, they were able to get at us individually and one young lad was slapped in the face with some force. But there was little fighting and we moved away as peacefully as we could.........About a fortnight later, some fourteen of us received summonses to appear in court to answer over fifty charges in all." [52]

The author subsequently describes how the police beat him up on his way to court:

"I fought and struggled, giving up only when my trousers were in danger of being dragged off me. I do not know how many or who were the policemen carrying me, but I did know that I was being punched in the kidneys I was being carried, stomach facing the road, so that my mouth was open as I gasped for breath. As we entered the police station, I was given a hefty punch in the mouth which smashed my upper dentures, scattering them to the floor as they dropped me."

The young Will Paynter was then just a rank and file communist militant who had only recently been elected to his first union post, as checkweighman at the Cymmer colliery in the Rhondda. In later life, he was to become the General Secretary of the National Union of Mineworkers. For his part in the demonstration, Paynter received four months of hard labour. [53] The sacrifice of Paynter and his comrades was due to their commitment to international working-class solidarity and their innate dislike of imperialism. It was a sacrifice that was to find even greater expression a few years later when Paynter, along with over two thousand others, mainly communists, risked their lives to fight against fascism in Spain.

Two years following Paynter's imprisonment the party announced that May 17, 1932, was to be an Anti-Empire Day of Youth. The youth wing of the League against Imperialism had organised demonstrations in opposition to colonialism in all major localities. May 17 had been chosen because it was one week before Empire Day. The Party's London District had made arrangements for a youth demonstration in Stepney. Young communists from Hackney would march down to Stepney, and there would-be an anti-imperialist rally at Valance Road. [54] A few days later Saklatvala spoke at an anti-Empire Day rally at Rotherhithe Town Hall in London. Another of the speakers at the CPGB organised event, who had come especially from Ireland, was Jim Larkin junior. The communists at their meetings repeatedly emphasised the international dimension to the struggle for socialism, both with their choice of speakers and their propaganda.

Ireland at that time was still looked upon as a colony. Ireland's freedom and unity even after the signing of the partition treaty in 1921 was an accepted goal of many of the organisations of the Labour movement. Ireland was regarded, along with India and Britain's other 'possessions', as a colony. At a rally in Sheffield City Hall six months after the news of the Meerut Prisoners sentences had been announced, Saklatvala called for their immediate release, and Jim Larkin junior from the same platform demanded Irish independence. It was a twin set of demands that were approved of by the more than 2000 communist supporters in the audience.

Even towards the end of the new line when some have argued that the focus on the struggle against fascism in Europe blunted the communists drive against colonialism, the CPGB continued with its by now established anti-Empire Day crusade. At a meeting called by the League Against Imperialism, the veterans, Saklatvala and Reginald Bridgeman, spoke alongside a relative newcomer, Arnold Ward, a Caribbean communist who was a CPGB activist. Once again internationalism, both in the line up of the speakers and the message was the theme. [55] It was a fitting tribute coming as it did at the end of what have been described as the party's wilderness years.

The struggle against colonialism in the nineteen twenties and thirties was no easy task.

The racist ideas that underpinned the colonial system were strong, and support for colonial freedom movements was weak. The CPGB, despite its own internal difficulties, and its marginalisation in the Labour movement, decided to tackle both these issues head-on. Through its propaganda, the party provided a continual critic of colonialism. It informed both the party membership and sympathisers about what was happening not just in Britain's colonies, but the colonial possessions of other major powers as well. It was information that was difficult to obtain elsewhere. Apart from reporting on these events, the CPGB also gave support to the various national liberation movements through its publicity. This support, although in conformity with the new line strategy of communist leadership, did provide valuable insights into the agitation that was taking place in Africa, India and the rest of the Empire. In this sense, it was unique. No other daily paper was prepared to devote resources to such an enquiry. The Indian National Congress, the struggle for land rights in Kenya, labour disputes in the West Indies, all these aspects and more were given a sympathetic hearing in the communist press.

Apart from informing its circle of supporters about events in the Empire, the party also played a pioneering role in trying to rouse British workers to give active support to their colonial comrades. Had it not been for the CPGB's almost single-handed agitation on behalf of the prisoners of Meerut it is unlikely that their fate would have been noticed in Britain. As it was, the communists succeeded in raising it as an issue of some significance. If it were not for their continued agitation, it is unlikely that the prisoners would have had such an early release. Of course had it not been for the communists and their acts of solidarity with their Indian comrades, it is unlikely that the Meerut Trial would ever have been necessary. The efforts of Saklatvala, Bradley, Allison and others in helping to forge the Indian Labour movement and its communist component, was very much a product of the party's internationalist aspirations and its new line period commitment to independent communist leadership.

Finally, credit is also due to those thousands of rank and file communists who throughout the difficult years of anti-colonialism kept alive the ideas of freedom and colonial liberation - ideas that had all but been extinguished in the Labour Party whose forlorn efforts while in power had so antagonised the anti-colonialist CPGB. If it had not been for the likes of the young Will Paynter, or the even younger Tottenham Young Pioneers, and the thousands of others who responded to the communists' anti-colonial call, it is doubtful if the flame of militant anti-imperialism would have continued to glow. The novelty of the anti-Empire day demonstrations by the small band of communists and their protestations against indoctrinating children with the ideas of Empire all had an effect. So too did the message conveyed to the many thousands who never joined the party but attended their numerous anti-imperialist rallies. Above all, there was a steady drip of anti-colonial propaganda emanating from the Daily Worker and its predecessor. This all helped create a climate of opinion which stretched outside the party's ranks, that was both informed about colonial matters, and was prepared to unite with workers of a different colour in a worldwide effort to overthrow imperialism. It was an over-ambitious project, but it can be said of the class against class period, unlike any other in CPGB history, that it did place the colonial revolution at centre stage.

Notes

1 *Report of the Sixth World Congress of the CI*, CPGB, page 1678
2 *Speeches and Documents of the Sixth Conference of the CPGB*, p 42
3 *Report of the Seventh National Congress CPGB*, pp196-197.
4 *Ibid*
5 Speeches and Documents of the Sixth Congress of the CPGB 6 *Daily Worker*, June 7, 1931
7 *Daily Worker*, October 15, 1931
8 Resolutions of the 11th Congress of the CPGB, 1929, p45
9 Resolutions of the Tenth Congress of the CPGB, 1929, p110
10 Resolutions of the Eleventh Congress of the CPGB November 30 – December 3, 1929 p45
11 Documents of the Tenth Congress, CPGB p111
12 *The Road to Victory,* Harry Pollitt's opening speech to the Twelfth Congress of the CPGB November 1932,p33
13 'A Call to All Workers', Harry Pollitt's Report to Thirteenth Congress of the CPGB, Feb 2nd- 5th

	1935,p76
14	10th Congress of the CPGB, p31.
15	*Ibid*,p113
16	*Daily Worker*, May 17, 1930
17	*Daily Worker*, June 26, 1930
18	*Daily Worker*, April 28, 1930
19	*Daily Worker*, April 3, 1930
20	*Daily Worker*, May 14 1930
21	11th Congress of the CPGB, p45
22	11th Congress of the CPGB, p16.
23	11th Congress of the CPGB, p16
24	*Workers Life* June 28 1928
25	*Workers Life*, November 30, 1928
26	See, resolution on the Present Situation and Tasks of the Party, 10th Congress CPGB.
27	*Workers Life*, June 21, 1929
28	*Daily Worker*, April 19, 1930
29	*Daily Worker*, April 16, 1930
30	*Daily Worker*, February 4, 1931 31. *Ibid*
32	*Ibid*
33	*Ibid*
34	*Daily Worker*, February 4, 1931
35	*Ibid*
36	*Daily Worker*, May 6, 1930
37	*Daily Worker*, May 5, 1931
38	*Daily Worker*, May 15, 1931
39	*Daily Worker* March 1, 1930
40	*Daily Worker*, December 16, 1930
41	*Ibid*
42	*Daily Worker*, April 22, 1930
43	*Daily Worker*, January 20, 1930
44	See, *Daily Worker* January 17, and *Daily Worker* January 20, 1933
45	*Daily Worker*, January 17, 1933
46	*Daily Worker*, February 6, 1930
47	*Daily Worker*, March 7, 1930
48	*Daily Worker*, March 11, 1930
49	*Daily Worker*, February 25, 1932
50	Report of the 9th Congress of the CPGB,p59
51	*Daily Worker*, May 20, 1930
52	*My Generation*, Will Paynter, Allen and Unwin 1972, pp39-40
53	*Daily Worker*, July 19, 1930
54	*Daily Worker*, May 7, 1932
55	*Daily Worker*, April 11, 1934

8 'Down with the Colour Bar'
Anti-Racism and the New Line

THE ISSUE of building unity between black and white workers during the new line was a cause of concern for Britain's communists. Although many have come to associate the Communist Party of Great Britain's fight against racism, namely anti-Semitism, with the period of the party's greatest popularity, from 1936-1946; the struggle against racism was already an established feature of communist politics well before the onset of the popular front in 1936. Although Britain's black population was tiny far less than the Jewish community, there were still attempts to create divisions and even half-hearted and localise efforts to blame black people for any economic shortcomings. Having said that, it must be remembered that the main thrust of any racist political party during the years under review was against Jews and not against people of colour. Jews were seen as the main enemy, racist propaganda against them both in Britain and on a world scale was intense. In Britain, Jews were more visible, more numerous and certainly since the days of the British Brothers League at the turn of the century, that section of the community that was most likely to be physically attacked.

Despite the numerical insignificance of Britain's black population, the CPGB did make attempts to recruit amongst black workers. What it also did, to a much larger extent and using a variety of methods, was to try and dispel any racist ideas that may have been gaining credence in the working-class movement. Once again using its new weapon the *Daily Worker* the CPGB worked to show the labour movement that racial differences were not important and that the oppression of black people anywhere in the world was of immediate concern to white workers here in Britain. Whether it be in what the party called 'boss sport' in Britain, or in the attempted frameup of black youths in the USA, the communists aimed to show to their supporters and others in the labour movement that it was class and not colour that should unite workers.

The agenda for this anti-racist approach had been set in the days before the new line. At the party's Seventh Congress in 1925, the CPGB had committed itself to a resolute struggle against racism, or, what it called 'imperialist prejudices'. These prejudices, which were it claimed a product of Empire, were, according to the CPGB, widespread amongst the British working class and it was the duty of communists to combat them and win the labour movement for a strategy of anti-racism. The Congress resolution declared:

> "every party member must actively take up the fight against the Imperialist prejudice still existing amongst large sections of the working class in Great Britain."[1]

This commitment made in 1925 set the pattern for the CPGB's struggle against racism during the class against class period.

In this fight against racist ideology, the CPGB was almost alone amongst political parties in Britain. The largest of the working-class parties, the Labour Party, had, in the view of the communists, acquiesced to racism by refusing during their two terms of office, to give any of Britain's black colonies independence. The Second Labour Government, much to the communists' indignation, had not even intervened and stopped the Meerut Conspiracy Trial in India. It had been left to the communists, through their satellite organisations principally the League Against Imperialism to wage this lonely fight both against colonialism and racism. It could be argued that the first of these was an easy option. To support the rights of subject nations abroad to self-determination was not the same as combating racist ideas at home. The daily battle against incipient and overt racism was a much more difficult one to wage, than the relatively cost-free call for colonial freedom. Anti-imperialism was an established and respected trend, not just in the labour movement but also amongst Liberals and some Tories. Whereas, to win over workers who had been fed a constant diet of the British race's superiority, and who had had minimal contact with other ethnic groups, apart from the Irish, was considerably more difficult. That the communists attempted to take on this momentous task, given their small numbers and lack of resources, was a credit to their internationalism.

For many historians of the labour movement, the battle of Cable Street in East London in 1936 is considered to have been a turning point in the struggle against Oswald Mosley and his British Union of Fascists. After this street battle, the danger of using anti-Semitism as a means to divide the working class began to recede. The tactics of the communists in the build-up to that epic day were two-fold. It was to rouse the London labour movement in defence of the East End's Jewish community and not to allow them to be used as a scapegoat by fascists, for what the CPGB saw as the ills of capitalism. Secondly, the communists sought to exert what influence they had, which was not inconsiderable, amongst the Jewish population of the East end in order to bring them out onto the streets in order to stop Mosley's march. For their efforts, the communists incurred the wrath not just of the labour movement leadership but also of the Jewish establishment, both of which implored their supporters to stay at home. However, the tactics of the CPGB prevailed, and Mosley suffered a setback from which he never recovered.

This strategy used with such success in 1936 was nothing new. The communists throughout the class against class years employed similar devices for uniting workers. Although the Jewish population of East London was considerable, particularly in Stepney and Whitechapel and was continually being harassed by fascist elements and their sympathisers, it was not the only ethnic group that was subject to attack. During the early 1930s, before the advent of the popular front, the communists had attempted to rally support for other minorities who were being, in their view, scapegoated. The tactics they used in rousing support for these persecuted elements was very similar to that tried a few years later. Combating racism may have been perfected in the party's period of most significant popularity. However, its origins lay in the earlier years when the struggle against racial prejudice was considered by many not to be a priority.

Not only did the communists take practical steps in their attempts to confront those using racism as a tool to divide the working-class movement, but they also challenged racist ideology Once again it was their newly founded daily paper that was in the forefront of this ideological confrontation. the *Daily Worker* in many different ways fed its readers a constant diet of anti-racism and anti-Semitism. Its interpretation of events in Britain and abroad, where the racial dimension was a significant factor, was to encourage and supports those elements that were attempting to unite workers rather than divide them. It played up these positive features and was scathing of those who used race or ethnicity to create divisions. In its coverage of cultural events, particularly sport, the paper was well ahead of its time in denouncing any attempt to portray non-whites as inferior. Even the paper's children's corner was used as a vehicle to combat racial prejudice amongst the paper's younger readers-often the sons and daughters of party members and their supporters. Whatever its weaknesses may have been in other areas, the party paper, with its steadily increasing readership, did pioneering work during the class against class period in combatting racist ideas at a time when all other *daily* newspapers were in support of the Empire and did nothing to counter suggestions that the white race was superior.

During the new line, the communists not only declared that social democracy was the mainstay of colonialism; they were also convinced that social democrats would do nothing to combat racism. It, therefore, came as no surprise to the CPGB when the Labour Government banned a CI inspired International Negro Workers Conference that was due to be held in Britain on July 1 1930. Publicity for the conference had already got underway, and the CPGB was using the forthcoming event to make contact with the small number of black people that were resident in the UK. The party was particularly concerned that racism was being used by an alliance of the National Union of Seamen and the ship owners, to divide black and white seamen. There had already been an outbreak of fighting between black and white seafarers in the North East over the signing on of an Arab crew, and the communists were keen to ensure that this did not reoccur and that all seafarers should be united against the bosses union and the employers. [2] This was the background to a report for the party paper from one of the worker correspondent's covering the port area of Cardiff. Worker correspondents were either party members or sympathisers, and this one claimed to have talked to West African seamen in the Tiger Bay area of the city. They described to the reporter their conditions and had also expressed an interest in the forthcoming Negro Conference. The conference, according to the report in the paper, was 'important in connection with the West African seamen's concern about the colour bar, which is being put up by the joint efforts of the Board of Trade, the National Seamen's Union and the Labour Party.' [3]

At one stroke, black seamen's worries about racial prejudice allowed the communists to attack, both racism, and its supporters, the Labour Party. Probably the most crucial revealing thing about this small news item was that the CPGB, at a time when its membership was at an all-time low, could still concern itself with issues of race. It was to prove not the first, nor the last time, that the CPGB would turn its attention to the colour bar.

The International Negro Conference, which had been planned since 1929, was banned by J R Clynes in May 1930. Delegates were in transit for the conference, and its location was then switched at the last minute to Hamburg in Germany from where reports of its deliberation were conveyed to party members in Britain. [4] A strong supporter of the event was the Communist Party of the United States of America, where issues of race had already been examined thoroughly by the American party membership. CPGB members in Britain were aware of the American party's attitude towards black liberation through reports in the party press. [5] The decision by the CPUSA at its Seventh Congress in 1930 to advocate self-determination for black Americans and the option for them to live in, and rule, an independent 'black belt' area in the South, was reported in the *Daily Worker*. [6]

If the CPGB perceived the banning of the conference as evidence of racism, then of even more significant concern was a renewed outbreak of fighting between black and white seafarers in South Shields in the North East. Although the CPGB had focused on the cause of the seamen's discontent some two months before they were somewhat taken aback by the sudden turn of events. The communists soon recovered, and the party was actively involved in the dispute from the start, and its propaganda played down any racial differences. It emphasised the common interest that existed between workers of all colours.

The first that party members, apart from those in the North East and those involved in the NUS, knew about a strike involving seafarers of all colours, was when it was reported in the *Daily Worker* under the banner headline, 'seamen united against PC5.'[7] The paper explained that the PC5 was a document that had to be signed by all seamen whether or not they were union members, at a cost to them of £2, every time that they signed on for work on a ship.

The communists declared that seamen have to pay to belong to, 'a union which is openly a company union.' Two thousand seafarers had struck work in South Shields against the issuing of the documents and those involved in the stoppage included twelve hundred British sailors and nine hundred Arab seamen. The strike was particularly pleasing for the communists because not only was it a strike that united black and white but also because it was a blow against the notoriously right-wing National Union of Seamen which in their view was in league with the ship-owners. The strike was applauded by the British party who welcomed 'the magnificent solidarity of white and coloured seamen.' [8]

The stoppage spread to other ports and involved seafarers of all nationalities. In Cardiff, with its established black community there was a rally in solidarity with the South Shields seamen. The rally called for the unity of white and Arab seamen. [9] The next day there was a lightning strike in Liverpool against the imposition of the PC5 and a mass picket of the port which was led by the communist Minority Movement.[10] A few days later, when fighting again broke out in South Shields between seamen, it was portrayed by the communists as a struggle between striking black and white seamen and scabs. the *Daily Worker* accused those, particularly other newspapers, who portrayed the strike as a racial riot as lying. Their headline said it all, 'seamen Fight the Police – Attempt to break South Shields Strike – Arab and White seamen solid.' The headline concluded with 'Racial Riot – Lie' The party presented the fighting in South Shields as a clash between strikers and scabs who were being assisted by the police to break the strike. Their presentation was very little different to that of any other dispute. The communists, in their attempts to build black and white unity, publicised a black seamen's rally in Liverpool in support of the strike. One of the party's lasting achievements as a result of the stoppage was its involvement in the establishment of Negro self-help organisations in Liverpool and London. [11]

In a further effort to build bridges to Britain's small black community the CPGB gave publicity to Frank Macauly, the editor of the *Lagos Daily News*. Macauly was to make a visit to Britain and address meetings in Liverpool and Cardiff. By publicising Macauly, and the reason for his visit, the communists, had a dual purpose, they would again focus attention on the Empire. At the same time, try to combat racism in the British working-class movement. Macauly, who was described in the party press as, 'a militant Nigerian trade unionist' was responding to numerous stories in the British press of the dangers of mixed-race relationships, particularly in Liverpool. One such report had been headlined, 'Half-Caste Evil in Liverpool.' [12] There were in the port city about one hundred and fifty, of what was described by Macauly as Anglo/Negroid families. Apart from this adverse publicity in the press, there were also calls for the replacement of the black fathers by white men. There were besides demands that black peoples right of access to Britain be withdrawn.

The port of Liverpool was home to many African seamen and Macauly, through the *Daily Worker* contrasted the treatment, of what he called, 'half caste children', in Nigeria, with those in Liverpool, and in so doing brought out not only the differing treatment the children received from the different races, but he also managed to inject into the article a class analysis:

> "The great difference that exists between the half-castes in Liverpool and those in Nigeria is that those in Liverpool are being taken care of by the coloured seamen, whilst in Nigeria the fathers of these half-castes, who are either white Provincial Commissioners, Resident Magistrates, Assistant Colonial Secretaries or white merchants, never subscribe a single penny for the maintenance of these children."[13]

This kind of approach by Macauly that united race and class was one welcomed by the communists. It reflected the CPGB's growing interest in the national question and how it related to social class and was one of the essential by-products of the class against class period. Previously the communists' commitment to a broad class alliance in the national liberation movement left little room for discussion about the national question and its relationship to class forces. This new interest was reflected in several articles in the *Communist Review* early in 1933 on the Scottish National Question along with an analysis of the growth of anti-Irish sentiment in Scotland. [14] Nigeria was a long way from Scotland, and the issues were very different but that the communists were beginning to grapple with them says something for the intellectual rigour that the application of the new line necessitated.

The communists again turned their attention to Liverpool, with its established black community, the following year. Research was undertaken by the Liverpool branch of the League against Imperialism into the living and working conditions of the city's 'three hundred Negroes'. It revealed that black workers were discriminated against by the employers and that the violation of their civil rights was a cause for concern. What is significant is that the communists, who could not have numbered more than a dozen militants in the city, should have made efforts into finding out about this small but neglected group of workers. The report revealed that black workers who worked in the stoke-holds of boats were paid £6.10s a month compared to their white counterparts who received £9 a month. One shipping company demanded that black workers in their employ carry identity cards with a photograph and that each card carry an impression of the employee's left thumb. Such injustices were publicised in the party paper in order to win sympathy for black workers and to show how employers were using this most vulnerable section of society as cheap labour. In case there were any doubts about the party's position, the *Daily Worker* carried news of the research under the headline 'Negro Slavery in Liverpool'. [15]

The CPGBs efforts in Liverpool and the North East to recruit amongst black seamen were not the first time that the communists had been involved in attempts to recruit black workers. The party had sent one of its leading members, Andrew Rothstein, to address a meeting of black workers in Barry, near Cardiff, in October 1929. The subject of the meeting was, 'the position of Negroes and the attitude of the Communist Party'. According to reports, almost thirty black people were in attendance which was an excellent turn out given the party's small membership. That such a meeting even took place was an indication that the CPGB must have had some contact with South Wales' tiny black community in order to organise such an event. There were attempts to recruit black workers throughout the new line. In 1932 Saklatvala was sent to South Wales to address meetings. At two of these in Cardiff, special efforts were made to recruit amongst the city's black community, a project that seems to have met with some success and some black recruits were made for the party. [16] How many members of the CPGB at this time were black it is impossible to say -no figures are available. However, given reports in the party press and knowing the numbers of active black party members, it can be said with some certainty that the CPGB had a disproportionate number of non-white members in its ranks.

The party's leading non-white was Saklatvala although there seems to have been no notable attempt by the party to use his racial origin as a means of recruiting amongst the black community. Saklatvala may have spoken to black people in Cardiff about their need to join the CP, but he also addressed Jews in Whitechapel about the same issue. [17] If anything Saklatvala was perhaps not the best person to advocate workers unity on the party's behalf – he had after all been condemned by the Central Committee of the CPGB of which he was a member a few years before, for allowing his five children to be initiated at a Parsee religious ceremony at Caxton Hall in London. Saklatvala's action was censored by the party leadership precisely because it might encourage religious differences and discord in Saklatvala's country of birth.

The CPGB was careful that its leading protagonists should, in their personal as well as their political lives, encourage tolerance of other races and culture.

Where there was evidence of racial discrimination and the CPGB was able to make a contribution towards its eradication it did so. In May 1931 in Edinburgh in Scotland, there was an attempt to introduce a colour bar. There were many Indian students in attendance at the university, and two of Edinburgh most prestigious cafes decided to ban Indian students from entering the premises. This discrimination was taken up and reported on in the *Daily Worker*, and from the article, it is evident that similar attempts at a colour bar had been tried in the city before, when there were concerted efforts to ban Indians, and other non-whites, from the city's dancehalls. On the first occasion Saklatvala, who was at that time a prominent MP, acting at the party's behest, had led a campaign against this racial intolerance. The campaign was successful, and the colour bar was dropped. [18]

Recruitment amongst the black community, the endorsing of black organisations, the sympathetic portrayal of people of colour in Britain, were all priorities on the CPGB's anti-racist agenda. One of the party's most successful campaigns was that around the imprisoned Scottsboro Boys. These were a group of black American youths who were accused of raping two white women while travelling on a train in the southern state of Tennessee. The case was quickly taken up by the communist-controlled International Labour Defence who provided the initial legal aid. Before the Scottsboro case was widely known, the CPGB in 1931 had tried to arouse interest in the affair and through the League Against Imperialism had ensured that resolutions were passed condemning the death sentences imposed on the defendants. The party made special efforts to recruit amongst black workers and through the ILD petitions were launched demanding the boys' release. There was also a pamphlet published entitled 'stop Legal Lynching'. In July 1931, with only a few days to go before the date set for the boys execution the party was keen to mobilise what support it could to win a stay of execution. In the mobilisation of public opinion it was obvious that the CPGB was keen to involve as many black workers as possible. One party member reported that, 'a comrade came into the ILD office and took away a couple of petition forms. In the space of two hours he returned with the forms completed, with 66 signatures, every one being that of a Negro worker'. [19] The CPGB was also at pains to explain that Scottsboro was not just the result of a class system, but that race inequality also played a part. In an urgent appeal to its supporters, the party made its position clear, 'there are only four days left in which to do our utmost for these victims of American white terror'. [20] The ILD, as might be expected of the party's subsidiary, had a similar approach. It organised a series of meetings to coincide with the boys' possible execution, all of which were to be addressed by Negro comrades. These black party members, whom it did not name, appealed for workers unity in the face of 'capitalist white terror'. [21]

Apart from the civil liberties angle of wrongful imprisonment, British communists were also fully aware of all the prejudices that were likely to arise in a case of this nature -where black men were accused of sexually assaulting white women. In order to tackle these preconceived ideas, the party warned that the 'experience of both British and American imperialism leads us to view a sexual charge, especially when brought against coloured working men by white men......with grave suspicion'. [22] The party's assessment of the case, which remained consistent was that it was one more attempt to create prejudice. [23]

To counter this intolerance and as part of the worldwide campaign to win the accused release, the following year, at the invitation of the British ILD under the leadership of Bob Lovell, a prominent member of the CPGB, Mrs Wright, the mother of one of the accused came over to Europe on a speaking tour. At first, she was denied a visa, this was later granted, and she came to Britain in June 1932. Some months before this the CPGB had organised a protest meeting about the Scottsboro Boys in the cosmopolitan Limehouse area of London. What was interesting about this meeting, as with so many other anti-racist meetings organised by the CPGB at the time, was that it included a non-white speaker, on this occasion Chris Jones a black CPGB member from the Caribbean. [24]

The arrival of Mrs Wright gave a focus to the campaign. She was meet at Waterloo Station by Saklatvala on behalf of the CPGB, and Bob Lovell. Later, at the first rally of the tour, Saklatvala, at his oratorical new line best, welcomed Mrs Wright to Britain and called for, 'capitalism to be given the electric chair'. He condemned the Labour leaders in the reformist trade unions in the USA who barred Negroes from their unions and had not lifted a finger to help the boys, just as the British trade union leaders refused to help the Indian workers to organise in unions.

He also highlighted the fate of a 'native boy' in Honolulu who had been murdered by an American naval officer who was then found not guilty in court. He claimed that 'only the Communist International had fought for the oppressed races, such as the Negroes.' [25]

His speech may have been sectarian in today's terms, but it did deal with neglected issues of racial prejudice. It showed, for all the rhetoric, that the party to which Saklatvala belonged was prepared to take these issues on and what was equally as important it was prepared to mount what may have been unpopular campaigns against what it called 'imperialist prejudices.'

Just before Mrs Wright's arrival, there was a Scottsboro protest rally at Trafalgar Square at which another black member of the CPGB spoke, Arnold Ward. He represented the short-lived Negro Workers Defence League, yet another communist-inspired black organisation. [26]

Mrs Wright addressed many meetings during her two weeks stay in Britain. She left to continue her European tour on July 7 and at a farewell rally at Liverpool Street Station attended by over a thousand people it was Saklatvala who wished her well on behalf of the Communist Party. Once again he used the occasion to e mphasise the party's commitment to the fight against racism He told the audience that, 'the British workers have shown by their reception to Mrs Wright that they have broken down the barriers dividing them from the Negro races.' [27] He then went on to commit the party to continue with its campaign until the Scottsboro boys were released. He told the audience that the departure of Mrs Wright did not mean that the fight for the release of the Scottsboro boys had ended, it meant that the fight must go on till the boys were set free. [28]

The CPGB did continue with the campaign, and it is doubtful that if it had not been for the communists, the Scottsboro case would have received the publicity it did. Despite the communists' reservations, there was even some attempt at local united front work around the issue. A meeting was organised in Camberwell in South London jointly by the communist Negro Welfare Association and the Independent Labour Party. The speakers though, according to the publicity, appeared to have been mainly CPGB members. These were Bob Lovell from International Labour Defense, and Arnold Ward and Chris Jones from the Negro Welfare Association. [29] Jones and Ward were very active in the party's Scottsboro campaign, and both were prominent speakers at meetings called by the CPGB. Chris Jones was a Barbadian and President of the Colonial Seamen's Association. He left the CPGB in 1933, according to the historian CLR James, because the Comintern embraced the Popular Front which according to James downplayed the struggle against imperialism and led to the disenchantment of many black people with communism. Jones was a docker who had come to Britain after the First World War and a period in the Merchant Navy. He lived with his white wife in Stepney and had been an organiser for the National Union of Seamen during the 1920s. Because of his militancy, he used the pseudonym Braithewaite to avoid being discriminated against at work by employers. Arnold Ward was also Barbadian and a member of the CPGB. He too left the party with the finish of class against class although in his case it was not until 1935 that he resigned. Ward and Jones were the CPGBs two most active black members – there could well have been others.

Although the campaign around the release of the Scottsboro boys highlighted the Communist Party's commitment to fighting racism, this was by no means the party's only endeavours in this field. In many other significant ways, the CPGB during the class against class period tried to eradicate racism as an ideology from the thinking of the working class. This was no mean task given Britain's pivotal role at the centre of an empire – an empire that was sustained by the notion that the subject black races were inferior, and needed the mother country's skill and guidance to prepare them for citizenship. The party fought these pervading ideas by concentrating in its campaigns on those issues that united workers across the world – wages, conditions, hatred of the common enemy the employers. But it also fought in other ways, the party attempted, through its propaganda, to portray black people in Britain in a positive way. The CPGB constantly publicised incidents of racial intolerance, particularly in the USA. The communists even appreciated the necessity of rearing children in the ideas of anti-racism, and some of their propaganda was used in this way Even in the arena of culture, whether it be cinema or sport, the communists tried hard to battle against the prevailing ideas. They spoke out against racism, whether it was overt or clandestine.

The establishment of the Negro Welfare Association by the two black communists Ward and Jones was something of an achievement for the CPGB. The new group, which was affiliated to the League against Imperialism, was described by the party as a 'militant organisation of Negro workers'.[30] Party branches were urged to invite speakers from the new association, and the communists gave coverage to its events and activities, which were a mixture of the social and political. The NWA organised several outings for black children, and the *Daily Worker* often carried pictures of the events. Always these portrayals were sympathetic. One such outing warranted a front-page photograph and the headline 'Negro Kiddies – having a good time'. It concerned a day out for black children living in London and was arranged by the London branch of the NWA.[31] It emphasised the importance that the party attached to developing amongst its membership and supporters a sympathetic awareness of other races. It was not just sympathy that was encouraged, but integration as well. Party members were made aware of NWA social functions which were regularly advertised in the *Daily Worker*. How many white party members attended what were predominantly black functions are not known, but at least the will to break down barriers was there. It is unlikely that during the new line period any other political parties, even on the left, made such an effort at attempting to recruit amongst Britain's tiny black minority.

After the Nazis came to power in Germany and the class against class period was drawing to a close, the communists were particularly keen to promote racial tolerance towards those of different colours. Combating anti-Semitism was increasing the primary pre occupant of the party, but black issues were not neglected. The CPGB continued with its Scottsboro campaign and Saklatvala, and Arnold Ward spoke at a big meeting at the Grand Palais in Commercial Road in the heart of the East End of London, which was one of the most multi-racial areas of the country.[32] This was at the end of 1933 when Scottsboro had been forgotten by many, and the threat was emanating from Nazi Germany was beginning to occupy centre stage. Neither was anti-colonialism relegated to second place in importance by the British party. To draw attention to its iniquities and at the same time confronts racial intolerance in Britain the CPGB sent Saklatvala to address a Negro Forum in London on, 'The New Sedition Bill in West Africa'.[33] It was yet another initiative by the CPGB to extend its links with the black community.

The communists, in their campaign around the Scottsboro Boys, had focused attention on racism in the United States, while at the same time attacking racist ideas in general. In the campaign, which was international and had been initiated by American communists, the CPGB tried to win over the black community, arouse the labour movement to the injustice that had taken place, and at the same time expose the inherent racism of US capitalism. The party was keen to use any opportunity to attack US imperialism and in this attack to try and foster unity with those whom it saw as imperialism's foremost victims, namely black people and workers. It needs to be emphasised that during the new line period American imperialism was considered by Britain's communists to be one of the greatest threats to peace – a role only later ascribed to Germany. Throughout class against class, the British party repeatedly warned of the war danger emanating from across the Atlantic. Although the USSR may have posed the most significant threat to capitalism, the rivalry between the United States and Britain was the primary source of war danger. The communists, in their class against class analysis, considered that fascist Italy and pre-Hitler Germany were pawns of the newest imperialist predator the United States. At the first of their new line congresses, the CPGB made its position clear:

> "America aims at destroying Britain's monopoly of oil and rubber and is fighting for a re-distribution of the colonies. She already holds a more powerful position in China, is driving Britain out of Latin America and gradually bringing Canada and Australia under her economic influence. In Europe, both Germany and Italy are heavily mortgaged to America." [34]

The communists warned that in the drive to war attempts would be made by the ruling classes of Britain and America to instil chauvinistic attitudes into their respective working classes.

The 10th Congress statement declared 'that ties of blood and language will in no way hold back the ruling class when profit is at stake. Already on both sides of the Atlantic the working class are being cunningly aroused to fly at one another's throats'.[35]

The line that the conflict between American and British imperialism posed the greatest threat to world peace was reiterated at the 11th Congress, where delegates were told that 'the principal antagonism between the Imperialist powers is between Great Britain and America. All minor imperialist antagonism revolve around this fundamental antagonism'. [36]

Barely four months before Hitler's assession to power the final CPGB Congress of the class against class period still committed the party to this analysis. If anything, in the party's view, the drive to war between the two contenders had accelerated, and capitalism was 'leading with breakneck speed towards a new world war.'[37]

Given this analysis, which was dropped after the new line, it is not surprising that Britain's communists should home in on any class or race conflicts and injustices which beset America. The CPGB's primary objective, however, was, as always, to build working-class unity. The campaign around the Scottsboro Boys went some way towards achieving this but so did other initiatives, particular the communists' long-running exposure during the new line of racism in the USA. They attacked the idea that somehow the United States in its development was any different from that of any other capitalist country. The American employers' treatment of workers, particularly black workers, was, the party argued, no different to that of British employers. America may not have been one of the first imperialist powers, but its record towards its indigenous population was on a par with that of any of the other colonial conquerors.

As part of this campaign to expose the United States as a capitalist, and therefore a racist state, just like any other, the *Daily Worker* carried extensive reports of the lynching of black Americans. These were a regular occurrence and took place in both the northern and the southern states The paper in its coverage of these killings could be quite graphite, and effectively conveyed to the readership some of the lengths that racists would go to in order to exact their toll on black Americans. For example, during 1930 a report of a killing in Texas was headlined 'Negro Worker hacked to death in Texas lynching' It described how a black man who was awaiting trial had been hacked to death by a white mob after the prison in which he was being kept was set on fire. [38] 'Another Negro Lynched ' was how the paper some months later reported yet another murder, this time in Georgia. Once again, a black man awaiting trial was taken out of prison and lynched after the jail in which he was being held was attacked by white locals. [39]

The regular coverage of such events had the intention of bringing home to communists, and their supporters, the iniquities of racism worldwide. It also helped foster a spirit of tolerance. In their own small way, the communists tried to build bridges between the races – they may have seen it as all part of a grander scheme of international working-class solidarity, but the effect was the same -it ensured that the seeds of racism could not be so easily be planted in a working-class that had for years been fed on the glories of Empire.

While campaigning against blatant forms of racial discrimination, whether in Britain or abroad, was the main thrust of the communists' agitation on this issue, they also conducted an ideological offensive against racism. In the developing media of cinema, with its increasing dominance by the United States, the party was not reticent in pointing out the dangers of allowing racism to go unchallenged. Cinema going was on the increase, and the communists were keen to ensure that the mainly working-class audiences were made aware of the racism that infected many films. Nowhere was this apparent than with the American blockbuster film *Birth of a Nation*.

This W G Griffiths classic was, in 1931, making a return appearance at London cinemas after a seventeen years absence – it was first made in 1914. The *Daily Worker* condemned the film as a piece of 'vicious propaganda against the Negro people.' [40]

Birth of a Nation had won acclaim as a masterpiece because of its technical merit, but this did not detract the communists argued from the film's underlying racist message, which was that black people were inferior. The party's paper described it as 'the most vicious anti-social equality propaganda film in the entire history of the American cinema. [41] In the film 'Negroes are represented as a people who have no claim to equality, who must remain the willing slaves to the lordly whites'. This view of black people as subhuman was, the communists claimed, nothing more than an ideological defence of colonialism. The entire film in the words of the *Daily Worker* attempted to justify,'the imperialist philosophy of the domination of the white man over the coloured races.' [42]

It was not just the portrayal of black Americans that was attacked by the British party; communists also sprang to the defence of the original inhabitants of the United States. Once again, this challenge was made through a film review. A sympathetic interpretation of the life of the Ojibwa Indians of the American Northeast before the coming of the white man was the subject of a film *The Silent Enemy*. Despite the apparent good intentions of the filmmaker, the communists could not resist the opportunity of using the film to lambast the treatment of native Indians by their new conquerors. 'Having robbed the Red Indians of most of their land, driven them into barren reservations, degraded and corrupted them, American imperialism can afford to sentimentalise over their nobility.' [43] At a time when the common conception of native Americans as gleaned through the cinema was of scalping savages thesentiments of the reviewer were well ahead of their time. This sympathetic interpretation of other cultures was an intrinsic part of the communists ideological offensive against racism. It was to stand them in good stead when a few years later, attacks on Jewish cultural habits became a staple diet for the British Union of Fascists.

Racism was not just an issue for 'grown ups' – the communists also tried to instil an anti-racist ideology into their younger followers. The party had its separate youth organisation, the Young Communist League, and there was also, for even younger members, the Young Pioneers It was these groups that were instrumental in initiating campaigns against Empire Day. Apart from this direct action, the CPGB, through the *Daily Worker*, carried on with its ideological offensive against racism and tried to win over the papers younger readers, most of whom were the sons and daughters of party members or sympathisers. Within the second month of publication, the paper carried its own Children's Column, the first issue of which contained a letter attacking caning. A popular cartoon character in the early days of the paper was Micky Mongrel. Micky, a dog, was a communist militant, who was constantly embroiled in the struggle, particularly with the dogs who went to the 'snob school'. But Micky was also used to promote internationalism and in one feature meets some 'Indian comrades' while attending a conference. [44] It was with some disappointment amongst the readership that Micky left the paper at the end of 1931 for a 'long stay in the USSR'. [45] However, Micky's adherents were reassured that the cartoonist who created Micky would continue with two new characters, Mike and Mary, who would appear early in the new year.

If anything the new arrivals were even better at getting across the party's message about racism than was Micky, as a series of cartoons in the January 1932 edition of the paper shows. The two children, Mike and Mary, are militants. Mike's father is a lighterman who is on strike, and the two children offer their services to the strike committee, to go and collect money and clothes in the neighbourhood for the strikers. Whilst out collecting Mike and Mary are mocked by Sam Silver, whom Mike refers to as, 'that rotten yid'. Mike and Mary are in the same class at school as Sam Silver and Mike, and he are always fighting and making fun of each other. We are told, through the cartoon, that Mike's father is Irish, and that he has been brought up to believe that Jews are dirty, funny, and foreign, and are a different sort of people. The day after the collection Mike and Mary are watching an unemployed demonstration when they are shocked to see Sam Silver collecting money for the strikers. Mary turns to Mike and says, 'are you sure he is such a horrid boy', which is rather a strange turn of phrase for a supposed working-class militant. The next day Mike confronts Sam about his support for the strikers, only to discover that Sam's dad is unemployed. They then realise that they are both on the same side-they shake hands and in the next cartoon, Mike, Mary and Sam all join the Young Pioneers.

The cartoon may not, in today's terms, have been seen as a subtle means of propaganda, but at least the communists were consistent, they saw racism as a means of dividing workers. Anything that they could do to promote the commonality of workers interests was in their view, beneficial in defeating racist ideas. That they should try and develop non-racist attitudes amongst children was all part of their new line strategy of winning over the working class, be it indigenous, black or Jewish.

Another area worth looking at is the CPGBs agitation during the period against racism in sport. This was conducted mainly through the party controlled British Workers Sports Federation, and the main focus of attention was the breaking down of racial barriers in boxing. That the party should even have been concerned with the sport was something of an anomaly. The communists had taken control of the BWSF in 1926/7 when George Sinfield was elected secretary. The Federation, which flourished during the new line, was a campaigning organisation that attracted a considerable measure of support. In London alone, at the start of 1931, over one hundred football teams were competing in BWSF leagues.[46] The ethos of the Federation was one of cooperation and equality. There was active encouragement of women, and team members were urged to help one another. At the first meeting of the Federation's newly formed London swimming group, it was stressed how important it was for Federation swimmers to teach non-swimmers how to swim.[47] Even the presentation of trophies was controversial, and one participant in the 1931 BWSF pre-Congress discussion was opposed to their display and thought instead that certificates 'should be hung up in the club room' to emphasise the cooperative nature of sport.[48]

For the early *Daily Worker* the coverage of what was referred to as, 'boss sport', was something of a conundrum. Readers were evenly divided over whether it should be dealt with or not. After some discussion racing tips and results were quickly dropped, but there was agreement that although emphasis should be placed on the BWSF, there should be some sports news. Sinfield, along with Dutt, was sceptical of this position and thought that all bourgeois sport should be boycotted. Fortunately, as it transpired, for the struggle against racism, sport news remained a part of the paper, and throughout the new line, the CPGB carried on a steady vendetta against the colour bar, particularly in that most working-class of sports-boxing.

One of the most important of spin-offs of this campaign was the recruitment, long after the new line had been forgotten, of Len Johnson, the famous mixed-race boxer from Manchester. Johnson, who in his boxing heyday during the 30s, was championed by the party because of his abilities was never allowed, because of his colour, to compete for a British title-an injustice highlighted continuously by the CPGB. After the war, Johnson joined the Communist Party and was a communist local candidate in Manchester on several occasions. [49]

It is only relatively recently in Britain that boxers of different colours have been allowed to compete for championship titles. During the period under review, black and non-white boxers were very much treated as second class citizens by the boxing establishment. The National Sporting Club which awarded Lonsdale belts did not allow black and white boxers to compete with each other for these trophies. This ban, according to the *Daily Worker* had been in force since the days of Jack Johnson, the early twentieth-century black American fighter. The paper, which campaigned against this discrimination, was pleased to tell its readers early in 1931 that at last the ban had been lifted and that for the first time a black and white fighter could contend under the auspices of the NSC. The ban the paper pointed out had been particularly discriminating against Len Johnson, who was described as 'beyond question the cleverest middleweight in England.' [50] The communists, through their paper, made their anti-racist position clear, 'because of his colour, Johnson was never permitted to fight for the English title or to hold a Lonsdale Belt. The plums of English boss boxing were not for a negro. [51] The paper also referred to the black American boxer, Godrey, who was never allowed to meet the world heavyweights, Gene Tunney or Jack Dempsey who were both white.

The communists returned to the attack on racism in boxing the following month, when the *Daily Worker* declared, 'Down with the Colour Bar in Sport'. [52] It was alleged that the Labour Government would ban a possible contest between a black fighter, Larry Gains, and Phil Smith, a white boxer, for the heavyweight championship of England. In condemning any such ban, the paper pointed out that there was already precedence and that promising non-white fighters in the past had been refused permission to compete against white opponents.

Daily Worker readers were told that 'rumours are already flying around that the Labour Government's Home Office would ban any match between a white man and a negro for the championship of England. Since the Home Office put up the bar against Siki, after the Senegalese had battered 'Gorgeous' George Carpentier to unconsciousness, no attempt has been made to stage a championship fight between principals of different colour'. Workers were encouraged to contrast this approach of 'boss sport' with the equality of all working-class sportsmen enrolled in the Red Sport International, whatever their race, creed or colour. [53]

Once again, the message was clear and reflected the party's clear commitment to anti-racism. Who can say what effect it had? One thing we know for sure is that at least one black sportsman belatedly responded and joined the CPGB. There was certainly no other campaign like it in the thirties by any of the political parties, even those of the left. Its almost modern parallel would be the Football Association sponsored 'Kick Racism out of Football', but that is supported by a well-funded organisation and takes place in a different political climate, one where racism is frowned upon in official circles The CPGBs campaign took place against a backdrop of innate prejudice. It was initiated by an organisation that at the time, had less than three thousand members.

The *Daily Worker* in its coverage of BSWF events, which were numerous, was keen to show the anti-racist content of some of the Federation's activities. For example, the Hackney Workers Sports Club in London, which was one of hundreds of local workers sports clubs that were established during the period, invited along Arnold Ward from the Negro Welfare Association to address the club on 'Negro Problems'. After hearing him speak the club members who were certainly not all communists, condemned racism and called for the release of the Scottsboro Boys. Interestingly enough, the same edition of the paper which carried this report also had an article in Yiddish, about the conditions of clothing workers. The Communist Party may be accused of sectarianism during the new line, one thing it cannot be accused of is a lack of commitment to multiculturalism.

The campaign against racism conducted by the Communist Party during the class against class period was many-faceted. With single-issue campaigns, like that of the Scottsboro Boys, the communists strove to focus attention on the international dimension of racism, and how the ruling class used it to deny rights to sections of workers. In the course of the campaign, the party hoped to break down any racial prejudices that existed amongst the British working class. They did this by attempting to show the unifying factors that affected workers everywhere. For the party during this period the class struggle was everything-race, religion, creed were not factors that needed to be taken into account-the slogan 'workers of the world unite' meant just that, and it was the duty of every party member to see that it was implemented. It was narrow in its conception, but at least the communists were attempting to raise the consciousness of the working class over racial issues. If it were not for the CPGB, the plight of nine black youths languishing in jail in Georgia in 1931 would never have become an issue in Britain.

On the home front too, the CPGB was prepared to commit itself to an anti-racist agenda. Through its subsidiary organisations the League against Imperialism and the British Workers Sports Federation the party paid attention to eradicating racist ideas. Its role in exposing racism in sport, whether it be in boxing, or the denial of black athletes admittance to the Empire Games in South Africa, was pioneering. Where there were incidents of a colour bar and the party was able to do something about it, it did. It publicised the plight of mixed-race children in Liverpool. They were the subjects of racist abuse in the press and elicited the services of a Nigerian Trade Unionist to argue their case in its newspaper. When ramblers were arrested at the BWSF initiated mass trespass of Kinder Scout in 1932, it was the communists that through their newspaper pointed out that all six of those arrested had Jewish names.

Readers of the new *Daily Worker* were regularly treated to articles that had an international dimension. There was coverage of news of liberation movements in all of the British colonies, and attention was also give to freedom struggles in every part of the globe. Whether it was in the children's corner, in its coverage of sport, or its interpretation of issues of race or colonialism, the *Daily Worker* pushed the party line, and that line was that racism divides workers. Every incident, whether it be in South Africa, India or Britain that showed that workers could unite, and break down the barriers of race, was sympathetically portrayed. Equally, whenever there were differences between black and white workers, as in the seamen's dispute, these were interpreted as a conflict between strikers and scabs. The strikers were black and white seamen, and the scabs, on the bosses behalf, were trying to divide them along racial lines. It may not have been the whole truth, but the intention was an excellent one-to minimalise any hostilities amongst the working class based upon skin colour.

Finally, we are not just talking about a party that was somehow or other above the racial divide. As referred to earlier, there are no reliable figures for the number of black people resident in Britain, but we can safely assume that it was tiny. As for non-white members of the CPGB that too is open to speculation. What we do know is that the party's leading orator and its sole representative in Parliament from 1924-29 was Indian. The party's foremost theoretician, and according to many historians of British communism, the manipulator, and power behind the throne of the party leadership, was half Indian. During the time of Scottsboro, and afterwards, in the heart of the new line, two of the party most prominent spokesmen on the issue of race were black. We know from recruitment reports published in the party press that there were black people present at party meetings-How many joined it is impossible to say. It is also well documented that the CPGB made special efforts to recruit black workers with meetings specifically about issues of race. Given this evidence, it seems a fair assumption to make that black representation in the CPGB was probably higher than in the country at large.

Probably the greatest significance of the CPGB's onslaught on racism during the new line is that it laid the basis for the much better know campaigns against anti-Semitism a few years later, during the period of the popular front. The battle of Cable Street is well recorded and remembered but not the communist's lone initiative around Scottsboro yet the party's methods of confronting racism were much the same during both periods. the *Daily Worker* was used to spotlight racism and arouse workers against those individuals, or parties that were using racism to disunite the working-class movement. Party branches and sympathetic organisations were then mobilised to isolate and condemn the racists, whether they be in Britain or abroad, and to implement the party line, which was common throughout both periods, that is, that racism is a tool of the employers and is used by then to divide and destroy the labour movement. Apart from this confrontation of racism, the communists also used their propaganda to pose an alternative to racist ideology. Of paramount importance in this battle of ideas was their daily paper which from the time of its first appearance carried on an invective against racist ideology and attempted to counter the ideas of Empire and racial superiority. It did this in many ways. These included the favourable reporting of black people living in Britain, the exposure of the appalling living conditions of black families in Liverpool, condemnation of the oppression of people of colour in the Empire, coverage of the activities of national liberation movements in Africa. All this and more contributed towards the development of cultural and racial awareness and tolerance amongst communists and their supporters. This is not surprising given that communists were after all members of an organisation committed to world revolution and internationalism.

Notes

1 Report of the 7th Congress of the CPGB, pp196-197
2 *Daily Worker*, May 2, 1930
3 *Daily Worker*, May 14 1930
4 *Daily Worker*, July 12, 1930
5 *Daily Worker*, July 2, 1930
6 *Ibid*
7 *Daily Worker*, July 24, 1930
8 *Ibid*
9 *Daily Worker*, August 1, 1930
10 *Daily Worker*, August 2, 1930
11 *Daily Worker*, August 5, 1930
12 *Daily Worker*, October 25, 1930
13 *Ibid*
14 *Communist Review*, April/May 1933
15 *Daily Worker*, February 20, 1931
16 *Daily Worker*, April 15, 1932
17 *Daily Worker*, April 2, 1931
18 *Daily Worker* May 4, 1931
19 *Daily Worker* July 6, 1931
20 *Ibid*
21 *Ibid*
22 *Daily Worker*, July 15, 1931
23 *Ibid*
24 *Daily Worker*, April 16, 1932
25 DailyWorker, June 30, 1932
26 *Daily Worker*, June 21, 1932
27 *Daily Worker*, July 9, 1932
28 *Ibid*
29 *Daily Worker*, October 8, 1932
30 *Daily Worker*, August 22, 1932
31 *Ibid*
32 *Daily Worker*, December 14, 1933
33 *Daily Worker*, March 16, 1934
34 *The New Line-Documents of the Tenth Congress of the Communist Party of Great Britain* held at Bermondsey, London on Jan 19th-22nd 1929, p115
35 *Ibid*
36 *Resolutions of the 11th Congress of the Communist Party of Great Britain* Leeds, Nov 30th - Dec 3rd 1929 p30
37 *Resolutions adopted by the Twelfth Congress of the Communist Party of Great Britain* Held at Latchmere Baths Battersea Nov 12th-15th 1932, p15
38 *Daily Worker*, May 12, 1930
39 *Daily Worker*, October 3, 1930
40 *Daily Worker*, May 18, 1931

41 *Ibid*
42 *Ibid*
43 *Daily Worker*, February 9, 1931
44 *Daily Worker*, April 20, 1931
45 *Daily Worker*, December 31, 1931
46 *Daily Worker*, January 20, 1931
47 *Daily Worker*, April 9, 1930
48 *Daily Worker*, December 5, 1930
49 See, *Never Counted Out*, Michael Herbert
50 *Daily Worker*, February 6, 1931
51 *Ibid*
52 *Daily Worker*, March 19, 1931
53 *Ibid*

9 The end of the New Line.

FOR THOSE who see British communists as mere tools of Moscow, the jettisoning of the class against class strategy poses a problem. Hitler came to power in Germany in February 1933 and almost immediately, the Communist International issued a united front statement to all its member parties. The statement urged Communist parties to seek maximum unity with the forces of social democracy and to present a common front against fascism. In line with this directive, the British party duly issued its united front statement that was sent to the Labour Party, the Trades Union Congress and the Independent Labour Party. Apart from the ILP, the communists' appeal met little positive response.

Although the Communist Party of Great Britain may have paid lip service to the International's change of line, it was to be almost two years before the party fully embraced the united front strategy and over a year and a half before it could even bring itself reluctantly, and with qualifications, to urge its members to vote Labour. During these two years, the party was in a kind of limbo-the leadership may have announced its adherence to the new strategy but still, its language and that of the rank and file was that of class against class. It was only after much internal discussion and some reluctance amongst the membership that the new line was finally laid to rest at the party's 13th Congress in 1935. There was undoubtedly no sudden about-turn

The experiences of the British Party do not bear out the idea that communists only became aware of fascism after Hitler came to power.

The difference between the pre- and post-Hitler period for the CPGB was merely one of tactics. Pollitt pointed out the dangers of German fascism at the Party's Twelfth Congress held in November 1932, four months before Hitler came to power. Pollitt's answer to the growth of fascism, however, was not a united front, but the destruction of Social Democracy. He told the delegates that, 'the position of the German Working Class today is a position which we must explain to the British Working Class, and show that this country will also travel the same way unless we are able to destroy the influence and power of the social democratic leaders in the Working Class Movement in this country.' [1]

Despite this strategy, British communists did attempt to alert the working class to the dangers of fascism and war, and during 1932, a year before the Nazis came to power, these twin dangers were very much at the centre of their campaigns.

The party initiated several regional conferences to unite the movement around the war danger. At a Manchester anti-war conference in July 1932, there were sixty-six delegates present, representing thirty-two local organisations – a comprehensive section of Manchester opinion. [2] This conference had set itself, as one of its aims, the exposure of the manufacture of ammunition for Japan by a local factory. The danger of Japanese militarism was an early target for the Communist Party, and it was almost alone on the Left in pointing to the danger from this quarter.

The *Daily Worker* argued that the capitalist class was using Japan to crush the USSR and the Communist-controlled areas of China.

A similar kind of argument was used by the communists a few years later. However, this time concerning Germany, which they also claimed was being used by the capitalist class as a bulwark against Bolshevism.

Although the main thrust of the CPGB's activity, before Hitler came to power, was against the danger of war, British communists were well aware of events taking place in Germany. Throughout 1932, there were several meetings called by the party to expose the dangers of German fascism. In the period immediately preceding the Nazis taking power, the communists initiated a number of united front anti-fascist activities.

There is no denying, however, the traumatic effect that the success of Nazism had on the World Communist Movement. After the Nazis seizure of power in March 1933, there were wholesale arrests of German communists and social democrats. In the new situation, the communists began to reappraise their 'Social Democrat equals Social Fascist' approach. The Communist International's instructions to its member parties to work for unity with the Social Democrats meant that in Britain the communists gradually discarded the view that the Labour Party was another capitalist party. However, it was not just an external directive that made the CPGB change its tactics, internally as well there were forces at work that made the old strategy redundant. Chief among these were Oswald Mosley's, British Union of Fascists. The 'Black Shirts', supported by some sections of the establishment, and encouraged by Hitler's success, were becoming increasingly strident. From mid-1933 onwards, British communists began to urge a United Front both against the dangers of fascism at home, and to thwart the growth of fascism in Europe. But just as the new line had been a gradual process for the British Party, so too was the Popular Front. It was to take over two years after that first Communist International directive before the CPGB would again give critical support to the Labour Party and as with the new line, the adoption of the Popular Front, for British communists, was as much due to their own experiences, as to any 'Orders from Moscow'.

The reasons for the demise of the class against class strategy after 1933 are similar to the reasons why it was accepted in the first place, namely, a combination of external factors and internal conditions. Externally, these were a series of directives from the Communist International to all the member Parties, while internally, the experiences of British communists themselves in combating fascism, helped the new line's decline. After Hitler came to power in Germany in February 1933, the Executive Committee of the Communist International immediately issued instructions to all the Communist parties of the world to work for an Anti-Fascist United Front with their own Social Democrats. At the international level, the CI made a similar appeal to the Socialist International.

Hitler s example was being followed in Britain by Oswald Mosley and his British Union of Fascists. The 'Blackshirts' were in the ascendancy, and they were mounting a challenge to the organisations of the labour movement. In this situation, the communists began to look around for allies, and they were prepared to unite with others on the Left in the face of this new danger. While Mosley and his followers were the overt form of fascism, after 1932 the National Government became increasingly right-wing. In order to mount a campaign against the Government s policies, the communists were once again pushed into a position where they needed to build alliances. This combination of the rise of fascism abroad and the CI's response, and the need to combat fascism at home, led British communists to rethink their class against class strategy. The policy did not change overnight – it was much more of a gradual process, but from 1933 onwards, the signs were there that the strategy would ultimately be abandoned.

Throughout 1933 and much of 1934 the new line remained virtually intact, although through the pages of the *Daily Worker* it was possible to detect a certain change of emphasis. The Labour Party still remained a capitalist party, but the communists were keen to unite with others on the Left. 1934 was to prove a watershed. Just as one year,1928, had seen the transition to the new line, so six years later, one year effectively ushered in its decline. At the beginning of the year, the communists were still saying much the same thing, but twelve months later, their strategy had changed in all but name. Just as the gradual adoption of the new line had been fraught with contradictions, so too was the acceptance of the United Front. Throughout much of 1934, the British Party had no clear line. It might still proclaim its adherence to the old strategy, but by its policy and actions, it was clear that a change was on the way.

A year after the CI's appeal for unity, and the CPGB's own unsuccessful overtures to the Labour Party, British communists still viewed Social Democracy as an ally of fascism. An article in *Communist Review*, entitled, 'Has the Labour Party Changed?' proclaimed, 'no, the Labour Party has not changed in a Socialist Direction. Its surface demagogy is adapted to using the danger of war and fascism to catch votes, but its fundamental policy of co-operation with the capitalist class, forces it to attempt to disrupt the workers struggle against fascism and war, to help its own Government in war preparations and to clear the way for fascism. [3]

Nevertheless, for all the communist claims about social democracy it was becoming increasingly apparent in 1934, that the most dangerous, and overt form of fascism, was not the Labour Party, but Mosley's Black Shirts. The British Union of Fascists had reached a membership of forty thousand and had opened their own Training Barracks in Chelsea. [4] They were disrupting labour movement meetings, and their organised Defence Corps posed a real problem for the entire Left. Something of the new sense of urgency felt by the communists can be gleaned from a report in the *Daily Worker*, about a Communist Party meeting in Battersea. It was a big meeting with over 1200 in attendance but, the paper reported,' that during the singing of the International a disturbance was started by a group of about 30 Fascists who had managed to get into the meeting'. The aim of the report, however, was not to show that the communists could attract large crowds but to expose the danger of Fascist disruption. The paper went on to urged vigilance in future and that precautions should be taken to prevent fascist disruption at all future working-class meetings. [5] The Communist Party was concerned that not just communist meetings should be protected, but the meetings of all labour movement organisations. This itself was a significant development from the old approach, which viewed all Social Democrats as Social Fascists.

During the first few months of 1934, the BUF continued to make headway. Mosley was supported by many in the establishment and by some sections of the press. The *Daily Mail*, owned by a Mosley sympathiser, Lord Rothermere, proclaimed in a famous headline on June 15, 'Hurray For The Black Shirts'. Mosley held successful rallies in Manchester and the Albert Hall in London. The Communist Party, through the *Daily Worker*, urged opposition to the Mosleyites and called for counter-demonstrations wherever the Fascists tried to meet. The high spot of Mosley's crusade was to be a mass meeting at the Olympia in June 1934. It was to be an all-ticket affair, with the emphasis on winning over sympathetic sections of the ruling class. The Communist Party, virtually alone of the left, called for a counter-demonstration outside the hall and managed to get some of its members inside the building. Phil Piratin, later to be elected as a Communist M.P. for Stepney, described what happened,

> "... the Communist Party rallied thousands of workers to go to Olympia. Previously, some hundreds of communists and other anti-fascists had been able to obtain tickets for the meeting. The thousands who rallied outside, however, could obtain no access to the meeting, the way being barred by a thousand police. Inside the meeting hundreds of courageous anti-fascists, men and women, exposed Mosley though they were battered and mauled by the Black Shirt thugs for the slightest interruption or protest ..." [6]

The violence at Olympia appalled even some of Mosley's supporters, and afterwards, they withdrew their support. The Labour Party, which had throughout adopted an attitude of telling its members to keep away from Fascist meetings, condemned the Communist Party for its organised opposition. Writing in the *Daily Herald*, Mr T West, the Labour M.P. for North Hammersmith, summed up the Labour Leadership's view and condemned the communists, 'for smashing Black Shirt Meetings' and accused them of,' aiding the Fascists and gaining public sympathy for them. We of the Labour Party do not fear the affect of Mosley's speeches. In any event let them be heard, for free speech is still precious today, although the communists are such opponents of it.'[7]

The events at Olympia led to Mosley's steady decline. For the Communist Party, which was pleased with the role it had played in organising the counter-demonstration, it exposed some contradictions. On the one hand, the party urged maximum opposition to Mosley, a stance that won it increasing support in the Labour and anti-fascist movement. However, on the other hand, it still clung to the view that the Labour Party was a social fascist organisation. This came through clearly in an article in *Communist Review* written just after Olympia. Referring to the failure of the Labour Party to respond to the Communist Party's call for a joint demonstration against Mosley's meeting, the article argued:

> "here is a living example of what is meant by social fascism. The Mosley Movement finds itself surrounded and attacked on all sides by the militant workers. The National Government seizes this situation to add once more to its already fairly numerous fascist measures, and the Labour Party rushes to support measures which can only aid Mosley against the workers. But we are asked to believe that the strengthening of this Labour Party is a guarantee against the coming of fascism in England." [8]

This was not just an isolated example, written in the heat of the moment after Olympia. The Communist Party, as if to dispel any idea that the rise of fascism meant that it might retract its new line policy, issued a policy statement in September 1934. The Executive Committee Resolution entitled, 'On The Fight For The United Front', stated, 'there is still confusion in many quarters on the role of social fascism. It is not yet sufficiently understood that the reformist leaders who verbally denounced fascism do not merely fail to organise any opposition to fascism, but in practice directly assist the advance of fascism. [9] Some eighteen months after Hitler had come to power, and the Communist International had urged tentative steps towards unity, despite all the United Front action on the ground to stop fascism, the CPGB's class against class policy remained, towards the end of 1934, very much intact. It was to be, yet again, in the field of electoral struggle that the first policy breakthrough was to occur.

At the London County Council Elections in March 1934, the communists decided to contest widely and put up candidates in eight boroughs.[10] When they published their election manifesto, it was a significant departure from past practice. Previously Communist election material, particularly during the class against class period, had confined itself to making general statements about the need for the revolutionary overthrow of capitalism; now there was a much more realistic approach. The Communist Party issued a list of demands for London that were both practical and well thought out. (See Chapter 5) They had been costed and were a realisable set of reforms that could be implemented without revolutionary change.

Apart from a welcome change in their propaganda, the communists at this election were much more even-handed in their attacks on the two main parties. Previously, much of their venom had been reserved for the Labour Party, but now they were equally scathing of the Tories. These were both small but significant changes in Communist Party tactics.

On the day of the election, *Daily Worker* readers were urged, in a front-page article to, 'Vote Communist in London Today'. [11] Then, as if to dispel any possible illusions that may have been gathering about the imminent demise of the new line, the article went on to reaffirm the Communist Party's class against class strategy. London electors were told:

> "the Communist Candidates are also challenging the anti-working class policy of

the Labour Party, which had been so strikingly demonstrated by the actions of Labour County Councils in Monmouthshire and Glamorganshire – Councils which have operated the infamous means tests. Every London Worker should support the communist fight against the parties of capitalism by going to the Poll today and unhesitatingly voting Communist ." [12]

The Labour Party was still referred to as anti-working class and as a party of capitalism, and there was no call to vote Labour where no communist candidate was standing. In the final analysis, very little seemed to have altered but by the way the election was conducted, it was apparent that there was some change of thinking taking place in the Communist Party.

By November 1934, this change of thinking had gathered momentum. Despite numerous Party statements that the Labour Party were the allies of fascism, in the Borough Council Elections that month the communists decided, for the first time in six years, to give grudging support to Labour. The news must have come as something of a shock to Party members, who had only three months before been told in the Executive Committee Statement that, 'the whole policy of reformism in practice prepares the way for fascism' The news of the change in the electoral line, was first publicly revealed to the membership through the *Daily Worker*. The communists were contesting sixty seats in London and agreement had been reached with the ILP to support each other's candidates. If no Communist or ILP candidate was standing, the voters were told to vote for those Labour Candidates who pledge themselves to build up the united front of struggle. [13]

The new line in the electoral field had been effectively broken. Although the communists were not yet prepared to give unequivocal support to Labour Candidates, the fact that they recognised differences within the Labour Party was itself a turn away from the old strategy.

Once the breach had been made, the trickle soon became a flood. Less than a month later in a discussion in the *Daily Worker*, entitled, 'Should We Support Labour Candidates', Gallacher said that only in constituencies where there is a chance of breaking through would the party stand candidates. In all others, it would support for Labour Candidates.' [14] It was not yet Party policy, but when someone of Gallacher's standing on the Executive Committee was making such statements, it would certainly not be long before there was a full discussion about a change of line. One reader of the paper argued for the continuance of the old policy,' there is no implication however, that we communists should say to the workers Vote Labour indiscriminately where there are no Communist Candidates and regardless of programmes and policy.'[15]

The discussion continued until the Communist Party's Thirteenth Congress in February 1935. At this Congress can be seen all the elements of the old and new policy. It was a kind of 'halfway house', while the Communist Party recognised the significant developments that had taken place, it was not yet prepared to throw overboard completely its new line strategy. The Labour leadership was still accused of effectively sabotaging the fight against fascism. The Congress Resolution stated that both the Labour Party leadership and the leadership of the Trade Union Congress despite their verbal declaration of opposition to fascism was trying to paralyse all active working class resistance to fascism. The communists needed to expose the entire policy of the Labour Party and TUC leadership. [16]

Yet despite this demand for an all-out struggle against the Labour Party, at this Congress, the communists decided to work for unity to defeat the National Government. They dropped their slogan calling for a 'Revolutionary Workers Government' and returned to their pre-new line strategy of maximum support for Labour. Yet another essential bastion of the new line had been effectively toppled.

The Seventh Congress of the Communist International in August 1935 brought to an end the World Communist Movement's Class against Class phase. Dimitrov called for a United Front against fascism, and this became the policy of the world's communist parties. In Britain, it put the seal of approval on a policy line that had changed some months before. Pollitt, at the Congress, reiterated the demand made at the Party's Thirteenth Congress, for maximum unity against the National Government. At a report back meeting, he called this the party's most important task and that the communists must ensure that the National Government was swept out of office and a Labour Government returned. [17] Abe Moffat, writing in the *Daily Worker*, as the Seventh Congress was meeting, proposed that there should be discussions between the Labour Party and the Communist Party about joint candidates at the forthcoming General Election. He proposed that in order to avoid any divisions in the ranks of the workers, the Communist Party would only contest in constituencies where the party had mass influence. In these constituencies, the Communist Party asked that the Labour Party withdraw their Candidates. [18]

Although no figure was mentioned, from the discussion that took place at the Thirteenth Congress, it was the Communist Party's intention to stand in some constituencies. Saklatvala had been re-adopted for Battersea North at an Executive Committee meeting in June 1934, and so had several other Communist candidates. [19] There was no public retraction of these commitments until the eve of the General Election, which took place in November 1935. The communists, despite their electoral offer to the Labour Party being rejected out of hand, decided to stand in just two constituencies, Rhondda East and West Fife, everywhere else they urged maximum support for Labour.

In many areas, the communists were again giving their active assistance to the Labour Candidates. In a letter to the Labour Party NEC written just after the election, Pollitt claimed that during the General Election there was a united front between branches of the Labour and Communist Parties all over the country. He claimed that many Labour candidates and successful members of parliament had publicly testified that this united front was of considerable help to them in winning a victory over the National Government candidate or a substantially increased vote. [20]

The General Election of 1935 brought to a close the class against class period.

Even its finale was something of a mixture of success and failure. At the General Election six years before, which ushered in the period, the communists, as part of their new strategy had contested on a wide scale. Now their candidates were reduced to two, but these two did remarkably well. In Rhondda East, Harry Pollitt polled over thirteen thousand votes and in West Fife Gallacher won the seat to become the first elected Communist MP since Saklatvala in 1924. Although the communists' electoral challenge had been small, it nevertheless resulted in their winning a parliamentary representative who was to hold his seat for the next fifteen years.

Just after the election, the new line received its deathblow when the Communist Party applied for Labour Party affiliation. The communists, in their application, argued that the rise of fascism made the unity of the labour movement all-important. In reply, the Labour Party NEC used the arguments they had used some thirteen years before and claimed that there were irreconcilable differences between the two parties that made affiliation impossible. What was significant, apart from indicating the communists' new approach to the Labour Party, was the response their application received from the labour movement. After six years of an unmitigated onslaught on the Labour Party, in which it was accused of 'propping up capitalism' and of being 'an agent of fascism', the communists could still gain broad appeal for their attempts at affiliation. The *Daily Worker* reported that over one thousand Labour and trade union organisations supported this application.[21] When it was discussed at the 1936 Annual Labour Party Conference, the motion for affiliation was rejected by 1,728,000 votes to 593,000.[22] Although this was a substantial vote against, it compared very favourably with the results achieved by the communists during the early '20s. The highest vote in favour of Communist Party affiliation was at the 1923 Labour Party Conference when a similar motion was rejected by 2,880,000 to 366,000 votes. The communists had made remarkable progress since then. Clearly, external factors had played a part, and the rise of fascism had affected the thinking of large sections of the labour movement. Apart from communists, many Labour Party members and others on the Left saw the necessity of a United Front. Yet, even so, it was the case that the new line had struck a chord amongst some sections of the organised working class. The communists' continuous attacks on the Labour Party had won them some sympathy, particularly after the debacle of the 1929/31 Labour Government. Despite all their sectarianism, the communists came out of the new line period a good deal closer to achieving Labour Party affiliation than at any time during the 1920s. If this was to be a measure of the policy's success, then it compared very favourably with the earlier phase.

The adoption by the CI of the class against class strategy in 1928, coincided with the British Party rethinking its policy. Already by that year, the CPGB had made several significant policy changes and had revised its previous assessment of the Labour Party. The new line continued a trend that was already taking place in the Communist Party, and this trend became an accepted part of the international perspective of the world communist movement. During the two years of discussions that took place in the CPGB before the strategy became accepted policy, there were three factors at work. These were the Executive Committee of the Communist International, the Executive Committee of the Communist Party of Great Britain, and the Party rank and file, and there was a relationship between all three. The universal contemporary view is that the ECCI was the dominating force in the situation. It played a part, but so too did the British Party leadership and the Party rank and file. At times the ECCI was more in tune with the feelings inside British Party than was the party's own Executive Committee. It was not merely a question of the CI deciding a strategy and this being imposed on the CPGB. There was much more of a dialectical relationship. The new policy of the CI fitted in very well with the experiences of British communists, and that was why it was so readily acceptable.

Apart from looking at why the new line became the official party policy, the book has also attempted to point out some of the positive and long-term features of the strategy. The party's new independent role led to the establishment of a *daily* paper, which has continued, albeit with a name change, until this day. The emphasis on winning a group of Communist M.P.'s led to a concerted electoral challenge and resulted at the end of the period in a Communist victory at West Fife. Gallacher, the victor, retained the seat for fifteen years and became the longest ever serving Communist M.P. Although there was no comparable victory in the Rhondda, there was a high Communist vote, and there have been communist councillors in the Valley until recently. Finally, the Communist Party's new aim of replacing the Labour Party as the party of the working class led to a redoubling of its activity. It initiated many campaigns, and the drive for increased membership dominated the period. By 1935 the party was three times as large as it had been at the beginning of the period. If the rate of recruitment is the sole criterion by which to judge the new line, then it was not unsuccessful. There were, of course, disadvantages to the new policy, and these have been amply outlined by other historians of the period. One of the purposes of this book has been to redress the balance and to show that the new line was not quite the disaster for British communists that has hitherto been maintained.

Notes

1 Harry Pollitt, *The Road to Victory*. Opening and concluding speeches at the Twelfth Congress of the CPGB, Battersea, November 1932
2 *Daily Worker,* July 12, 1932
3 *Communist Review,* April 1934
4 See, Mike Power, *The Struggle Against Fascism and War in Britain, 1931-39*. Our History Pamphlet No 70, CPGB
5 *Daily Worker,* February 13, 1934
6 Phil Piratin, *Our Flag Stays Red,* Thames Publications, 1945,pp6-7.
7 *Daily Herald,* June 9, 1934
8 *Communist Review,* July 1934
9 Executive Committee, CPGB Statement, *On the Fight for the United Front,* contained in *Communist Review,* September 1934
10 *Daily Worker,* January 13, 1934
11 *Daily Worker* March 8, 1934

12 *Ibid*
13 *Daily Worker*, October 27, 1934
14 *Daily Worker*, November 21, 1934
15 *Daily Worker*, November 24, 1934
16 The Draft Resolution on 'The Communist Party and the United Front', submitted to the Thirteenth Party Congress, Manchester, February 2-5,1935. CPGB,1935,pp4-5
17 *Daily Worker*, September 9, 1935
18 *Daily Worker* August 20, 1935
19 *Daily Worker*, June 14, 1934
20 Letter from Central Committee of the CPGB to the Labour Party NEC. Contained in Report of the Thirty Sixth Annual Conference of the Labour Party, Edinburgh, 5-9 October 1936. The Labour Party, p 50.
21 *Daily Worker*, August 8, 1936
22 *Report of the Thirty Sixth Annual Conference of the Labour Party*, Edinburgh, 5-9 October 1936. The Labour Party, p211

10 Class against Class:
The formative years of British communism

THE PURPOSE of this book has been twofold. To refute the standard bourgeois account that British communists were merely dupes of Moscow and that the strategy that they adopted was determined solely by the Communist International, which itself was in thrall to the USSR. This has been, to a greater or lesser extent, the interpretation put on the course of events that led to the new line. By this account British communists were little more than playthings in the global power struggle that was taking place between the USSR and the capitalist world and an internal struggles taking place in the USSR.

The second message contained in these pages is that far from being a bleak period, the class against class era produced great advances for Britain's communists and for the working class. The new line too, like its method of adoption, has been universally condemned by the Establishment historiography of the period. Even some sympathetic to the CPGB have joined in with writing off the seven years as the least productive period in the party's history.

By highlighting some of the communists' campaigns during class against class, the author has tried to show the positive achievements. These included the upturn in membership, the establishment and subsequent growth of sales of the *Daily Worker*, the electoral fight to achieve the new line aim of communist representation in parliament and the communists almost lone struggle against racism and colonialism. This was a period in which a tough and experienced cadre of communist militants in the unemployed movement and in industry – in factory, depot, mine and mill – established a deep penetration in the working class.

It is not an exaggeration to state that the new line recruits for the CPGB formed the backbone of the party during the post war years of its greatest success.

For the information on many of the following individuals printed below many thanks to the late Graham Stevenson for his meticulous encyclopedia of British communists. One of the best resources for anyone looking at the history of the CPGB.

It was during the class against class years that many of those those who fought in Spain had been recruited. Bill Alexander, son of a carpenter and subsequently Battalion commander of the British section of the International Brigade joined the party during the height of the new line in 1932. After the war he worked full time for the CPGB and was for a period its assistant general secretary.

Amongst mineworkers the lone support of the communists after the 1926 lockout proved fruitful to recruitment and the adherents won then provided the future leadership of the National Union of Mineworkers. A prime example is Will Paynter, who joined the Communist Party during the Parliamentary election campaign in 1929 in support of Arthur Horner in Rhondda East. Paynter became a member of the Central Committee of the Communist Party and was one of its organisers in South Wales. For five years until 1936, he was a full time activist for the Communist Party and the National Unemployed Workers' Movement. In 1931 he was victimised and then imprisoned in Cardiff jail for his trade-union and political activities. Paynter then studied for a time at the Lenin School in Moscow and was involved in underground activities in Nazi Germany, assisting the escape of communists and socialists.

He led three major Hunger Marches, in 1931, 1932 and 1936. On the 1932 March he was Treasurer of the South Wales contingent. He also volunteered for the International Brigade and fought in Spain.

In 1951 he became President of the South Wales Miners Federation and from 1959 to 1969 he was general secretary of the National Union of Mineworkers.

Another working class militant that rose to prominence at this time in the Transport and General Workers Union was Bert Papworth, 'Pappy'. He was rank and file leader amongst bus workers both before and after the war. He joined the CPGB in 1932 and had the distinction of being the first communist elected to the General Executive Committee of the Transport and General Workers Union in 1935.

In 1944 he was elected, in another first, to the Trades Union Congress General Council, again being the first CPGB member to hold such a post. Such was the threat from communists in the TGWU that Ernest Bevin, the union's right wing leader banned communists from holding office in the union in 1950.

Yet another, who was to become a prominent communist trade unionist was Tom Driver. He came from a poor family in Barnsley and was brought up in the South Yorkshire coalfield. His remarkable ability and intelligence saw him study English and Literature at Sheffield University, where he became the editor of 'Arrows', the university magazine. In 1933, he joined the Communist Party.

Driver became a teacher in further education and was elected to the National Council of the Association of Teachers in Technical Institutes in 1945 He was a key activist in the union becoming a member the NEC in 1960, President in 1961 and General Secretary in 1969. His greatest achievement was to be the decisive force in talks to form one college lecturers' union. This came about in 1976 when ATTI merged with the Association of Teachers in Colleges and Departments of Education, to form the National Association of Teachers in Further and Higher Education. Driver became the new union's first president.

Jessie Eden (later McCulloch) made famous by the TV series Peaky Blinders was born in Birmingham in 1902. She was employed at Joseph Lucas' motor components factory, where she worked filing shock absorbers. In January 1931, Jessie went down in history by leading ten thousand women out on a week's strike, an extraordinary thing to do in those times.

What led to the walkout was the Lucas company management's attempt to bring in a time and motion scheme at the plant. Unfortunately for the directors they chose Jessie Eden, probably because she was a fast worker, as their guinea pig. She realised she was being timed and immediately took action Already, complaints about being timed on toilet visits were especially offensive to female workers and this was the final straw. Under Eden's leadership a rank and file committee was formed and thousands of women at Lucas stopped work. The company, faced with such a complete stoppage capitulated and the Bedaux System, as it was called, was abandoned before it even started. "VICTORY! BEDAUX SYSTEM SMASHED!" ran the headline in the *Daily Worker* on 29 January 1932.

Jessie Eden was yet another new line recruit, joining the CPGB during the strike in early 1932. She subsequently spent time at the Lenin school and was a volunteer worker in the construction of the Moscow Metro, spending two and a half years in the USSR before returning to Britain.

Richard 'Dick' Seabrook was yet another post war trade union leader who joined the Communist Party during the class against class years, in 1931. He and his brother Alfred were both active in the Chelmsford Communist Party probably from its conception around 1933. Dick was a boot and shoe repairer with Chelmsford Co-op.

Both would later hold elevated positions in the shop workers union USDAW, Dick as a USDAW area organiser from 1937 and later as the president of the enlarged and merged shop workers' union, USDAW, and Alfred as a National Executive Committee member. Dick was elected national president of USDAW in 1965. Re-elected in 1967, he held this role for another six years.

Erik Rechnitz was yet another trade union activist recruited during the new line years. A was a prominent member of the TGWU rank and file up until his death in 2001. His work for the union earned him a Union Gold Badge, presented to him by Ron Todd, the then T&G general secretary.

Known mainly as a leading member of the Transport and General Workers' Union, Rechnitz was a long time member of the Communist Party. A Smithfield meat porter, he had once been a professional wrestler. Born on February 4th 1915 in Highbury, north London, Rechnitz was the son of Jewish immigrants from the Austro-Hungarian empire who arrived in England just two years before the outbreak of the first world war. His father went on to practice as a dentist in the East End. Erik, meanwhile, was educated at local schools in Stoke Newington and, as an 11-year-old, was fund-raising for workers during the 1926 General Strike.

After leaving school, he began training as a metallurgist. However, after the factory where he worked closed, he entered, in 1930, the industry that was to be his life – meat haulage at Smithfield, where he entered as an 'offal boy'. Two years later he was in the TGWU. After a time in the Independent Labour Party, he joined the CPGB in 1932. He volunteered for the International Brigade but was not allowed to go as he was the sole family breadwinner. After the war he returned to work in Smithfield and was a key figure behind the scenes in the 1958 nine-week strike at Smithfield markets, which involved 58,000 workers. Rechnitz at the time, like all Communist Party members in the TGWU was banned from holding office

After the bans on Communists holding office were lifted, he was became a senior lay representative in the T&G. He was chairman of the T&G's Region 1 (London and the South East) Regional Road Transport Commercial (RTC) trade group committee and the national RTC representative to the TGWU's general executive council from 1968.

Not everything can be covered. Important areas require more detailed study, the trade unions, the unemployed movement and the role of factory and community newspapers in particular.

Alongside the deep roots in the working class and the trade unions three areas of achievement that must not go without a brief mention are the growth of communist student branches at universities, the attraction of communist policy for artists, musicians, poets and writers, and the advances of the communist-initiated British Workers Sports Federation. It was this organisation that fronted the most famous and long-reaching action of the new line communists; the mass trespass of Kinder Scout.

The event, like Cable Street, has entered into, not just Labour history, but has become part of the national narrative. It was led by Benny Rothman, a member of the Cheetham branch of the Manchester Young Communist League which he had joined in 1929. He was also active in the British Workers Sports Federation. The importance of this particular action during the new line is that the mass trespass organised by Rothman and the young communists had national ramifications. Thanks to the publicity received in 1932 around open access to the countryside; national parks became an objective, and the post-war Labour government created the first one. The long-distance walk, the Pennine Way, which starts, or finishes, at Kinder Scout, has also been attributed to the new line activities of Rothman and his comrades.

No study of the new line would be complete without a brief reference to the recruitment amongst students during the period. It was at this time that communist groups emerged at three important universities, Oxford, Cambridge and the LSE.

John Cornford, a Cambridge graduate and militant by his seventeenth year, galvanised the emerging Cambridge group of communists. In his short but dynamic life, he achieved more than most. Writer, activist, theoretician, and poet of the new line, he sacrificed his life in Spain fighting against fascism. Along with many others recruited during the period, it is somewhat of an irony that they gave their lives supporting the implementation of the new united front strategy.

Cornford's poems written before his untimely death in Spain are eclectic. They cover all the emotions. He had been writing poetry since his school days. A lesser-known one written during his Cambridge years is a vindication of the communists' go it alone approach that was a hallmark of the period. Entitled, *Keep Culture out of Cambridge*, it is a bitter attack on figures like T S Elliot, Salvador Dali and their fashionable contemporaries. It concludes with what could be a ringing endorsement of class against class.

> "There's none of these fashions have come to stay,
> And there's nobody here got time to play,
> All we've brought are our party cards
> Which are no bloody good for your bloody charades"

Another Cambridge communist intellectual who joined the party in 1931 was David Guest. Son of a Labour MP he too responded to the call to go to Spain and join the International Brigade. He died in 1938 at the battle of the River Ebro. The battalion commander of the British volunteers in Spain was Bill Alexander. Not part of the Cambridge group but an industrial chemist he too had been recruited in 1932. He went on to play a leading role in the Communist Party for many year.

Two other, who were to become leading party theoreticians, James Klugmann and Victor Kiernan were also part of the communist cell at Cambridge. They, too, were recruited during the new line. Another communist historian, Christopher Hill, also joined the party at Oxford during its class against class phase. Like his Cambridge contemporaries, he too volunteered for the International Brigade but was turned down. Arthur Leslie Morton, AL Morton, penned the most popular alternative history of England, *A People's History of England*. First published in 1938, updated editions are still in print today. Morton, who was to become a stalwart of the post-war Communist Party historians group and its chair joined the party in 1929, yet another new line convert.

There were others, Noreen Branson, Margot Heineman, Robert Browning, Rodney Hilton all joined the party during the new line years. Like Morton, they were all to become associated with the historians' group. That Marxism was, post-war, to play such an influential role in the teaching of history was in part due to these adherents to the Communist Party made during its class against class phase.

Other areas too gained from those who had become converts during those few years. In the field of literature, the poet Randell Swingler became a communist and joined the party in 1934. Hugh MacDiarmid who was in later years to become Scotland's national poet, joined at the same time. The author Edward Upward, who later was to become famous for his trilogy on life in the Communist Party joined the Bethnal Green branch in 1931. Another recruit who was to become famous was Ewan McColl, folk singer, author, playwright, and much more. He wrote the 'Manchester Rambler' always associated with the Kinder Scout trespass.

Even the relatively newly found study or oral history, as an alternative to the narrative of history from the top, was inspired by a pioneering communist in the field, George Ewart Evans

Born on 1st April 1909 in Abercynon, a coal-mining village north of Cardiff, Evans was one of a family of eleven to Welsh-speaking parents. His parents ran a small grocery business. As a boy he assisted in the delivery rounds travelling by pony and trap through the neighbouring farms and villages until the business closed following the 1924-5 coal strike. The loss of his father's shop and the experience of bankruptcy was a strong influence on young George, although shopkeepers it seems his parents strongly identified with working class neighbours.

George went to Mountain Ash School and graduated from University College, Cardiff, in 1931, with an honours degree in Classics and a teaching certificate. During a long period of unemployment and after an unsuccessful attempt to move to London, he joined the Communist Party in 1934, which he stayed in it for the rest of his life.

George was secretary to the Cambridge branch of the Communist Party for three years, although he was briefly also a dual member of the Labour Party in the very late 1930s, when many Communists felt it imperative to seek to draw Labour activists away from their leadership-inspired anti-communism and draw them into anti-fascist work.

He was called up in December 1941 and served in the Royal Air Force working with wireless equipment during the Second World War. Because his hearing was poor, he was consigned to routine duties and moved around a lot; it was a difficult and unhappy time for him. Nonetheless he began to write and produced a number of short stories and poetry, some of which were republished in 1975 in a collection titled *Let Dogs Delight*. He also wrote an account of his childhood in the South Wales valleys.

In 1947, they moved to the remote Suffolk village of Blaxhall, where his wife taught in the school and he became a tutor for the Workers Education Association. He then began to write – first off, mainly stories, poetry and film scripts for the BBC, especially about the people of the village of Blaxhall. This was eventually published as *Ask The Fellows Who Cut The Hay* in 1956. Evans wrote another ten books of this kind over the next three decades.

Most of his neighbours were agricultural labourers, born before the turn of the century, who had worked on farms before the arrival of mechanisation. He found that the speech men and women who were born after 1890 differed substantially from those born earlier. Their language had lost a great deal of its visual imagery, which commanded long attention spans by virtue of its vitality.

George began to record the dialect and to collect details of rural customs, traditions and folklore. By the 1960s George had become influential in persuading many people to start collecting oral history in 1969 he became a founding member of the Oral History Society. His tape recordings formed the basis of radio scripts for features broadcast on the BBC Third Programme. George also became a tutor for the Extramural Department of the University of Cambridge and the WEA in East Anglia. In 1982 his contribution to oral history and education was acknowledged by the Universities of Essex and Keele, both of whom awarded him honorary doctorates.

Having published some fourteen books by the time he died in 1988, George had also become almost infamous as a folklorist and collector of oral history (or 'spoken history' as he preferred to call it) in the East Anglian countryside from 1956 and 1977.

His collection is maintained by the British Library, and consists of 250 recordings of interviews and songs made mainly in Suffolk, with a smaller number in Wales, Ireland and Scotland. The recordings document rural life and agricultural work in the late nineteenth and early twentieth century, folk beliefs about animals, medicine and witchcraft, folk and popular songs.

The subtitle of the book is 'the formative years of British communism'. Given the disparaging dismissal as disastrous – by almost all 'mainstream' historians – of this short period in communist history, how can the new line be described as formative? Formative means to have a 'lasting influence.' The class against class years did just that not only in establishing a daily press and a deep industrial impantation but on the development of communist strategy in Britain in which independent electoral work is conceived of as part of the struggle to win working class state power. Its after-effects are still with the party today.

As we have seen, in the period before the new line Labour Party affiliation was a strategic aim. Acting in conformity with Lenin's advice much was subordinated to this objective. In the face of every demand by the Labour leadership, the communists backed down to achieve this goal. This even included withdrawing their candidates where they may be in opposition to Labour candidates. It failed. Even when communists were deprived of their Labour Party membership they refused to accept the decision and tried hard, with their allies, to get it reversed. In this too they were unsuccessful. Faced with the hard reality of exclusion from the federal party of the workig class, the communists underwent a massive reappraisal of their role. It was a reappraisal they still adhere to today.

After class against class, the communists entered the electoral arena against all comers. They stood candidates in competition for working class votes with Labour, and this policy – with the brief intereggnum brought about by Jeremy Corbyn's election as leader of the Labour Party and the adoption of an electoral programme that included many of the policies long advocated by the communists – is still part of the party's armoury. The communist programme, now *Britain's Road Socialism*, much revised, envisages a mixture of parliamentary and extra-parliamentary struggle that will result in a progressive government consisting of Labour and Communist MPs. Had it not been for the new line and its concentration on winning communist votes and electing MPs, the party's present programme may never have seen fruition. After 1928 and up until the present time communists contest parliamentary seats where there are Labour candidates. Had they not, neither Willie Gallacher in West Fife nor Phil Piratin in Stepney would have become MPs.

The lasting monument to the period is, of course, the *Morning Star*. Established as the *Daily Worker* and first published on 1 January 1930 it has survived government bans, persecution, fines, imprisonment of staff, and a damaging 1980s division between communists that was only resolved by a decisive intervention by the broad labour movement acting through the democratic structures of the cooperative.

It survived all that, and since the post war period transfer of ownership from the Communist Party to a cooperative has been open to every legitimate trend in the Labour movement. It is invariably the platform of choice for trade union leaders in struggle and the voice of liberation and freedom from every kind of oppression.

Alongside material from the most staunch of Labour's left wing MPs it carries features from Green and nationalist politicans and the environmental movement. Editorially it is guided by the unity project that underpins the Communist Party's programme. Its editor is a member of the party's leadership while its staff represent the full spectrum of progressive labour movement opinion.

As we have seen, from the earliest days of the CPGB's creation, there were demands for a daily party newspaper. These demands were both external, from the CI, and internal from the party leadership and the membership. They had little effect. Given that the CPGB was expending much of its energy on Labour Party affiliation; that should not come as a surprise.

It was only after the new line, and the party's attempt to gain the leadership of the Labour movement that a daily voice becomes a necessity.

The Communist Party was created on the wave of revolution that started in 1917 after the Bolsheviks took state power in Russia. After the establishment of the Communist International in 1919, Communist parties were formed in all parts of the globe, either as new creations, or as in Britain from existing socialist parties. And despite the collapse of the USSR and the East European states, the Communist tradition lives on. Communist parties exist still in virtually every country in the world.

Today the Communist Party in Britain carries on the struggle for a fundamental change in society with an ideology entirely consistent those in came together in 1920 at the party's first foundation congress in London.

Marxism, as an ideology is resurgent and millions in Britain, particularly the young, are searching for answers to problems that were not recognised in the 1920s and early 30s. That climate change could destroy the planet was then unknown. Had it been Britain's communists then, as they do now, would have argued that only a fundamental change in society can halt the rush to destruction.

The communist message lives on, and party activists still champion 'the good old cause' of socialism and carry that message into all arenas of struggle. In the nearly hundred years since the period under review, much has changed. Britain's communists today are no longer overwhelmingly male, and neither are the bulk of them unemployed. They still agitate in their places of work, still sell the paper, the *Morning Star*, issue pamphlets, leaflet, and most important of all still exert an influence far above their numbers on the broader labour movement. They still keep alive the hope of a new society, one based on human need rather than private profit.

Index

African National Congress   133, 141
Ainley, David   106
Allen, William   84, 88
Allison, George   86, 114
Ancrum, Jim   84
Arnot, Robin Page   456
Beauchamp, Kay   115
Bell, Tom   42, 48, 49, 50, 59, 77, 124, 60, 61, 62, 64, 65, 72, 82
Birth of a Nation (DW Griffiths)   155
Bond Ralph   43
Bradley, Ben   128, 131
Branson, Noreen   30, 175
Brennan Ward, F   110
Bright, Frank   51
British Road to Socialism   96, 175
British Socialist Party   9, 10, 12, 29
British Workers Sports Federation (BWSF)   105, 159
Brown, Isobel   76

Cable Street   144, 159, 173
Campbell, JR   19, 44, 47, 48, 51, 52, 76, 77, 80, 84, 85, 96, 100, 101, 102, 109
Citriani, AA   139
Clynes, JR   147
Cook, AJ   12, 19, 46,
Communist Review   49, 55, 63, 70, 73, 87, 88, 97, 103, 106, 116, 119, 147, 160, 164, 165, 170,
Cox, Idris   52, 61, 62, 65, 66, 67, 68, 70, 71, 112
Crawfurd, Helen   76

Daily Herald   99, 100, 101, 110, 117, 165, 170
Daily Worker   7, 44, 59, 60, 64-69, 80-88, 90-95, 98 *Illustration*, 100-113, 116, 117, 124, 126,129, 130, 132, 134-139, 142, 144, 146-150, 153, 155, 156-160, 163, 165-170, 175,179,
Deakin, Fanny   35
Dutt, Rajani Palme   33-35, 37, 57, 104-107, 117, 118, 132, 157

Ferguson, Aitken   39, 49, 76,
Ferguson, Maurice   49
Flanagan, Chris   86
Frow, Edmund   84

Gallacher, William   16, 46, 48, 49, 52, 64, 66, 75, 76, 78, 81, 82, 88, 93, 94, 104, 167, 169, 175

Gerhardt (of the Communist International)   87, 88, 97
General Strike   4, 22, 23, 24, 28, 31, 33, 38, 53, 58, 62, 66, 73, 87, 99

Hannington, Wall   49
Hardy, George   113
Henderson,   Arthur 12, 92
Hodges, Frank   18
Horner, Arthur   44, 46, 47, 48, 51, 52, 55, 78, 89, 92, 101, 102, 111
Hutt, Allen   116

Independent Labour Party   10, 29
Inkpin, Albert   52, 53, 57
International Labour Defence (ILD)   150
International Negro Conference   147, 181

Jackson, TA   49, 52
James, CLR   151
Jones, Chris   150,   151, 152

Kenyatta, Jomo   138,
Kerrigan, Peter   81, 84
Khitarov, RM   50
Klugman,   James   24, 31, 73, 96, 174

Larkin, Jim   141
Labour Monthly   132
League Against Imperialism   123, 127, 130, 137, 140, 141, 145, 149, 150, 153, 159
Lovell, Bob,   150, 151

MacDonald Ramsay   12, 62, 86,87, 124
Manuilsky, Dmitri Z   48, 52, 86
Mason, Clarence   114
Massey, Alex   64
Maxton, James   123, 128
Mcauly,   Frank (*Lagos Daily News*)   147
McGovern, John,   81, 92, 93
McIlhone R   110
McIntyre, Hugh   91
McLaughlan, Jack   80
McManus, Arthur   10, 11, 14
Meerut Trial   6, 86, 128, 129, 130, 133, 141, 142, 144
Minority Movement   36, 38, 67, 100, 102, 114, 146
Moffat, Abe   100, 168
Moore, Bill   6
Morning Star   175, 176

Mosley, Sir Oswald 144, 163, 164, 165, 166
Murphy, JT 49, 51, 77, 78, 80, 97

Negro Welfare Association (NWA), 151, 152, 158
Newbold, Walton 75
Nkosi, JW 136, 137

Patterson Frank 110
Paul, William 18
Paynter, Will 140, 142,143,173,174, 182
Piratin, Phil 165, 170, 175
Pollitt, Harry 15, 18, 20, 33, 35, 37, 43, 47, 50, 52, 53, 57, 59, 61, 63, 64, 71, 75, 76, 78, 82, 83, 87, 88, 89, 91, 92, 95, 96, 100, 103, 109, 110, 116, 127, 143, 163, 170, 171, 182
Priestley, Frank 110

Robson, RW 71, 86
Rothstein, Andrew 45, 52, 148
Rothmere, Lord 165
Roy, MN 121, 122, 123, 131
Rust, William 37, 39, 43-45, 47, 49, 51, 52, 59, 61, 63, 64, 76, 77, 90, 102, 104, 105, 109, 116-119

Saklavala, Shapurji 15, 21, 22, 29, 31, 46, 48, 60, 67, 68, 75, 76, 81, 82, 83, 85, 89, 92, 100, 114, 121, 123, 124, 125, 127, 129, 130, 131, 132, 141.149, 150, 169
Scottsboro Boys 125, 149, 150, 151, 152, 159, 160
Simon, Sir John 128
Shields, Jimmy 117
Snowden, Phillip 86
Spratt, Phil 128
Springhall, Dave 67
Stewart, Bob 59, 78, 86

Tapsell, Walter 44, 49, 51, 52, 61
The Communist 11
Thomas, JH 86
Turner, Beth 52

Usmani, Shaukat 86, 128
Usher, Nellie 62

Ward, Arnold 139, 141, 151, 153
Webb, Lily 103
Wheatley, John 81
Williams, Bert 86
Wilson, JR 49, 53, 76, 88

Wintringham, Tom 100
Workers Bulletin 22, 23 (Councils of Action)
Workers Life 36, 38, 39, 40, 41, 43, 44, 45, 47, 49, 54, 55, 96, 97, 100, 103, 108, 115, 117, 118, 119, 128, 132, 133, 134, 143, 183
Workers Weekly (Illustration) ii
Wright, Mrs (Scottsboro Boys) 125, 150, 151

Young Communist League 40, 44, 48, 64, 65, 81, 85, 110, 139, 173

www.ingramcontent.com/pod-product-compliance
Lightning Source LLC
Chambersburg PA
CBHW060836190426
43197CB00040B/2628